Where do I go for answers to my travel questions?

What's the best and easiest way to plan and book my trip?

frommers.travelocity.com

Frommer's, the travel guide leader, has teamed up with **Travelocity.com,** the leader in online travel, to bring you an in-depth, easy-to-use resource designed to help you plan and book your trip online.

At **frommers.travelocity.com**, you'll find free online updates about your destination from the experts at Frommer's plus the outstanding travel planning and purchasing features of Travelocity.com. Travelocity.com provides reservations capabilities for 95 percent of all airline seats sold, more than 47,000 hotels, and over 50 car rental companies. In addition, Travelocity.com offers more than 2,000 exciting vacation and cruise packages. Travelocity.com puts you in complete control of your travel planning with these and other great features:

> **Expert travel guidance from Frommer's** - over 150 writers reporting from around the world!

> **Best Fare Finder** - an interactive calendar tells you when to travel to get the best airfare

> **Fare Watcher** - we'll track airfare changes to your favorite destinations

> **Dream Maps** - a mapping feature that suggests travel opportunities based on your budget

> **Shop Safe Guarantee** - 24 hours a day / 7 days a week live customer service, and more!

Whether traveling on a tight budget, looking for a quick weekend getaway, or planning the trip of a lifetime, Frommer's guides and Travelocity.com will make your travel dreams a reality. You've bought the book, now book the trip!

Travelocity.com
A Sabre Company

Frommer's

A New Star-Rating System & Other Exciting News from Frommer's!

In our continuing effort to publish the savviest, most up-to-date, and most appealing travel guides available, we've added some great new features.

Frommer's guides now include a new star-rating system. Every hotel, restaurant, and attraction is rated from 0 to 3 stars to help you set priorities and organize your time.

We've also added seven brand-new features that point you to the great deals, in-the-know advice, and unique experiences that separate travelers from tourists. Throughout the guide, look for:

Finds	Special finds—those places only insiders know about
Fun Fact	Fun facts—details that make travelers more informed and their trips more fun
Kids	Best bets for kids—advice for the whole family
Moments	Special moments—those experiences that memories are made of
Overrated	Places or experiences not worth your time or money
Tips	Insider tips—some great ways to save time and money
Value	Great values—where to get the best deals

Frommer's®

PORTABLE

Paris

2002

*by Darwin Porter &
Danforth Prince*

Hungry Minds™

Best-Selling Books • Digital Downloads • e-Books
Answer Networks • e-Newsletters • Branded Web Sites • e-Learning
New York, NY • Cleveland, OH • Indianapolis, IN

ABOUT THE AUTHORS

Veteran travel writers **Darwin Porter** and **Danforth Prince** have written numerous best-selling Frommer's guides, notably to France, Italy, England, and Germany. Porter, who was bureau chief for the *Miami Herald* when he was 21, has lived in Paris periodically and written about the city for many years. Prince lived in the city for several years as a member of the Paris bureau of the *New York Times*.

Published by:

HUNGRY MINDS, INC.

909 Third Ave.
New York, NY 10022

ISBN 0-7645-6479-X
ISSN 1520-5541
Editor: Lisa Torrance
Production Editor: Suzanna R. Thompson
Photo Editor: Richard Fox
Cartographer: John Decamillis
Production by Hungry Minds Indianapolis Production Services

SPECIAL SALES

For general information on Hungry Minds' products and services, please contact our Customer Care department; within the U.S. at 800-762-2974, outside the U.S. at 317-572-3993, or fax 317-572-4002. For sales inquiries and reseller information, including discounts, bulk sales, customized editions, and premium sales, please contact our Customer Care department at 800-434-3422.

Manufactured in the United States of America

5 4 3 2 1

Contents

List of Maps

Here's what critics say about Frommer's:

"Amazingly easy to use. Very portable, very complete."

—*Booklist*

"The only mainstream guide to list specific prices. The Walter Cronkite of guidebooks—with all that implies."

—*Travel & Leisure*

"Complete, concise, and filled with useful information."

—*New York Daily News*

"Hotel information is close to encyclopedic."

—*Des Moines Sunday Register*

"Detailed, accurate, and easy-to-read information for all price ranges."

—*Glamour Magazine*

Planning Your Trip to Paris

The discovery of the City of Light and the experience of making it your own are—and always have been—the most compelling reasons to visit. If you're a first-timer, everything in Paris, of course, will be new to you. If you've been away for a while, expect changes: Taxi drivers may no longer correct your fractured French but address you in English—and that's tantamount to a revolution. More Parisians have a rudimentary knowledge of English, and France, at least at first glance, seems less hysterically xenophobic than in past years—spending your much-needed francs or euros, you likely won't be looked at as an "ugly American" anymore. Part of this derives from Parisians' interest in music, videos, and films from foreign countries, and part is caused by France's growing awareness of its role within a united Europe.

Yet France has never been more concerned about the loss of its identity, as it continues to attract an increasing number of immigrants from its former colonies. Many have expressed concern that the country will lose the battle to keep its language strong, distinct, and unadulterated by foreign (particularly American) slang or catchwords (*le weekend,* for example). In fact, the rancor of France's collective xenophobia has been increasingly redirected toward the many immigrants seeking better lives in Paris, where the infrastructure has nearly been stretched to its limits.

Though Paris is in flux culturally and socially, it lures travelers for the same reasons it always has. You'll still find grand old sights like the Eiffel Tower, Notre-Dame, the Arc de Triomphe, Sacré-Coeur, and all those atmospheric cafes, as well as trendy new projects like La Grande Arche de La Défense, the Cité des Sciences et de l'Industrie, and the Bibliothèque François-Mitterrand. And don't forget the parks, gardens, and squares; the Champs-Elysées and other grand boulevards; and the river Seine and its quays. Paris's beauty is still overwhelming, especially in the illumination of night, when it certainly is the City of Light.

This chapter provides the nuts-and-bolts details you need before setting off for Paris—everything from information sources to money matters to the major airlines and how to save money on your flight.

1 Visitor Information

TOURIST OFFICES

Your best source of information is the **French Government Tourist Office,** which you can reach at the following addresses:

IN THE UNITED STATES   444 Madison Ave., 16th Floor, New York, NY 10022 (© **212/838-7800**); 676 N. Michigan Ave., Suite 3360, Chicago, IL 60611 (© **312/751-7800**); 9454 Wilshire Blvd., Suite 715, Beverly Hills, CA 90212 (© **310/271-6665;** fax 310/276-2835). To request information at any of these offices, call the **France on Call** hot line at © **410/286-8310.**

IN CANADA   Maison de la France/French Government Tourist Office, 1981 av. McGill College, Suite 490, Montréal, PQ H3A 2W9 (© **514/288-4264;** fax 514/845-4868); 30 St. Patrick St., Suite 700, Toronto, ON M5T 3A3 (© **416/491-7622;** fax 416/979-7587).

WEBSITES

You can contact the French Government Tourist Office through its website at **www.francetourism.com**. Other Paris-based sites worth checking out include:

- Bonjour Paris, www.bparis.com
- Paris Digest, www.parisdigest.com
- Paris France Guide, www.parisfranceguide.com
- Paris Free Voice, www.parisvoice.com
- Paris Pages, www.paris.org
- Paris Tourist Office, www.paris-touristoffice.com

2 Entry Requirements & Customs Regulations

PASSPORT & VISAS

All non-French nationals need a **valid passport** to enter France (check its expiration date). The French government no longer requires visas for **U.S. citizens,** providing they're staying less than 90 days. For longer stays, they must apply for a long-term visa, residence card, or temporary-stay visa. Each requires proof of income or a viable means of support in France and a legitimate purpose for remaining in the country. Applications are available from the **Consulate Section of the French Embassy,** 4101 Reservoir Rd.

NW, Washington, DC 20007 (✆ **202/944-6000**), or from the **Visa Section of the French Consulate,** 10 E. 74th St., New York, NY 10021 (✆ **212/606-3689**). Visas are required for students planning to study in France even if the stay is less than 90 days.

At the moment, citizens of Australia, Canada, New Zealand, Switzerland, Japan, and European Union countries do not need visas.

If your passport is lost or stolen, head to your consulate as soon as possible for a replacement.

CUSTOMS REGULATIONS

WHAT YOU CAN BRING INTO FRANCE   Customs restrictions differ for citizens of European Union (EU) countries and citizens of non-EU countries.

For Non-EU Nationals   You can bring in, duty-free, 200 cigarettes, 100 cigarillos, 50 cigars, or 250 grams of smoking tobacco. These amounts are doubled if you live outside Europe. You can also bring in 2 liters of wine and either 1 liter of alcohol over 22 proof or 2 liters of wine under 22 proof. In addition, you can bring in 50 grams (1.75 oz.) of perfume, a quarter liter (250ml) of eau de toilette, 500 grams (1 lb.) of coffee, and 200 grams (0.5 lb.) of tea. Visitors 15 and over may also bring in other goods totaling 1,200F (182.40€, $174); the allowance for those 14 and under is 600F (91.20€, $87). (Customs officials tend to be lenient about general merchandise, realizing the limits are unrealistically low.)

For EU Citizens   Visitors from fellow European Union countries can bring into France any amount of goods as long as it's intended for their personal use—not for resale.

WHAT YOU CAN BRING HOME FROM FRANCE   For U.S. Citizens   If you've been out of the country for 48 hours or more, you can bring back into the States $400 worth of goods (per person) without paying a duty. On the first $1,000 worth of goods over $400 you pay a flat 10%. Beyond that, it works on an item-by-item basis. There are a few restrictions on amount: 1 liter of alcohol (you must be over 21), 200 cigarettes, and 100 cigars. Antiques over 100 years old and works of art are exempt from the $400 limit, as is anything you mail home. Once per day, you can mail yourself $200 worth of goods duty-free; mark the package "For Personal Use." You can also mail to other people up to $100 worth of goods per person per day; label each package "Unsolicited Gift." Any package must state on the exterior a description of the contents and their values. You can't mail alcohol, perfume (it contains alcohol), or tobacco products.

For more details on regulations, check out the **U.S. Customs Service** website at www.customs.ustreas.gov or contact the office at P.O. Box 7407, Washington, DC 20044 (© **202/927-6724;** www. customs.ustreas.gov), to request the free "Know Before You Go" pamphlet.

For Canadian Citizens   For a clear summary of Canadian rules, write for the booklet "I Declare," issued by **Revenue Canada,** 2265 St. Laurent Blvd., Ottawa K1G 4KE (© **506/636-5064**), or check out www.ccra-adrc.gc.ca. Canada allows its citizens a $750 exemption if you're gone for 7 days or longer (only $200 if you're gone between 48 hr. and 7 days), and you're allowed to bring back—duty-free—200 cigarettes, 50 cigars, and 1.5 liters of wine *or* 1.14 liters of liquor *or* 8.5 liters of beer or ale. In addition, you're allowed to mail gifts to Canada at the rate of $60 a day, provided they're unsolicited and aren't alcohol or tobacco. (Write on the package "Unsolicited Gift, Under $60 Value.")

3 Money Matters

CURRENCY

During part of the life of this edition, France will have two currencies—the old French franc and the new euro adopted by 11 nations of the European Union. French currency is based on the **franc (F),** which consists of 100 **centimes (c).** Coins come in units of 5c, 10c, 20c, and 50c and 1F, 2F, 5F, and 10F. Notes come in denominations of 20F, 50F, 100F, 200F, 500F, and 1,000F. The front of the 200F note honors Gustave Eiffel, creator of the Eiffel Tower, father of experimental aerodynamics, and co-designer of New York's Statue of Liberty.

The franc will remain France's currency only until March 1, 2002. At that time, the **euro,** which has already been introduced, will take over completely. See "The Euro & You" box, below.

All banks are equipped for foreign exchange, and you'll find exchange offices at the airports and airline terminals. Banks are open Monday to Friday, from 9am to noon and from 2 to 4pm. Major bank branches also open their exchange departments on Saturday, from 9am to noon.

When converting your home currency into French francs or euros, be aware that rates vary. Your hotel will probably offer the worst exchange rate. In general, banks offer the best rate, but even banks charge a commission for the service (often $5, depending on

The Euro & You

The **euro** (€), the new single European currency, became the official currency of France and 10 other countries on January 1, 1999. You'll likely see prices in restaurants, shops, and so on listed in both French francs and euros. However, the franc will remain the only currency for cash transactions until December 21, 2001. (You can also use it in non-cash transactions, as with checks and credit cards.) At that time, euro banknotes and coins will be introduced, and franc banknotes and coins will be withdrawn from circulation during a maximum 2-month transition period. On March 1, 2002, the euro will become the only currency.

For more details on the euro, check out www.europa.eu.int/euro.

the transaction). Whenever you can, stick to the big Paris banks, like Crédit Lyonnais, which usually offer the best exchange rates and charge the least commission.

At press time, $1 is equivalent to 6.89F (or 1F = 14.5¢)—this exchange rate was used to calculate the dollar values in this guide—and £1 equals about 10.34F (or 1F = 9.7p). Here's a rough guideline that, undoubtedly, will be subject to multiple revisions as Europe's newest currency increases in usage: 1€ equals about 91¢, 6.57F, or 63p.

ATMS

Using ATMs is the fastest, easiest, and least expensive way to change money. You can take advantage of the bank's bulk exchange rate (better than anything you'll get on when exchanging cash or traveler's checks on your own), and unless your home bank charges you for using a non-proprietary ATM, you won't have to pay a commission.

Both the **Cirrus** (© 800/424-7787; www.mastercard.com) and the **PLUS** (© 800/843-7587; www.visa.com) networks have automated ATM locators listing the banks in Paris that will accept your card. Or just search out any machine with your network's symbol emblazoned on it. Be sure to check the daily withdrawal limit before you depart and ask whether you need a new PIN (see the "A PIN Alert" box, below).

Tips A PIN Alert

Make sure the PINs on your bankcards and credit cards will work in Paris. You usually need a four-digit code. (Six digits often won't work.) Also, keep in mind that you're usually able to access only your checking—not your savings—account from ATMs abroad.

CREDIT CARDS

Credit cards are invaluable when traveling. They're a safe way to carry money, they provide a convenient record of all your expenses, and you can withdraw cash advances from your credit cards at any bank (though you'll start paying hefty interest on the advance the moment you receive the cash—and you won't receive frequent-flyer miles on an airline credit card). At most banks, you don't even need to go to a teller; you can get a cash advance at the ATM with your PIN. (See the "A PIN Alert" box, above.)

Almost every credit-card company has an emergency toll-free number that you can call if your wallet or purse is stolen. The company may be able to wire you a cash advance off your credit card immediately and, in many places, can deliver an emergency card in a day or two. The issuing bank's toll-free number is usually on the back of the credit card—though that doesn't help you if the card is stolen. Citicorp Visa's U.S. emergency number is © **800/336-8472** or 410/581-3836. American Express cardholders and traveler's check holders should call © **800/233-5439** for all money emergencies. MasterCard holders should call © **800/307-7309.**

TRAVELER'S CHECKS

These days, traveler's checks seem less necessary than they used to because most cities have 24-hour ATMs that allow you to withdraw small amounts of cash as needed. Many banks, however, impose a fee every time a card is used at an ATM in a different city or bank. If you're withdrawing money every day, you may be better off with traveler's checks—provided you don't mind showing ID every time you want to cash a check.

American Express (© **800/221-7282;** www.americanexpress. com) is one of the largest issuers, and its checks are the most commonly accepted. It'll also sell checks to holders of certain types of American Express cards at no commission. **Thomas Cook** (© **800/ 223-7373** in the U.S. and Canada, 0800/622-101 in the U.K., or

44-1733/294-451 collect from other parts of the world; www.thomascook.com) issues MasterCard traveler's checks. **Citicorp** (© **800/645-6556** in the U.S. and Canada or 813/623-1709 collect from anywhere else in the world; www.citicorp.com) and many other banks issue checks under their own name or under MasterCard or Visa.

4 When to Go

In August, Parisians traditionally leave town for their annual holiday and put the city on a skeleton staff to serve visitors. July has also become a popular vacation month, with many a restaurateur shuttering up for a month-long respite.

Hotels, especially first-class and deluxe, are easy to come by in July and August. Budget hotels, on the other hand, are likely to be full during these months of student invasion. You might also try to avoid the first 2 weeks in October, when the annual auto show attracts thousands of enthusiasts.

THE WEATHER: APRIL IN PARIS?

Balmy weather in Paris has prompted more popular songs and love ballads than weather conditions in any other city. But the weather here is actually quite fickle. Rain is much more common than snow throughout the winter, prompting many longtime residents to complain about the occasional bone-chilling dampness.

In recent years, Paris has had only about 15 snow days a year, and there are only a few oppressively hot days (over 86°F) in midsummer. What will most likely chill a Parisian heart, however, are blasts of rapidly moving air—wind tunnels sweep along the city's long boulevards, channeled by bordering buildings of uniform height. Other than the occasional winds and rain (which add an undeniable drama to many of the city's panoramas), Paris offers some of the most pleasant weather of any capital in Europe, with a highly tolerable average temperature of 53°F.

HOLIDAYS

Holidays in France are known as *jours feriés*. Shops and banks are closed, as well as many (but not all) restaurants and museums. Major holidays include January 1, Easter, Ascension Day (40 days after Easter), Pentecost (seventh Sunday after Easter), May 1, May 8 (VE Day), July 14 (Bastille Day), August 15 (Assumption of the Virgin Mary), November 1 (All Saints' Day), November 11 (Armistice Day), and December 25 (Christmas).

5 Getting There

BY PLANE FROM NORTH AMERICA
THE MAJOR AIRLINES

One of the best choices for travelers in the southeastern United States and the Midwest is **Delta Airlines** (© **800/241-4141;** www.delta.com). From cities like New Orleans; Phoenix; Columbia, S.C.; and Nashville, Delta flies to Atlanta, connecting every evening with a nonstop flight to Paris. Delta also operates daily nonstop flights to Paris from Cincinnati and New York.

Another excellent choice is **United Airlines** (© **800/538-2929;** www.ual.com), with nonstop flights from Chicago; Washington, D.C.; and San Francisco to Paris. United also offers discounted fares in the low and shoulder seasons to London from five major North American hubs. From London, it's an easy train and hovercraft or Chunnel connection to Paris, a fact that tempts many passengers to spend a weekend in London either before or after their visit to Paris.

Another good option is **Continental Airlines** (© **800/ 231-0856;** www.flycontinental.com), serving the Northeast and much of the Southwest through its busy hubs in Newark and Houston. From both of those cities, Continental provides nonstop flights to Paris.

TWA (© **800/221-2000;** www.twa.com), operates daily nonstop service to Paris from New York and, in summer, several flights a week from Boston and Washington, D.C. In summer, TWA also flies to Paris from St. Louis several times a week, nonstop, and from Los Angeles three times a week, with connections in St. Louis or New York. In winter, flights from Los Angeles and Washington, D.C. are suspended and flights from St. Louis are routed with brief touchdowns en route to Paris in New York or Boston.

The French flag carrier, **Air France** (© **800/237-2747;** www.airfrance.com), offers daily or several-times-a-week flights to Paris from Newark; Washington, D.C.; Miami; Chicago; New York; Houston; San Francisco; Los Angeles; Boston; Cincinnati; Atlanta; Montréal; Toronto; and Mexico City.

American Airlines (© **800/433-7300;** www.aa.com), provides daily nonstop flights to Paris from Dallas/Fort Worth, Chicago, Miami, Boston, and New York. American Airlines now flies into Charles de Gaulle (Roissy) instead of Orly Airport. Facilities at its new terminal 2A include a deluxe Admirals Club, plus a mammoth Arrivals Lounge complete with 10 showers. And **US Airways**

(© **800/428-4322;** www.usairways.com) offers daily nonstop service from Philadelphia to Paris.

Canadians usually choose **Air Canada** (© **888/247-2262** from the U.S. and Canada; www.aircanada.ca) for flights to Paris from Toronto and Montréal. Nonstop flights from Montréal and Toronto depart every evening. Two of the nonstop flights from Toronto are shared with Air France and feature Air France aircraft.

PARIS AIRPORTS

Paris has two major international airports: **Orly** (© **01-49-75-15-15**), 14 kilometers (8½ miles) south of the city, and **Charles de Gaulle (Roissy)** (© **01-48-62-22-80**), 23 kilometers (14¼ miles) northeast. An 80F (12.15€, $11.60) Air France shuttle operates between the two airports about every 30 minutes, taking 50 to 75 minutes.

CHARLES DE GAULLE (ROISSY) AIRPORT   At Charles de Gaulle, foreign carriers use Aérogare 1 and Air France uses Aérogare 2. From Aérogare 1, you take a moving walkway to the passport checkpoint and the Customs area. The two terminals are linked by a **shuttle bus** (*navette*).

The free shuttle bus connecting Aérogare 1 with Aérogare 2 also transports passengers to the Roissy rail station, from which fast **RER trains** leave every 15 minutes for such Métro stations as Gare du Nord, Châtelet, Luxembourg, Port Royal, and Denfert-Rochereau. The train fare from Roissy to any point in central Paris is 69F (10.50€, $10) in first class or 49F (7.45€, $7.10) in second. You can also take an **Air France shuttle bus** to central Paris for 75F (11.40€, $10.90). It stops at the Palais des Congrès (Porte Maillot), then continues on to place Charles de Gaulle–Etoile, where underground lines can carry you farther along to any other point. Depending on traffic, the ride takes between 45 and 55 minutes. The shuttle departs about every 12 minutes from 5:40am to 11pm.

Another option, the **Roissybus** (© **01-48-04-18-24**), departs from a point near the corner of the rue Scribe and place de l'Opéra every 15 minutes from 5:45am to 11pm. The cost for the 50-minute ride is 48F (7.30€, $6.95).

Taxis from Roissy into the city run about 350F (53.20€, $50.75) on the meter. At night (8pm–7am), fares are about 40% higher. Long queues of both taxis and passengers form outside each of the airport's terminals in a surprisingly orderly fashion.

Tips **The New Airport Shuttle**

Cheaper than a taxi for one or two people but more expensive than airport buses and trains, the new **Airport Shuttle,** 2 av. Général-Leclerc, 14th arr. (© **01-43-21-06-78;** fax 01-43-21-35-67; www.paris-anglo.com/clients/ashuttle.html), will pick you up in a minivan at Charles de Gaulle or Orly and take you to your hotel for 120F (18.25€, $17.40) for one person or 89F (13.55€, $12.90) per person for parties of two or more. It'll take you out to the airports from your hotel for the same price. The **Paris Airport Service,** BP 41, CEDEX 94431 Chennevières (© **01-49-62-78-78;** fax 01-49-62-78-79), offers a similar service costing 145F (22.05€, $21.05) for one person or 180F (27.35€, $26.10) for two or more persons from Charles de Gaulle, and 115F (17.50€, $16.70) for one person or 135F (20.50€, $19.60) for two or more persons from Orly. Both companies accept Visa and MasterCard, with 1-day advance reservations required.

ORLY AIRPORT   Orly has two terminals: Orly Sud (south) for international flights and Orly Ouest (west) for domestic flights. A free shuttle bus links them together.

Air France buses leave from exit E of Orly Ouest and from exit F, Platform 5 of Orly Sud every 12 minutes from 5:45am to 11pm, heading for Gare des Invalides in central Paris at a cost of 45F (6.85€, $6.55) one-way. Other buses depart for place Denfert-Rochereau in the south of Paris at a cost of 35F (5.30€, $5.10).

An alternative method for reaching central Paris involves taking a free shuttle bus that leaves both of Orly's terminals at intervals of about every 15 minutes for the nearby **RER train station** (Pont de Rungis/Aéroport d'Orly), from which RER trains take 30 minutes to reach the city center. A trip to Les Invalides, for example, costs 47F (7.15€, $6.80).

A **taxi** from Orly to the center of Paris costs about 200F (30.40€, $29) and is higher at night and on weekends. Returning to the airport, **buses** to Orly leave from the Invalides terminal to either Orly Sud or Orly Ouest every 15 minutes, taking about 30 minutes.

Caution: Don't take a meterless taxi from Orly Sud or Orly Ouest—it's much safer (and usually cheaper) to hire a metered cab from the taxi queues, which are under the scrutiny of a police officer.

BY TRAIN FROM EUROPE

If you're already in Europe, you might decide to travel to Paris by train, especially if you have a Eurailpass. For example, a one-way first-class fare between Paris and London is $279 ($199 in second). Rail passes or individual rail tickets within Europe are available at most travel agencies, at any office of **Rail Europe** (© 800/848-7245 in the U.S., 800/361-RAIL in Canada; www.raileurope.com), or at **Eurostar** (© 800/EUROSTAR in the U.S., 0990/300-003 in London, 01-44-51-06-02 in Paris; www.eurostar.com).

There are six major train stations in Paris: **Gare d'Austerlitz,** 55 quai d'Austerlitz, 13th arr. (serving the southwest, with trains from the Loire Valley, the Bordeaux country, and the Pyrénées); **Gare de l'Est,** place du 11 Novembre 1918, 10th arr. (serving the east, with trains from Strasbourg, Nancy, Reims, and beyond to Zurich, Basel, Luxembourg, and Austria); **Gare de Lyon,** 20 bd. Diderot, 12th arr. (serving the southeast with trains from the Côte d'Azur, Provence, and beyond to Geneva, Lausanne, and Italy); **Gare Montparnasse,** 17 bd. Vaugirard, 15th arr. (serving the west, with trains from Brittany); **Gare du Nord,** 18 rue de Dunkerque, 15th arr. (serving the north, with trains from Holland, Denmark, Belgium, and northern Germany); and **Gare St-Lazare,** 13 rue d'Amsterdam, 8th arr. (serving the northwest, with trains from Normandy).

For general train information and to make reservations, call © 08-36-35-35-35 daily from 7am to 8pm. Buses operate between rail stations. Each of these stations has a Métro stop, making the whole city easily accessible. Taxis are also available at designated stands at every station. Look for the sign that says TÊTE DE STATION. Be alert in train stations, especially at night.

BY TRAIN UNDER THE CHANNEL

One of the great engineering feats of our time, the $15-billion Channel Tunnel (Chunnel) opened in 1994, and the **Eurostar Express** now has daily service from London to both Paris and Brussels. The 31-mile journey takes 35 minutes, though the actual time spent in the Chunnel is only 19 minutes. Duty-free stores, restaurants, service stations, and bilingual staffs are available to travelers on both sides of the Channel.

Eurostar tickets are available through **Rail Europe** (© 800/4-EURAIL; www.raileurope.com). In Great Britain, make reservations for Eurostar at © 0345/484950; in the United States, call © 800/EUROSTAR. Chunnel train traffic is roughly competitive with air travel, if you calculate door-to-door travel time. Trains leave from London's Waterloo Station and arrive in Paris at the Gare du Nord.

The tunnel also accommodates passenger cars, charter buses, taxis, and motorcycles, transporting them under the Channel from Folkestone, England, to Calais, France. It operates 24 hours a day, running every 15 minutes during peak travel times and at least once an hour at night. You can buy tickets at the tollbooth at the tunnel's entrance. With **Le Shuttle** (© **0990/353-535;** www.eurodrive.co. uk), gone are the days of weather-related delays, seasickness, and advance reservations.

Before boarding Le Shuttle, motorists stop at a tollbooth and pass through British and French immigration services at the same time. They then drive onto a half-mile-long train and travel through the tunnel. During the ride, motorists stay in bright air-conditioned carriages, remaining inside their cars or stepping outside to stretch their legs. When the trip is completed, they simply drive off. Total travel time is about an hour. Once on French soil, British drivers must remember to drive on the right-hand side of the road.

BY FERRY FROM ENGLAND
Despite competition from the Chunnel, services aboard ferries and hydrofoils operate day and night in all seasons, with the exception of last-minute cancellations during fierce storms. Many channel crossings are carefully timed to coincide with the arrival/departure of major trains (especially those between London and Paris); trains let you off a short walk from the piers. Most ferries carry cars, trucks, and massive amounts of freight, but some hydrofoils take passengers only. The major routes include at least 12 trips a day between Dover or Folkestone and Calais or Boulogne. Hovercraft and hydrofoils make the trip from Dover to Calais, the shortest distance across the Channel, in just 40 minutes during good weather; the slower-moving ferries might take several hours, depending on weather conditions and tides. If you're bringing a car, it's important to make reservations, as space below decks is usually crowded. Timetables can vary depending on weather conditions and many other factors.

The leading operator of ferries across the Channel is **P&O Stena Lines.** (Call BritRail for reservations at © **800/677-8585** in North America or 087/0600-0600 in England.) It operates car and passenger ferries between Portsmouth, England, and Cherbourg, France (three departures a day; 4¼ hr. each way during daylight hours, 7 hr.

each way at night); between Portsmouth and Le Havre, France (three a day; 5½ hr. each way). Most popular are the routes it operates between Dover and Calais, France (25 sailings a day; 75 min. each way), costing £25 ($37.50) one-way adults or £12 ($18) children.

The shortest and by far the most popular route is between Calais and Dover. **Hoverspeed** operates at least 12 hovercraft crossings daily; the trip takes 35 minutes. It also runs a SeaCat (a catamaran propelled by jet engines) that takes slightly longer to make the crossing between Boulogne and Folkestone; the SeaCats depart about four times a day on the 55-minute voyage. For reservations and information, call Hoverspeed (© **800/677-8585** for reservations in North America or 0870/5240241 in England). Typical one-way fares are £25 ($37.50) per person.

If you plan to transport a rental car between England and France, check in advance with the rental company about license and insurance requirements and additional drop-off charges. And be aware that many car-rental companies, for insurance reasons, forbid transport of one of their vehicles over the water between England and France. Transport of a car each way begins at £109 ($113.50).

BY PACKAGE TOUR FROM NORTH AMERICA

If you're interested in a package deal (which includes airfare plus hotel room), the best place to start your search is the travel section of your local Sunday newspaper. Also check the ads in the back of national travel magazines such as *Travel & Leisure, National Geographic Traveler,* and *Condé Nast Traveler.*

Liberty Travel (© **888/271-1584** to be connected with the agent closest to you; www.libertytravel.com), one of the biggest packagers in the Northeast, often runs a full-page ad in the Sunday papers. **American Express Travel** (© **800/446-6234;** www.americanexpress.com) is another option. Check out its **Last Minute Travel Bargains** site, offered in conjunction with **Continental Airlines** (www.americanexpress.com), with deeply discounted vacation packages and reduced airline fares that differ from the E-savers bargains Continental e-mails weekly to subscribers. **Northwest Airlines** (www.nwa.com) offers a similar service. Posted on Northwest's website every Wednesday, its **Cyber Saver Bargain Alerts** offer special hotel rates, package deals, and discounted airline fares.

Another good resource is the airlines themselves, which often package their flights together with accommodations. Among the airline packagers, your options are **American Airlines Vacations** (© **800/321-2121;** www.aavacations.com), **Delta Vacations**

(© **800/872-7786;** www.deltavacations.com), and **US Airways Vacations** (© **800/455-0123;** www.usairwaysvacations.com). Delta Dream Vacations offers a full package called Jolie France, lasting 10 nights and costing $3,850 to $4,280 for two, taking in not only Paris but also some of France's regional highlights, like Tours, Bordeaux, Carcassonne, Nice, Nîmes, and Dijon. All hotels, tours, and breakfasts are included, plus four dinners.

The **French Experience,** 370 Lexington Ave., Room 812, New York, NY 10017 (© **212/986-1115;** fax 212/986-3808; www.frenchexperience.com), offers inexpensive tickets to Paris on most scheduled airlines and arranges tours and stays in various types and categories of country inns, hotels, private châteaux, and B&Bs. In addition, it takes reservations for about 30 small hotels in Paris and arranges short-term apartment rentals in the city or farmhouse rentals in the countryside and offers all-inclusive packages in Paris as well as prearranged package tours of various regions of France. Any tour can be adapted to suit individual needs.

2

Getting to Know Paris

Ernest Hemingway called the many splendors of Paris a "moveable feast" and wrote, "There is never any ending to Paris, and the memory of each person who has lived in it differs from that of any other." It's this aura of personal discovery that has always been the most compelling reason to come to Paris. And perhaps that's why France has been called *le deuxième pays de tout le monde*—"everybody's second country."

The Seine not only divides Paris into the Right Bank and the Left Bank but also seems to split the city into two vastly different sections and ways of life. Depending on your time, interest, and budget, you may quickly decide which section of Paris suits you best.

1 Essentials

VISITOR INFORMATION

At the airports are small **info offices,** which, for a fee, will help you make a hotel reservation. But the prime source is the **Office de Tourisme de Paris,** 127 av. des Champs-Elysées, 8th arr. (© 08-36-68-31-12; fax 01-49-52-53-00; www.paris-touristoffice.com; Métro: Charles de Gaulle–Etoile or George V), where you can obtain info about both Paris and the provinces. It's open April to October daily from 9am to 8pm. November to March hours are Monday to Saturday from 9am to 8pm, Sunday from 11am to 7pm. The staff will make an accommodations reservation for you on the same day you want a room: 8F (1.20€, $1.15) for hostels and *foyers* ("homes"), 20F (3.05€, $2.90) for one-star hotels, 25F (3.80€, $3.65) for two-star hotels, and 40F (6.10€, $5.80) for three-star hotels. (Stars refer to government ratings, rather than those used in this book.) It's often very busy in summer, so you'll probably have to wait in line.

There is a tourist office, **Bureau Gare de Lyon,** at the major rail terminus, Gare de Lyon, 12th arr. (© 0143-43-33-24), serving rail passengers arriving by train. It is open Monday to Saturday from 8am to 8pm. Métro: Gare de Lyon.

Paris at a Glance

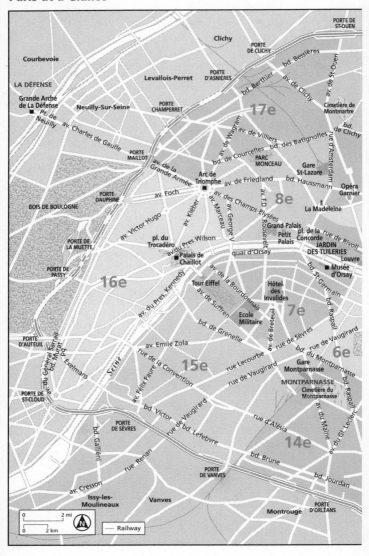

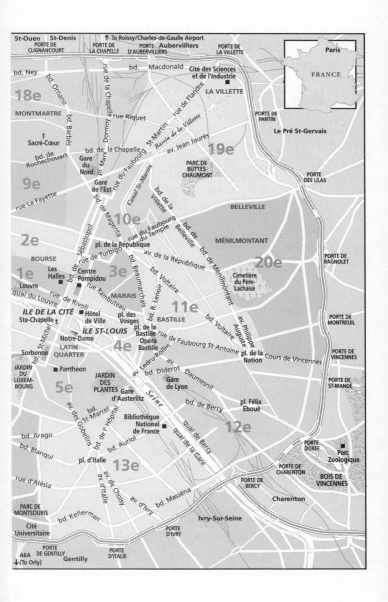

Tips **Country & City Telephone Codes**

The country code for France is 33. The city code for Paris (as well as for all cities in the Ile-de-France region) is 1; use this code if you're calling from outside France. If you're calling Paris from within Paris or from anywhere else in France, use 01, which is now built into all phone numbers in the Ile-de-France, making them 10 digits long.

There are **other branches** in the base of the Eiffel Tower (open May–Sept, daily 11am–6pm) and in the arrivals hall of the Gare de Lyon (open year-round Mon–Sat 8am–8pm). All these offices will give you free copies of the English-language *Time Out* and *Paris User's Guide.*

CITY LAYOUT

Paris is surprisingly compact. Occupying 1,119 square kilometers (432 sq. miles), it's home to more than 10 million people. The city is divided into 20 municipal wards called *arrondissements,* each with its own mayor, city hall, police station, and central post office. Some even have remnants of market squares.

The river Seine divides Paris into the **Right Bank** (Rive Droite) to the north and the **Left Bank** (Rive Gauche) to the south. These designations make sense when you stand on a bridge and face downstream; watching the water flow out toward the sea, to your right is the north bank, to your left the south. Thirty-two bridges link the banks of the Seine, some providing access to the two small islands at the heart of the city: **Ile de la Cité,** the city's birthplace and site of Notre-Dame, and **Ile St-Louis,** a moat-guarded oasis of sober 17th-century mansions. These islands can cause some confusion to walkers who think they've just crossed a bridge from one bank to the other, only to find themselves caught up in an almost medieval maze of narrow streets and old buildings.

As part of Napoléon III's massive urban redevelopment project, Baron Georges-Eugène Haussmann forever changed the look of Paris between 1860 and 1870 by creating the **legendary boulevards:** St-Michel, St-Germain, Haussmann, Malesherbes, Sébastopol, Magenta, Voltaire, and Strasbourg.

The "main street" on the Right Bank is, of course, the **Champs-Elysées,** beginning at the Arc de Triomphe and running to place de la Concorde. Haussmann also created avenue de l'Opéra (as well as the Opéra) and the 12 avenues that radiate star-like from the Arc de Triomphe and inspired the intersection's original name: place de l'Etoile (*étoile* means "star"). The intersection was renamed place Charles de Gaulle following the general's death and is often referred to as **place Charles de Gaulle–Etoile.**

Haussmann also cleared Ile de la Cité of its medieval buildings, transforming it into a showcase for Notre-Dame. Finally, he laid out the two elegant parks on the western and southeastern fringes of the city: the **Bois de Boulogne** and the **Bois de Vincennes.**

THE ARRONDISSEMENTS IN BRIEF

Each of Paris's 20 arrondissements possesses a unique style and flavor. You'll want to decide which district appeals most to you and then try to find accommodations there. Later on, try to visit as many areas as you can so you get the full taste of Paris.

1ST ARRONDISEMENT (MUSÉE DU LOUVRE/ LES HALLES) "I never knew what a palace was until I had a glimpse of the Louvre," wrote Nathaniel Hawthorne. Perhaps the world's greatest art museum, the **Louvre,** a former royal residence, still lures all visitors to Paris to the 1st arrondissement. Walk through the **Jardin des Tuileries,** Paris's most formal garden (originally laid out by Le Nôtre, gardener to Louis XIV). Pause to take in the classic beauty of **place Vendôme,** the opulent home of the Hôtel Ritz. Zola's "belly of Paris" (Les Halles) is no longer the food-and-meat market of Paris (traders moved to the new, more accessible suburb of Rungis); today the **Forum des Halles** is a center of shopping, entertainment, and culture.

2ND ARRONDISEMENT (LA BOURSE) Home to the **Bourse** (stock exchange), this Right Bank district lies mainly between the Grands Boulevards and rue Etienne-Marcel. Monday to Friday, brokers play the market until it's time to break for lunch, when the movers and shakers of French capitalism channel their hysteria into the area restaurants. Much of the eastern end of the arrondissement (**Le Sentier**) is devoted to wholesale outlets of the Paris garment district, where thousands of garments are sold (usually in bulk) to buyers from clothing stores throughout Europe. "Everything that exists elsewhere exists in Paris," wrote Victor Hugo in *Les Misérables,* and this district provides ample evidence of that.

3RD ARRONDISEMENT (LE MARAIS) This district embraces much of *Le Marais* ("The Swamp"), one of the best loved of the old Right Bank neighborhoods. (It extends into the 4th as well.) After decades of seedy decay, Le Marais recently made a come-back, though it may never again enjoy the prosperity of its 17th-century aristocratic heyday; today it contains Paris's **gay neighborhood,** with lots of gay/lesbian restaurants, bars, and stores, as well as the remains of the old Jewish quarter, centered on **rue des Rosiers.** Two of the district's chief attractions are the **Musée Picasso,** a kind of pirate's ransom of painting and sculpture the Picasso estate had to turn over to the French government in lieu of the artist's astronomical death duties, and the **Musée Carnavalet,** which brings to life the history of Paris from prehistoric times to the present.

4TH ARRONDISEMENT (ILE DE LA CITÉ/ILE ST-LOUIS & BEAUBOURG) At times it seems as if the 4th has it all: not only Notre-Dame on Ile de la Cité, but Ile St-Louis and its aristo-cratic town houses, courtyards, and antiques shops. **Ile St-Louis,** a former cow pasture and dueling ground, is home to dozens of 17th-century mansions and 6,000 lucky Louisiens, its permanent residents. Seek out **Ile de la Cité's** two glorious Gothic churches, **Sainte-Chapelle** and **Notre-Dame**—the latter a majestic structure that, according to poet E. E. Cummings, doesn't budge an inch for all the idiocies of this world. You'll find France's finest bird and flower markets along with the nation's law courts, which Balzac described as a "cathedral of chicanery." It was here that Marie Antoinette was sentenced to death in 1793. The 4th is also home to the freshly renovated **Centre Pompidou,** one of the top three attractions in France. After all this pomp and glory, you can retreat to **place des Vosges,** a square of perfect harmony and beauty where Victor Hugo lived from 1832 to 1848 and penned many of his famous masterpieces.

5TH ARRONDISEMENT (LATIN QUARTER) The Quartier Latin is the intellectual heart and soul of Paris. Bookstores, schools, churches, smoky jazz clubs, student dives, Roman ruins, publishing houses, and expensive and chic boutiques characterize the district. Discussions of Artaud or Molière over long cups of coffee may be more rare today than in the past, but they aren't at all out of place here. Beginning with the founding of the **Sorbonne** in 1253, the quarter was called Latin because all students and professors spoke the scholarly language. You'll follow in the footsteps of Descartes, Verlaine, Camus, Sartre, James Thurber, Elliot Paul, and Hemingway as you explore this historic area. Changing times have brought Greek, Moroccan, and Vietnamese immigrants, among others, hustling everything from couscous to fiery-hot spring rolls and souvlaki. The 5th borders the Seine, and you'll want to stroll along quai de Montebello, inspecting the inventories of the *bouquinistes,* who sell everything from antique Daumier prints to yellowing copies of Balzac's *Père Goriot* in the shadow of Notre-Dame. The 5th also has the **Panthéon,** built by a grateful Louis XV after he recovered from the gout and wanted to do something nice for Ste-Geneviève, Paris's patron saint. It's the resting place of Rousseau, Gambetta, Zola, Braille, Hugo, Voltaire, and Jean Moulin, the World War II Resistance leader whom the Gestapo tortured to death.

6TH ARRONDISEMENT (ST-GERMAIN/LUXEMBOURG)

This is the heartland of Paris publishing and, for some, the most colorful Left Bank quarter, where waves of earnest young artists still emerge from the famous Ecole des Beaux-Arts. The secret of the district lies in discovering its narrow streets, hidden squares, and magnificent gardens. To be really authentic, stroll with an unwrapped loaf of sourdough bread from the wood-fired ovens of **Poilâne** at 8 rue du Cherche-Midi. Everywhere you turn in the area, you'll encounter famous historic and literary associations, none more so than on **rue Jacob.** At no. 7, Racine lived with his uncle as a teenager; Richard Wagner resided at no. 14 from 1841 to 1842; Ingres once lived at no. 27 (now it's the office of the French publishing house Editions du Seuil); and Hemingway once occupied a tiny upstairs room at no. 44. The 6th takes in the **Jardin du Luxembourg,** a 60-acre playground where Isadora Duncan went dancing in the predawn hours and a destitute Ernest Hemingway went looking for pigeons for lunch, carrying them in a baby carriage back to his humble flat for cooking.

7TH ARRONDISEMENT (EIFFEL TOWER/ MUSÉE D'ORSAY)

Paris's most famous symbol, the **Eiffel Tower,** dominates Paris and especially the 7th, a Left Bank district of respectable residences and government offices. The tower is now one of the most recognizable landmarks in the world, despite the fact that many Parisians (especially its nearest neighbors) hated it when it was unveiled in 1889. Many of Paris's most imposing monuments are in the 7th, like the **Hôtel des Invalides,** which contains Napoléon's Tomb and the Musée de l'Armée, and the **Musée d'Orsay,** the world's premier showcase of 19th-century French art and culture, housed in the old Gare d'Orsay. But there's much hidden charm here as well. **Rue du Bac** was home to the swashbuckling heroes of Dumas's *The Three Musketeers* and to James McNeill Whistler, who moved to no. 110 after selling *Mother*. Auguste Rodin lived at what's now the **Musée Rodin,** 77 rue de Varenne, until his death in 1917.

8TH ARRONDISEMENT (CHAMPS-ELYSÉES/MADELEINE)   The prime showcase of the 8th is the **Champs-Elysées,** stretching grandly from the **Arc de Triomphe** to the purloined Egyptian obelisk on **place de la Concorde.** By the 1980s, the Champs-Elysées had become a garish strip, with too much traffic, too many fast-food joints, and too many panhandlers. In the 1990s, Jacques Chirac, then the Gaullist mayor, launched a massive cleanup, broadening the sidewalks and planting new rows of trees. Now you'll find fashion houses, elegant hotels, and expensive restaurants and shops. Everything in the 8th is the city's "best, grandest, and most impressive": It has the best restaurant (**Taillevent**); the sexiest strip joint (**Crazy Horse Saloon**); the most splendid square (**place de la Concorde**); the grandest hotel (**Hôtel de Crillon**); the most impressive triumphal arch (**Arc de Triomphe**); the most expensive residential street (**av. Montaigne**); the world's oldest subway station (**Franklin D. Roosevelt**); and the most ancient monument (the 3,300-year-old **Obelisk of Luxor**).

9TH ARRONDISEMENT (OPÉRA GARNIER/PIGALLE)
From the Quartier de l'Opéra to the strip joints of Pigalle (the infamous "Pig Alley" for World War II GIs), the 9th endures, even if fickle fashion prefers other addresses. Over the decades, the 9th has been celebrated in literature and song for the music halls that brought gaiety to the city. No. 17 bd. de la Madeleine was the death site of Marie Duplessis, who gained fame as the heroine Marguerite Gautier in Alexandre Dumas the younger's *La Dame aux camélias*. (Greta Garbo later redoubled Marie's legend by playing her in the film *Camille*.) At **place Pigalle,** gone is the cafe La Nouvelle Athènes, where Degas, Pissarro, and Manet used to meet. Today, you're more likely to encounter nightclubs in the area. Other major attractions include the **Folies Bergère,** where cancan dancers have been high-kicking it since 1868. More than anything, it was the rococo **Opéra Garnier** (home of the notorious Phantom) that made the 9th the last hurrah of Second Empire opulence. Renoir hated it, but several generations later, Chagall did the ceilings. Pavlova danced *Swan Lake* here, and Nijinsky took the night off to go cruising.

10TH ARRONDISEMENT (GARE DU NORD/GARE DE L'EST)   The **Gare du Nord** and **Gare de l'Est,** along with porno houses and dreary commercial zones, make the 10th one of the least desirable arrondissements for living, dining, or sightseeing. We always try to avoid it, except for one of our longtime favorite restaurants (see p. 81): **Brasserie Flo,** 7 cour des Petites-Ecuries, best known for its formidable choucroute, a heap of sauerkraut garnished with everything.

11TH ARRONDISEMENT (OPÉRA BASTILLE) The 1989 opening of the **Opéra Bastille** revitalized this previously rundown neighborhood. The facility, called the "people's opera house," stands on the landmark place de la Bastille, where on July 14, 1789, 633 Parisians stormed the fortress and seized the ammunition depot, as the French Revolution swept across the city. Over the years, the prison held Voltaire, the Marquis de Sade, and the mysterious "Man in the Iron Mask." The area sandwiched between the Marais, Ménilmontant, and République is now being called "blue-collar chic," as the *artistes* of Paris have been driven from the costlier sections of the Marais and can now be found walking the gritty sidewalks of rue Oberkamf. Hip Parisians in search of a more cutting-edge experience are now found living and working among the decaying 19th-century apartments and the 1960s public housing with graffiti-splattered walls.

12TH ARRONDISEMENT (BOIS DE VINCENNES/ GARE DE LYON) Very few out-of-towners came here until a French chef opened a restaurant called **Au Trou Gascon** (see p. 82). The 12th's major attraction remains the **Bois de Vincennes,** sprawling on the eastern periphery of Paris. This park has been a longtime favorite of French families, who enjoy its zoos and museums, its royal château and boating lakes, and most definitely its **Parc Floral de Paris,** a celebrated flower garden boasting springtime rhododendrons and autumn dahlias. The 12th, once a depressing urban wasteland, has been singled out for budgetary resuscitation and is beginning to sport new housing, shops, gardens, and restaurants. Many of these will occupy the site of the former Reuilly rail tracks.

13TH ARRONDISEMENT (GARE D'AUSTERLITZ) Centered around the grimy **Gare d'Austerlitz,** the 13th might have its devotees, but we've yet to meet one. British snobs who flitted in and out of the train station were among the first of the district's foreign visitors and in essence wrote the 13th off as a dreary working-class counterpart of London's East End. The 13th is also home to Paris's **Chinatown,** stretching for 13 square blocks around the Tolbiac Métro stop. It emerged out of the refugee crisis at the end of the Vietnam War, taking over a neighborhood that had held mostly Arab-speaking peoples. Today, recognizing the overcrowding that's now endemic in the district, the Paris civic authorities are imposing new, and not particularly welcome, restrictions on population densities.

14TH ARRONDISEMENT (MONTPARNASSE)   The northern end of this large arrondissement is devoted to **Montparnasse,** home of the "lost generation" and former stamping ground of Stein, Toklas, Hemingway, and other American expats of the 1920s. After World War II, it ceased to be the center of intellectual life, but the memory lingers in its cafes. One of the monuments that sets the tone of the neighborhood is **Rodin's statue of Balzac** at the junction of boulevard Montparnasse and boulevard Raspail. At this corner are some of the world's most famous **literary cafes,** including **La Coupole** (see p. 104). Though Gertrude Stein avoided them (she loathed cafes), all the other American expatriates, including Hemingway and Fitzgerald, had no qualms about enjoying a drink here (or quite a few of them, for that matter). Stein stayed at home (27 rue de Fleurus) with Alice B. Toklas, collecting paintings, including those of Picasso, and entertaining the likes of Max Jacob, Apollinaire, T. S. Eliot, and Matisse.

15TH ARRONDISEMENT (GARE MONTPARNASSE/ INSTITUT PASTEUR)   A mostly residential district beginning at **Gare Montparnasse,** the 15th stretches all the way to the Seine. In size and population, it's the largest quarter of Paris but attracts few tourists and has few attractions. In the early 20th century, many artists—like Chagall, Léger, and Modigliani—lived in this arrondissement in a shared atelier known as "The Beehive."

16TH ARRONDISEMENT (TROCADERO/BOIS DE BOULOGNE)   Originally the village of Passy, where Benjamin Franklin lived during most of his time in Paris, this district is still reminiscent of Proust's world. One of the largest of the city's arrondissements, it's known today for its well-heeled bourgeoisie, its upscale rents, and some rather posh (and, according to its critics, rather smug) residential boulevards. The arrondissement also has the best vantage of the Eiffel Tower, **place du Trocadéro.**

17TH ARRONDISEMENT (PARC MONCEAU/ PLACE CLICHY)   Flanking the northern periphery of Paris, the 17th incorporates neighborhoods of conservative bourgeois respectability (in its western end) and less affluent neighborhoods (in its eastern end).

18TH ARRONDISEMENT (MONTMARTRE)   The 18th is the most famous outer quarter of Paris, containing **Montmartre,**

the **Moulin Rouge, Sacré-Coeur,** and ultratouristy **place du Tertre.** Utrillo was its native son, Renoir lived here, and Toulouse-Lautrec adopted the area as his own. Today, place Blanche is known for its prostitutes, and Montmartre is filled with honky-tonks, too many souvenir shops, and terrible restaurants. You can still find pockets of quiet beauty, though.

19TH ARRONDISEMENT (LA VILLETTE) Today, visitors come to what was once the village of La Villette to see the much-publicized angular **Cité des Sciences et de l'Industrie,** a spectacular science museum and park built on a site that for years was devoted to the city's slaughterhouses. Mostly residential, and not at all upscale, the district is one of the most ethnically diverse in Paris, home to people from all parts of the former Empire.

20TH ARRONDISEMENT (PÈRE-LACHAISE CEMETERY) The 20th's greatest landmark is **Père-Lachaise Cemetery,** the resting place of Jim Morrison, Edith Piaf, Marcel Proust, Oscar Wilde, Isadora Duncan, Sarah Bernhardt, Gertrude Stein and Alice B. Toklas, Colette, and many, many others. Otherwise, the 20th arrondissement is a dreary and sometimes volatile melting pot comprising residents from France's former colonies. Though nostalgia buffs sometimes head here to visit Piaf's former neighborhood, **Ménilmontant-Belleville,** it has been almost totally bulldozed and rebuilt since the bad old days when she grew up here.

2 Getting Around

Paris is a city for strollers whose greatest joy in life is rambling through unexpected alleyways and squares. Only when you're dead tired and can't walk another step or have to go all the way across town in a hurry should you consider using the swift and dull means of urban transport.

For information on the city's public transportation, call ℂ **08-36-68-77-14.**

BY MÉTRO & RER

A century old, the **Paris Métro** will soon become one of the most modern and efficient in the world. At its centenary in the summer of 2000, the Métro announced a gigantic overhaul program that will refurbish some 200 of the system's nearly 300 stations by 2003. The **Métro** (ℂ **08-36-68-77-14)** is the easiest and most efficient way to get around Paris. Most stations display a map of the system at the entrance. Within Paris, you can transfer between the subway

Discount Passes

You can buy a **Paris Visite pass,** valid for 1, 2, 3, or 5 days on the public transport system, including the Métro, the city buses, the RER (regional express) trains within Paris city limits, and even the funicular to the top of Montmartre. (The RER has both first- and second-class compartments, and the pass lets you travel in first class.) The cost is 60F (9.10€, $8.70) for 1 day, 95F (14.45€, $13.83) for 2 days, 130F (19.75€, $18.85) for 3 days, or 185F (28.10€, $26.85) for 5 days. The card is available at the **Services Touristiques de la Régie Autonome des Transports Parisiens (RATP),** with offices at place de la Madeleine, 8th arr. (℡ **08-36-68-77-14** or 01-40-06-71-45; Métro: Madeleine; www.ratp.fr), and 54 quai de la Rapée, 12th arr. (℡ **01-44-68-20-20** or 08-36-63-77-14; Métro: Gare de Lyon); the tourist offices (see "Visitor Information" earlier in this chapter); or the main Métro stations.

Another more economical pass available to visitors is **Carte Mobilis,** allowing unlimited travel on all bus, Métro, and RER lines in Paris during a 1-day period for 32F to 74F (4.85€–11.25€, $4.65–$10.75), depending on the zone. You will need to provide a passport-size photo of yourself. You can buy the pass at any Métro station.

Most economical of all, for anyone who happens to arrive in Paris early (Mon, Tues, or even Wed) of any given week, is a **Carte Orange.** Sold at any large Métro station, it allows 1 full week of unlimited Métro or bus transit within central Paris (the 20 arr. and the nearby suburbs) for 85F (12.90€, $12.35). To get one, you'll have to submit a passport-size photo. They're valid from any Monday to the following Sunday, and they're sold only on Monday, Tuesday, or Wednesday of any given week.

and the RER regional trains for no additional cost. To make sure you catch the right train, find your destination, then visually follow the line it's on to the end of the route and note its name. This is the sign you look for in the stations and the name you'll see on the train. Transfer stations are known as *correspondances.* (Note that some require long walks—Châtelet–Les Halles is the most notorious.)

Few trips require more than one transfer. Some stations have maps with push-button indicators that help plot your route by lighting up when you press the button for your destination. A ride on the urban lines costs 8F (1.20€, $1.15) to any point within the 20 arrondissements of Paris, as well as to many of its near suburbs. A bulk purchase of 10 tickets (which are bound together into what the French refer to as a *carnet*) costs 58F (8.80€, $8.40). Métro fares to outlying suburbs on the Sceaux, the Noissy–St-Léger, and St-Germain-en-Laye lines cost more and are sold on an individual basis depending on the distance you travel. At the entrance to the Métro station, insert your ticket into the turnstile and pass through. Take the ticket back, because it may be checked by uniformed police officers when you leave the subway. There are also occasional ticket checks on the trains, platforms, and passageways. If you're changing trains, get out and determine which direction (final destination) on the next line you want, then follow the bright orange CORRESPON-DANCE signs until you reach the proper platform. Don't follow a SORTIE sign, which means "exit." If you exit, you'll have to pay another fare to resume your journey.

The Paris Métro runs daily from 5:30am to around 1:15am, at which time all underground trains reach their final terminus at the end of each of their respective lines. Be alert that the last train may pass through central Paris as much as an hour before that time. The subways are reasonably safe at any hour, but beware of pickpockets.

BY BUS

Bus travel is much slower than the subway. Most buses run from 7am to 8:30pm (a few operate to 12:30am, and 10 operate during the early-morning hours). Service is limited on Sundays and holidays. Bus and Métro fares are the same and you can use the same *carnet* tickets on both. At certain stops, signs list the destinations and numbers of the buses serving that point. Destinations are usually listed north to south and east to west. Most stops along the way are also posted on the sides of the buses. To catch a bus, wait in line at the bus stop. Signal the driver to stop the bus and board.

Most bus rides (including any that begin and end within Paris's 20 arr. and nearby suburbs) require one ticket (the same that's used within the Métro). For bus travel to some of the city's more distant suburbs, an additional ticket may be required. If you intend to use the buses a lot, pick up an **RATP bus map** at its offices on place de la Madeleine and quai de la Rapée (see the "Discount Passes" box, above) or at any tourist office. For details on bus and Métro routes, call ✆ **08-36-68-41-14.**

The same entity that maintains Paris's network of Métros and buses, the **RATP** (✆ **08-36-68-77-14**) has initiated a motorized mode of transport designed exclusively as a means of appreciating the city's visual grandeur. Known as the **Balabus,** it's a fleet of big-windowed orange-and-white motor coaches whose most visible drawback is their limited hours—they run only on Sunday and national holidays from noon to 9pm, from April 15 to October 30. The coaches journey in both directions between the Gare de Lyon and the Grande Arche de La Défense, encompassing some of the city's most monumental vistas and making regular stops. Presentation of two Métro tickets 16F (2.45€, $2.30), a valid Carte Mobilis, or a valid Paris Visite pass will carry you along the entire route (see the "Discount Passes" box, above, for Carte Mobilis and Paris Visite Pass). You'll recognize the bus and the route it follows by the "Bb" symbol emblazoned on each bus's side and on signs posted beside the route it follows.

BY TAXI

Taxi drivers are organized into an effective lobby to keep their number limited to around 15,000, and it's nearly impossible to get one at rush hour. You can hail regular cabs on the street when their signs read *libre.* Taxis are easier to find at the many stands near Métro stations.

The flag drops at 13F (2.03€, $1.94), and you pay 3.87F (.60€, 55¢) per kilometer. At night, expect to pay 6.32F (.95€, 90¢) per kilometer. On airport trips, you're not required to pay for the driver's empty return ride. You're allowed several small pieces of luggage free if they're transported inside and don't weigh more than 5 kilograms (11 lb.). Heavier suitcases carried in the trunk cost 6F (.90€, 85¢) apiece. Tip 12% to 15%—the latter usually elicits a *merci.* To radio cabs, call ✆ **01-44-52-23-86** or 01-44-52-23-58; you'll be charged from the point where the taxi begins the drive to pick you up.

BY BOAT

In April and mid-October, the **Batobus** (✆ **01-44-11-33-44**), a series of 150-passenger ferries with big windows for viewing the riverfronts, operates at 25-minute intervals daily from 10am to 7pm. Boats chug along between the quays at the base of the Eiffel

Tower and the quays at the base of the Louvre, stopping at the Musée d'Orsay, St-Germain-des-Prés, Notre-Dame, the Hôtel-de-Ville, the Louvre, and what the organizers of this affair refer to as the Champs-Elysées, but which is actually a stop at the base of the Pont Alexandre-III. Transit between any two stops costs 20F (3.05€, $2.90) for children and adults, and 10F (1.50€, $1.45) for transit between any additional stops, although passengers who intend to use the boat as a sightseeing opportunity usually opt to pay a flat rate (good all day) of 65F (9.90€, $9.45) for adults and 35F (5.30€, $5.13) for children under 19, and then settle back and watch the monuments. Photo ops are countless aboard this leisurely but intensely panoramic "floating observation platform."

 FAST FACTS: Paris

American Express From its administrative headquarters in the Paris suburb of Reuil-Malmaison, at 4 rue de Louis-Blériot, 92561 Rueil-Malmaison CEDEX, the largest travel service in the world operates a 24-hour hot line at ℂ **01-47-77-70-00**. Day-to-day services, like tours and money exchange, are available at 11 rue Scribe, 9th arr., 75009 Paris (ℂ **01-47-77-77-07**; Métro: Opéra), or the smaller branch at 38 av. Wagram, 8th arr., 75008 Paris (ℂ **01-42-27-58-80**; Métro: Ternes). Both are open Monday to Friday from 9am to 6:30pm, with money-changing services ending at 4:45pm. The rue Scribe office is open Saturday from 10am to 5pm (no mail pickup).

Banks American Express may be able to meet most of your banking needs. If not, banks in Paris are open Monday to Friday from 9am to 5pm. A few are open on Saturday. Ask at your hotel for the location of the bank nearest you. Shops and most hotels will cash your traveler's checks, but not at the advantageous rate a bank or foreign-exchange office will give you, so make sure you've allowed enough funds for *le weekend*.

Business Hours Opening hours in France are erratic, as befits a nation of individualists. Most museums close 1 day a week (often Tues) and national holidays; hours tend to be from 9:30am to 5pm. Some museums, particularly the smaller ones, close for lunch from noon to 2pm. Most French museums are open Saturday, but many close Sunday morning and reopen in the afternoon. (See museum listings in chapter 5 for specific times.) Generally, **offices** are open Monday to Friday from

9am to 5pm, but don't count on it. Always call first. **Large stores** and **chain stores** are open from 9 or 9:30am (often 10am) to 6 or 7pm without a break for lunch. Some **shops,** particularly those operated by foreigners, open at 8am and close at 8 or 9pm. In some **small stores,** the lunch break can last 3 hours, beginning at 1pm.

Electricity In general, expect 200 volts AC (60 cycles), though you'll encounter 110 and 115 volts in some older establishments. Adapters are needed to fit sockets. Many hotels have two-pin (in some cases, three-pin) sockets for electric razors. It's best to ask at your hotel before plugging in any electrical appliance.

Embassies/Consulates If you have a passport, immigration, legal, or other problem, contact your consulate. Call before you go, as they often keep strange hours and observe both French and home-country holidays.

The Embassy of the **United States,** at 2 av. Gabriel, 8th arr. (✆ **01-43-12-22-22;** Métro: Concorde), is open Monday to Friday from 9am to 6pm. Passports are issued at its consulate at 2 rue St-Florentin (✆ **01-43-12-22-22;** Métro: Concorde). Getting a passport replaced costs $55. The Embassy of **Canada** is at 35 av. Montaigne, 8th arr. (✆ **01-44-43-29-00;** Métro: F. D. Roosevelt or Alma-Marceau), open Monday to Friday from 9am to noon and from 2 to 4pm. The Canadian consulate is at the embassy. The Embassy of the **United Kingdom** is at 35 rue du faubourg St-Honoré, 8th arr. (✆ **01-44-51-31-00;** Métro: Concorde or Madeleine), open Monday to Friday from 9:30am to 12:30pm and from 2:30 to 5pm. The consulate is at 16 rue d'Anjou, 8th arr. (✆ **01-44-51-31-00;** Métro: Consulate), open Monday to Friday from 9:30am to 12:30pm and from 2:30 to 5pm. The Embassy of **Australia** is at 4 rue Jean-Rey, 15th arr. (✆ **01-40-59-33-00;** Métro: Bir Hakeim), open Monday to Friday from 9:15am to noon and from 2:30 to 4:30pm. The Embassy of **New Zealand** is at 7 ter rue Léonard-de-Vinci, 16th arr. (✆ **01-45-00-24-11;** Métro: Victor Hugo), open Monday to Friday from 9am to 1pm and from 2:30 to 6pm. The Embassy of **Ireland** is at 4 rue Rude, 16th arr. (✆ **01-44-17-67-00;** Métro: Etoile), open Monday to Friday from 9:30am to noon.

Emergencies For the police, call ✆ **17;** to report a fire, call ✆ **18.** For an ambulance, call the fire department at ✆ **01-45-78-74-52;** a fire vehicle rushes patients to the nearest emergency room. For **S.A.M.U.,** an independently operated, privately owned ambulance company, call ✆ **15.** For less urgent matters, you can reach the police at 9 bd. du Palais, 4th arr. (✆ **01-53-73-53-71** or 01-53-73-53-73; Métro: Cité).

Hospitals Open Monday to Saturday from 8am to 7pm, **Central Médical Europe,** 44 rue d'Amsterdam, 9th arr. (✆ **01-42-81-93-33;** Métro: Liège), maintains contacts with medical and dental practitioners in all fields. Appointments are recommended. Another choice is the **American Hospital of Paris,** 63 bd. Victor-Hugo, Neuilly (✆ **01-46-41-25-25;** Métro: Pont de Levallois or Pont de Neuilly; Bus: 82), which operates 24-hour medical and dental services. An additional clinic is the **Centre Figuier,** 2 rue du Figuier (✆ **01-49-96-62-70;** Métro: St-Paul). Call before visiting.

Internet Access To surf the Net or check your e-mail, try the **Cybercafé Latino,** 13 rue de l'Ecole Polytechnique, 5th arr. (✆ **01-40-51-86-94;** www.cybercafelatino.com; Métro: Maubert-Mutualité), open Monday to Saturday from 11:30am to 2am, Sunday from 3 to 9pm; or **Le Rendez-vous Toyota,** 79 av. des Champs-Elysées (✆ **01-56-89-29-79;** http://www. lerendez-voustoyota.com/; Métro: George V), open Monday to Thursday from 10:30am to 9pm and Friday and Saturday from 10:30am to midnight. See also **Le Web Bar** on p. 000.

Mail/Post Offices Most post offices in Paris are open Monday to Friday from 8am to 7pm and Saturday from 8am to noon. The **main post office (PTT)** for Paris is at 52 rue du Louvre, 75001 Paris (✆ **01-40-28-76-00;** Métro: Louvre). It's open 24 hours a day for the sale of stamps, phone calls, and sending faxes and telegrams, with limited hours (Mon–Fri 8am–5pm, Sat 8am–noon) for more esoteric financial services like the sale of money orders. Stamps can also usually be purchased at your hotel reception desk and at cafes with red TABAC signs. You can send faxes at the main post office in each arrondissement.

Airmail letters within Europe cost 3F (.45€, 45¢); to the United States and Canada, 4.40F (.65€, 65¢); and to Australia and New Zealand, 5.10F (.83€, 75¢). You can have mail sent to you *poste restante* (general delivery) at the main post office for a small fee. Take an ID, such as a passport, if you plan to pick up mail. American Express (see above) also offers a *poste restante* service, but you may be asked to show an American Express card or traveler's checks.

Newspapers/Magazines English-language newspapers are available at nearly every kiosk. Published Monday to Saturday, the *International Herald-Tribune* is the most popular paper with visiting Americans and Canadians; the *Guardian* provides a British point of view. For those who read French, the leading domestic newspapers are *Le Monde, Le Figaro,* and *Libération;* the top magazines are *L'Express, Le Point,* and *Le Nouvel Observateur.* Kiosks are generally open daily from 8am to 9pm.

Police Call ⓒ **17** for emergencies. The principal Préfecture is at 9 bd. du Palais, 4th arr. (ⓒ **01-53-71-53-71**; Métro: Cité).

Restrooms If you're in dire need, duck into a cafe or brasserie to use the lavatory. It's customary to make some small purchase if you do so. In the street, the domed self-cleaning lavatories are a decent option if you have small change; Métro stations and underground garages usually have public lavatories, but the degree of cleanliness varies.

Safety In Paris, be especially aware of child pickpockets. They roam the capital, preying on tourists around attractions like the Louvre, the Eiffel Tower, and Notre-Dame, and they also often strike in the Métro, sometimes blocking a victim from the escalator. A band of these young thieves can clean your pockets even while you try to fend them off. Their method is to get very close to a target, ask for a handout (sometimes), and deftly help themselves to your money or passport.

Although public safety is not as much a problem in Paris as it is in large American cities, concerns are growing. Robbery at gun- or knifepoint is uncommon here, but it's not unknown. Be careful.

Taxes See "Getting a VAT Refund" on p. 146 for an explanation of the value-added tax refund.

Telephone Public phones are found in cafes, restaurants, Métro stations, post offices, airports, and train stations, and occasionally on the streets. Finding a coin-operated telephone in France is an arduous task. A simpler and more widely accepted method of payment is the *télécarte,* a prepaid calling card available at kiosks, post offices, and Métro stations and costing 49F to 97.50F (7.45€–14.80€, $7.10–$14.15) for 50 and 120 units, respectively. A local call costs 1 unit, which provides you with 6 to 18 minutes of conversation, depending on the rate. Avoid making calls from your hotel, which might double or triple the charges.

Time France is usually 6 hours ahead of Eastern Standard Time in the United States. French daylight saving time lasts from around April to September, when clocks are set 1 hour ahead of the standard time.

Tipping By law, all bills show *service compris,* which means the tip is included; additional gratuities are customarily given as follows: For **hotel staff,** tip the porter 6F to 10F (.90€–1.50€, 85¢–$1.45) per item of baggage and 10F (1.50€, $1.45) per day for the chambermaid. You're not obligated to tip the concierge, doorman, or anyone else unless you use his or her services. In **cafes** and **restaurants,** waiter service is usually included, though you can leave a couple of francs. Tip **taxi drivers** 12% to 15% of the amount on the meter. In **theaters** and **restaurants,** give cloakroom attendants at least 5F (.75€, 75¢) per item. Give **restroom attendants** in nightclubs and such places about 2F (.30€, 34¢). Give **cinema** and **theater ushers** about 2F (.30€, 34¢). Tip the **hairdresser** about 15%, and don't forget to tip the person who gives you a shampoo or a manicure 10F (1.50€, $1.45). For **guides** for group visits to museums and monuments, 5F to 10F (.75€–1.50€, 75¢–$1.45) is a reasonable tip.

Water Drinking water is generally safe, though it has been known to cause diarrhea in some unaccustomed stomachs. If you ask for water in a restaurant, it'll be bottled water (for which you'll pay), unless you specifically request tap water (*l'eau du robinet*).

3

Where to Stay

Paris boasts some 2,000 hotels—with about 80,000 rooms— spread across its 20 arrondissements. They range from the Ritz and the Crillon to dives so repellent that even George Orwell, author of *Down and Out in Paris and London,* wouldn't have considered checking in. (Of course, you won't find any of the latter in this guide!) We've included deluxe places for those who can afford to live like the Sultan of Brunei as well as a wide range of moderate and inexpensive choices for the rest of us.

Most visitors, at least those from North America, come to Paris in July and August. Many French are on vacation then, and trade fairs and conventions come to a halt, so there are usually plenty of rooms, even though these months have traditionally been the peak season for European travel. In most hotels, February is just as busy as April or September because of the volume of business travelers and the increasing number of tourists who've learned to take advantage of off-season discount airfares.

Because hot weather rarely lasts long in Paris, few hotels, except the deluxe ones, provide air-conditioning. If you're trapped in a garret on a hot summer night, you'll have to sweat it out. You can open your window to get some cooler air, but open windows admit the nuisance of noise pollution. To avoid this, you can request a room in back when reserving.

WHICH BANK IS FOR YOU?

The river dividing Paris geographically and culturally demands that you make a choice. Are you more **Left Bank,** wanting a room in the heart of St-Germain, perhaps where Jean-Paul Sartre and Simone de Beauvoir once spent the night? Or are you more **Right Bank,** preferring sumptuous quarters like those at the Crillon, perhaps where Tom Cruise once slept? Would you rather look for that special old curio in a dusty shop on the Left Bank's rue Jacob or inspect the latest Lagerfeld or Dior couture on the Right Bank's avenue Montaigne? Each of Paris's neighborhoods has its own flavor, and your experiences and memories of Paris will likely be formed by where you choose to stay. If you desire chic surroundings, choose a Right Bank hotel. If you want less formality and tiny bohemian streets, head for the Left Bank, where prices are traditionally lower.

1 On the Right Bank

We'll begin with the most centrally located arrondissements on the Right Bank, then work our way through the more outlying neighborhoods and to the area around the Arc de Triomphe.

1ST ARRONDISSEMENT
VERY EXPENSIVE

Hôtel Costes 🔯🔯🔯   Grand style and a location close to the headquarters of some of Paris's most upscale shops, as well as the offices of *Harper's Bazaar*, attract lots of high-style fashion types. Don't expect the Ritz, but other than that, this is one of the shining stars of Paris hostelries. The town house–style premise was a *maison bourgeoise* for many generations, presenting a severely dignified facade. In 1996, it was richly adorned with jewel-toned colors, heavy swagged curtains, and lavish Napoléon III accessories. Today, everything about it evokes the rich days of the Gilded Age, especially the guest rooms. Some are small, but they're cozy and ornate, with one or two large beds, CD players, and fax machines. The best units are called Grandes Chambres, and they contain sitting areas. For the ultimate luxury, ask for one of the duplex units with split-level layouts.

239 rue St-Honoré, 75001 Paris. 📞 **01-42-44-50-50**. Fax 01-42-44-50-01. 83 units. 3,000F–3,500F (456€–532€, $435–$507.50) double; from 7,500F (1,140€, $1,087.50) suite. AE, DC, MC, V. Métro: Tuileries or Concorde. **Amenities:** Restaurant (French); bar; indoor pool; health club; car-rental desk; room service; massage; babysitting; laundry/dry cleaning. *In room:* A/C, TV, minibar, hair dryer.

Hôtel de Vendôme 🔯🔯   For a time the Embassy of Texas (when that state was a nation), this jewel box opened in 1998 at one of the world's most prestigious addresses. It is comparable and almost as good as Costes (see above). Though the guest rooms are only moderate in size, you live in opulent comfort. Most of the rooms are in classic Second Empire style with luxurious beds, tasteful fabrics, and well-upholstered, hand-carved furnishings. The security is fantastic, with TV intercoms. This new version of the hotel replaces a lackluster one that stood here for a century, and its facade and roof are classified as historic monuments by the French government.

1 place Vendôme, 75001 Paris. 📞 **01-55-04-55-00**. Fax 01-49-27-97-89. reservations@hoteldevendome.com. 29 units. 2,800F–3,200F (425.60€–486.40€, $406–$464) double; 4,500F–5,500F (684€–836€, $652.50–$797.50) suite. AE, DC,

Hotels in the Heart of the Right Bank
(Arrondissements 1–4, 9, 11–12 & 18)

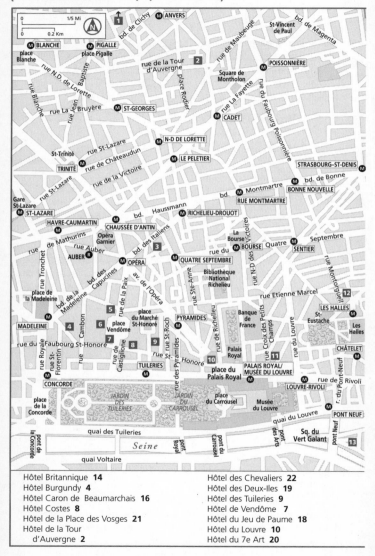

Hôtel Britannique **14**	Hôtel des Chevaliers **22**
Hôtel Burgundy **4**	Hôtel des Deux-Iles **19**
Hôtel Caron de Beaumarchais **16**	Hôtel des Tuileries **9**
Hôtel Costes **8**	Hôtel de Vendôme **7**
Hôtel de la Place des Vosges **21**	Hôtel du Jeu de Paume **18**
Hôtel de la Tour	Hôtel du Louvre **10**
d'Auvergne **2**	Hôtel du 7e Art **20**

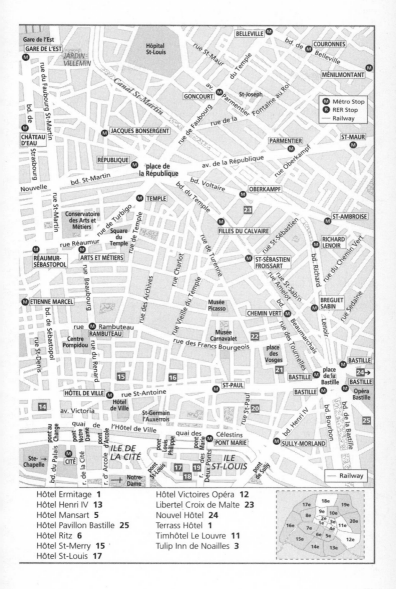

Gare de l'Est
GARE DE L'EST Ⓜ

BELLEVILLE Ⓜ

Ⓜ **COURONNES**
bd. de Ⓜ Belleville

JARDIN VILLEMIN

Hôpital St-Louis

rue St-Maur

du Temple

Ⓜ **MÉNILMONTANT**

rue du Faubourg St-Martin

Canal St-Martin

av. Ⓜ Parmentier Fontaine au Roi

GONCOURT Ⓜ

St-Joseph

rue de Faubourg

rue de la

bd. de Château d'Eau

Ⓜ **CHÂTEAU D'EAU**

JACQUES BONSERGENT Ⓜ

PARMENTIER Ⓜ

rue Oberkampf

ST-MAUR Ⓜ

Strasbourg

RÉPUBLIQUE Ⓜ

place de la République

av. de la République

Ⓜ Nouvelle

bd. St-Martin

bd. Voltaire

OBERKAMPF Ⓜ

rue St-Martin

bd. du Temple

TEMPLE Ⓜ

`23`

Conservatoire des Arts et Métiers

rue de Turbigo

Square du Temple

FILLES DU CALVAIRE Ⓜ

rue St-Sébastien

ST-AMBROISE Ⓜ

rue Réaumur

rue de Temple

rue de Turenne

Ⓜ **ST-SÉBASTIEN FROISSART**

RICHARD LENOIR Ⓜ

RÉAUMUR-SÉBASTOPOL Ⓜ

ARTS ET MÉTIERS Ⓜ

rue Beaubourg

rue Charlot

rue St-Sabin

rue du Chemin Vert

bd. Richard

BREGUET SABIN Ⓜ

Ⓜ **ETIENNE MARCEL**

bd. de Sébastopol

rue des Archives

rue Vieille du Temple

Musée Picasso

rue Amelot

CHEMIN VERT Ⓜ

bd. Beaumarchais

rue Sedaine

Lenoir

rue Ⓜ Rambuteau
RAMBUTEAU

Centre Pompidou

rue du Renard

rue des Francs Bourgeois

Musée Carnavalet

`22`

place des Vosges

rue des Tournelles

BASTILLE Ⓜ

place de la Bastille

BASTILLE Ⓜ

BASTILLE →

`15`   `16`

HÔTEL DE VILLE Ⓜ

rue St-Antoine

ST-PAUL Ⓜ

`21`

BASTILLE Ⓜ

Ⓜ **BASTILLE**

Opéra Bastille

`14`

av. Victoria

Hôtel de Ville

St-Germain l'Auxerrois

rue St-Paul

`20`

bd. Henri IV

bd. Bourbon

bd. de la Bastille

`25`

quai de l'Hôtel de Ville

quai des Célestins

PONT MARIE Ⓜ

Ste-Chapelle →

pont au Change

pont Notre Dame

pont d'Arcole

Ⓜ **CITÉ**

r. de la Cité

r. d' Arcole

ILE DE LA CITÉ

pont St-Louis

pont Louis Philippe

pont Marie

pont des Deux Ponts

ILE ST-LOUIS

pont de Sully

Ⓜ **SULLY-MORLAND**

bd. du Palais

→ Notre-Dame

`17` `19`
`18`

Ⓜ **Métro Stop**
Ⓡ **RER Stop**
— Railway

---- Railway

17e 18e 19e
9e 10e
8e 2e 3e 11e 20e
16e 1e 4e
6e 5e 12e
15e 14e 13e

MC, V. Métro: Concorde or Opéra. **Amenities:** Restaurant (French); bar; room service; laundry. *In room:* A/C, TV, minibar, hair dryer.

Hôtel du Louvre ✴✴   After a massive overhaul, the hotel is now in a neck-and-neck race with the Regina for neighborhood supremacy. When Napoléon III inaugurated the hotel in 1855, French journalists described it as "a palace of the people, rising adjacent to the palace of kings." In 1897, Camille Pissarro moved into a room with a view that inspired many of his landscapes. Between the Louvre and the Palais Royal, the hotel has a decor of marble, bronze, and gilt. The guest rooms are quintessentially Parisian, filled with souvenirs of the Belle Epoque. Most were renovated between 1996 and 1998. Some are small, but most are medium-size to spacious—with elegant fabrics and upholstery, excellent carpeting, double-glazed windows, comfortable beds, and traditional wood furniture.

Place André-Malraux, 75001 Paris. ✆ 800/888-4747 in the U.S. and Canada, or ✆ 01-44-58-38-38. Fax 01-44-58-38-01. www.hoteldulouvre.com. 195 units. 2,350F–5,280F (357.20€–802.55€, $340.75–$765.60) double; from 6,000F (912€, $870) suite. Ask about midwinter discounts. AE, DC, MC, V. Parking 120F (18.25€, $17.40). Métro: Palais Royal or Louvre-Rivoli. **Amenities:** 2 restaurants (both French); 2 bars; health club; room service; massage; laundry/dry cleaning. *In room:* A/C, TV, minibar, hair dryer, safe.

Hôtel Ritz ✴✴✴   The Ritz is Europe's greatest hotel, an enduring symbol of elegance on one of Paris's most beautiful and historic squares. César Ritz, the "little shepherd boy from Niederwald," converted the private Hôtel de Lazun into a luxury hotel that he opened in 1898. With the help of the culinary master Escoffier, he made the Ritz a miracle of luxury living.

   In 1979, the Ritz family sold the hotel to Egyptian businessman Mohammed al Fayed, who refurbished it and added a cooking school. (You may remember that his son, Dodi, and Princess Diana dined here before they set out on their fateful drive.) Two town houses were annexed, joined by a long arcade lined with miniature display cases representing 125 of Paris's leading boutiques. The public salons are furnished with museum-caliber antiques. Each guest room is uniquely decorated, most often with Louis XIV or XV reproductions; all have fine rugs, marble fireplaces, tapestries, brass beds, and more. The spacious marble bathrooms are the city's most luxurious, filled with deluxe toiletries, scales, private phones, cords to summon maids and valets, robes, full-length and makeup mirrors, and dual basins. Ever since Edward VII got stuck in a too-narrow bathtub with his lover of the evening, the tubs at the Ritz have been deep and big.

Tips Café and a Croissant?

Hotel breakfasts are fairly uniform and include your choice of coffee, tea, or hot chocolate; a freshly baked croissant and roll; and limited quantities of butter and jam or jelly. It can be at your door moments after you call for it and is served at almost any hour. (When we mention breakfast charges in our listings, we refer to continental breakfasts only.) Breakfasts with eggs, bacon, ham, or other items must be ordered from the a la carte menu. For a charge, larger hotels serve the full or "English" breakfast, but smaller hotels typically serve only the continental variety.

---

15 place Vendôme, 75001 Paris. ✆ 800/223-6800 in the U.S. and Canada, or ✆ 01-43-16-30-30. Fax 01-43-16-31-78. www.ritzparis.com. 175 units. 4,000F–4,560F (608€–693.10€, $580–$661.20) double; from 5,415F (823.13€, $785.23) suite. AE, DC, MC, V. Parking 230F (34.95€, $33.35). Métro: Opéra, Concorde, or Madeleine. **Amenities:** 2 restaurants (both French); 2 bars; indoor pool; health club; shopping arcade; room service; massage; laundry/dry cleaning. *In room:* A/C, TV, minibar, hair dryer, safe.

EXPENSIVE

Hôtel des Tuileries ⭐   On a quiet narrow street, this hotel occupies a 17th-century town house that Marie Antoinette used when she left Versailles for unofficial Paris visits. Don't expect mementos of the queen, as all the frippery of her era was long ago stripped away. But in honor of its royal antecedents, the hotel's public areas and guest rooms are filled with copies of Louis XV furniture—a bit dowdy, but still dignified and very comfortable. In 2001, major improvements were made to the building structure, including the elevators. Each unit has a full tub and shower bathroom.

10 rue St-Hyacinthe, 75001 Paris. ✆ 01-42-61-04-17. Fax 01-49-27-91-56. www.hotel-des-tuileries.com. 26 units. 1,090F–1,400F (165.70€–212.80€, $158.05–$203) double. AE, DC, MC, V. Parking 110F (16.70€, $15.95). Métro: Tuileries or Pyramides. **Amenities:** Room service (7am–10pm only); babysitting; laundry. *In room:* A/C, TV with cable, minibar, hair dryer, safe.

MODERATE

Hôtel Britannique *Value*   Conservatively modern and plush, this is a much-renovated 19th-century hotel near Les Halles, the Pompidou, and Notre-Dame. It was re-rated with three government stars after a complete renovation in the mid-1980s. The place not only is British in name but also seems to have cultivated an English style of graciousness. The guest rooms may be small, but they're immaculate and soundproof, with comfortable beds. A satellite receiver gets U.S. and U.K. television shows. The reading room is a cozy retreat.

20 av. Victoria, 75001 Paris. (℃) **01-42-33-74-59.** Fax 01-42-33-82-65. www. hotel-britannic.com. 40 units. 820F–1,130F (124.65€–171.75€, $118.90–$163.85) double. AE, DC, MC, V. Parking 100F (15.20€, $14.50). Métro: Châtelet. **Amenities:** Room service. *In room:* TV, minibar, hair dryer, safe.

Hôtel Burgundy ⸙ *(Value)*

The Burgundy is one of this outrageously expensive area's best values. The frequently renovated building began as two adjacent town houses in the 1830s, one a pension where Baudelaire wrote some of his eerie poetry in the 1860s and the other a bordello. They were linked by British-born managers, who insisted on using the English name. Radically renovated in 1992, with continued improvements in 2001, the hotel hosts many North and South Americans and features conservatively decorated rooms and comfortable beds, each with a full tub and shower in the bathroom. The Charles Baudelaire restaurant and its bar are open for lunch and dinner Monday to Friday.

8 rue Duphot, 75001 Paris. (℃) **01-42-60-34-12.** Fax 01-47-03-95-20. 89 units. 1,000F–1,150F (152€–174.80€, $145–$166.75) double; 1,600F–1,900F (243.20€–288.80€, $232–$275.50) suite. AE, DC, MC, V. Métro: Madeleine or Concorde. **Amenities:** Restaurant (French); bar; room service (breakfast); babysitting. *In room:* A/C, TV, minibar, hair dryer.

Hôtel Mansart *(Value)*

After operating as a glorious wreck for many decades, this hotel—designed by its namesake—was fully renovated in 1991 and offers some of the lowest rates in this pricey area. The public rooms contain Louis reproductions and startling floor-to-ceiling geometric designs inspired by the inlaid marble floors (or formal gardens) of the French Renaissance. The small- to medium-size guest rooms are subtly formal and comfortable, though only half a dozen of the suites and most expensive rooms actually overlook the famous square. Twenty rooms are air-conditioned, and all come with a tub and shower in the bathroom. Breakfast is the only meal served.

5 rue des Capucines, 75001 Paris. (℃) **01-42-61-50-28.** Fax 01-49-27-97-44. www. hotelinformation.com. 57 units. 650F–1,100F (99€–167€, $93–$160) double; 1,500F–1800F (228€–274€, $218–$261) suite. AE, DC, MC, V. Métro: Opéra or Madeleine. **Amenities:** Bar; room service (drinks); babysitting; laundry/dry cleaning. *In room:* TV, minibar, safe.

INEXPENSIVE

Hôtel Henri IV

This is our funky, fun selection. Four hundred years ago, this decrepit narrow building housed the printing presses used for the edicts of Henri IV. Today one of the most famous and most consistently crowded budget hotels in Europe sits in a dramatic location at the westernmost tip of Ile de la Cité, beside a formal park. The crowd is mostly bargain-conscious academics, journalists, and Francophiles, many of whom reserve rooms as much as 2 months in advance. The low-ceilinged lobby, a flight above street level, is cramped and bleak; the creaky stairway leading to the guest rooms is almost impossibly narrow. The rooms are considered romantically threadbare by many and run-down and substandard by others. Each contains a sink, but not even the five rooms with showers have toilets.

25 place Dauphine, 75001 Paris. ℂ **01-43-54-44-53.** 21 units (5 with shower only). 190F–220F (28.90€–33.45€, $27.55–$31.90) double without shower; 250F–290F (38€–44.10€, $36.25–$42.05) double with shower. Rates include breakfast. No credit cards. Métro: Pont Neuf. *In room:* No phone.

Timhôtel Le Louvre *Kids*   This hotel and its sibling, the Timhôtel Palais-Royal, are mirror images of each other, at least inside; they're part of a new breed of government-rated two-star family-friendly hotels cropping up around France. These Timhôtels share the same manager and the same temperament, and though the rooms at the Palais-Royal branch are a bit larger than the ones here, this branch is so close to the Louvre as to be almost irresistible. The ambience is standardized modern, with monochromatic guest rooms and wall-to-wall carpeting that was upgraded in 1998. The price and amenities, such as a full tub and shower in the bathroom of each room, make it a good bet for families.

The **Timhôtel Palais-Royal** is at 3 rue de la Banque, 75002 Paris (ℂ **01-42-61-53-90;** fax 01-42-60-05-39; Métro: Bourse).

4 rue Croix des Petits-Champs, 75001 Paris. ℂ **01-42-60-34-86.** Fax 01-42-60-10-39. Louvre@timhotel.fr. 56 units. 750F–850F (114.16€–129.38€, $108.85–$123.37) double. AE, DC, MC, V. Métro: Palais Royal. **Amenities:** Babysitting; laundry/dry cleaning. *In room:* A/C, TV.

2ND ARRONDISSEMENT
EXPENSIVE

Hôtel Victoires Opéra *☆*   Head to this little charmer if you want a reasonably priced place convenient to Les Halles and the Pompidou as well as to the Marais, with its shops and gay and straight restaurants. It's a classically decorated hotel, evoking the era of Louis Philippe. Recent renovations include the addition of a private bathroom for every room. Because a junior suite is priced about the same as a double, request a double suite—you'll enjoy the extra space. Most of the rooms are alike—comfortable, but a bit tiny. They're reached by elevator from the second floor. Twenty of its units come with a tub/shower combination; the others with a shower. Skip the hotel breakfast (which costs extra) and cross the street to Stohrer at no. 51, one of Paris's most historic pâtissèries, founded in 1730 by the pâtissier to Louis XV.

56 rue Montorgueil, 75002 Paris. © **01-42-36-41-08.** Fax 01-45-08-08-79. www. hotelvictoiresopera.com. 26 units. 1,400F (212.80€, $203) double; 1,800F (273.60€, $261) junior suite. AE, DC, MC, V. Parking 120F (18.25€, $17.40). Métro: Les Halles. **Amenities:** 24-hr. room service; babysitting; laundry/dry cleaning. *In room:* A/C, TV, minibar, iron/ironing board.

MODERATE

Tulip Inn de Noailles　If you're looking for a postmodern hotel in the style of Putman and Starck, book here. Proprietor Martine Falck has turned this old-fashioned place in a great location into a refined Art-Deco choice with bold colors and cutting-edge style. Yet the prices remain reasonable. The guest rooms come in various shapes and sizes, but all are comfortable; half are air-conditioned, and all but five come with a shower only. A favorite is no. 601 with its own terrace.

9 rue de la Michodière, 75002 Paris. © **800/344-1212** in the U.S., or © **01-47-42-92-90.** Fax 01-49-24-92-71. www.hoteldenoailles.com. 61 units. 1,200F (182.40€, $174) double; 1,400F (212.80€, $203) suite. Rates include breakfast if you book directly with the hotel. AE, DC, V. Parking 100F (15.20€, $14.50). Métro: 4 Septembre or Opéra. **Amenities:** Bar; health club; sauna; room service; massage; babysitting; laundry/dry cleaning. *In room:* A/C, hair dryer.

3RD ARRONDISSEMENT
MODERATE

Hôtel des Chevaliers　Half a block from the northwestern edge of place des Vosges, this renovated hotel occupies a dramatic corner building whose 17th-century vestiges have been elevated into high art. These include the remnants of a stone-sided well in the cellar, a sweeping stone barrel vault covering the breakfast area, half-timbering artfully exposed in the stairwell, and Louis XIII accessories that'll remind you of the hotel's origins. Each guest room is comfortable and well maintained, and all units come with a complete tub and shower in the bathroom. Rooms on the top floor have artfully exposed ceiling beams.

30 rue de Turenne, 75003 Paris. © **01-42-72-73-47.** Fax 01-42-72-54-10. 24 units. 680F–820F (103.35€–124.65€, $98.60–$118.90) double; 895F–995F (136.05€–151.25€, $129.80–$144.30) triple. Parking 60F (9.10€, $8.70). Métro: Chemin Vert or St-Paul. *In room:* TV, minibar, hair dryer, safe.

4TH ARRONDISSEMENT
EXPENSIVE

Hôtel du Jeu de Paume　　It's small-scale and charming, with a layout that includes an interconnected pair of 17th-century town houses accessed via a timbered passageway from the street outside. This hotel has rooms that are a bit larger than those within some of its nearby competitors on the Ile St-Louis. It originated as a "clubhouse" that was used by members of the court of Louis XIII who amused themselves with *Les jeux de paume* (an early form of tennis) on a vacant lot nearby. Bedrooms are outfitted in a simple and unfrilly version of Art Deco. In terms of mentality and aesthetics, here you'll feel more closely aligned with the pervasive ethic of the Marais than within the Latin Quarter to the south. There's an elevator on the premises, and scads of charm from the well-meaning staff.

54 rue St-Louis en l'Isle, 75004 Paris. ℂ **01-43-26-14-18.** Fax 01-40-46-02-76. www.jeudepaumehotel.com. 30 units. 1,365F–1,650F (207.50€–250.80€, $197.95–$239.25) double; 2,500F–2,750F (380€–418€, $362.50–$398.75) suite. AE, DC, MC, V. Parking 120F (18.25€, $17.40). Métro: Pont-Marie. **Amenities:** Exercise room; sauna; babysitting; laundry/dry cleaning. *In room:* TV, minibar, hair dryer, safe.

MODERATE

Hôtel Caron de Beaumarchais *(Value*   Built in the 18th century and gracefully upgraded in 1998, this good-value choice features floors of artfully worn gray stone, antique reproductions, and elaborate fabrics based on antique patterns. Hotelier Alain Bigeard likes his primrose-colored guest rooms to evoke the taste of the French gentry in the 18th century when the Marais was the scene of high-society dances or even duels. Most rooms retain their original ceiling beams. The smallest units overlook the interior courtyard, and the top-floor rooms are tiny but have panoramic balcony views across the Right Bank. Each of the bedrooms comes with a tub/shower combination.

12 rue Vieille-du-Temple, 75004 Paris. ℂ **01-42-72-34-12.** Fax 01-42-72-34-63. www.carondebeaumarchais.com. 19 units. 790F–870F (120.10€–132.25€, $114.55–$126.15) double. AE, DC, MC, V. Métro: St-Paul or Hôtel de Ville. **Amenities:** Babysitting; laundry/dry cleaning. *In room:* A/C, TV, minibar, hair dryer.

Hôtel des Deux-Iles *&*   This is a much-restored 18th-century town house. It was an inexpensive hotel until 1976, when an elaborate decor with lots of bamboo and reed furniture and French provincial touches was added. The result is an unpretentious but charming hotel with a great location. The guest rooms are on the small side, however. A garden of plants and flowers off the lobby leads to a basement breakfast room with a fireplace.

59 rue St-Louis-en-l'Ile, 75004 Paris. ℂ **01-43-26-13-35.** Fax 01-43-29-60-25. hotel2iles@free.fr. 17 units. 910F (138.51€, $132.08) double. AE, MC, V. Métro:

Pont Marie. **Amenities:** Garden; room service; laundry/dry cleaning. *In room:* A/C, TV, hair dryer.

Hôtel St-Louis *(Value)*

Proprietors Guy and Andrée Record maintain a charming family atmosphere at this small, antique-filled hotel in a 17th-century town house. Despite a full renovation completed in 1998, it represents an incredible value considering its prime location on Ile St-Louis. Expect cozy, slightly cramped rooms. With mansard roofs and old-fashioned moldings, the top-floor rooms sport tiny balconies with sweeping rooftop views. The breakfast room is in the cellar, with 17th-century stone vaulting.

75 rue St-Louis-en-l'Ile, 75004 Paris. ✆ **01-46-34-04-80.** Fax 01-46-34-02-13. www.hotel-paris-saintlouis.com. 21 units. 815F–1,300F (123.90€–197.60€, $118.20–$188.50) double. MC, V. Métro: Pont Marie. **Amenities:** Room service; babysitting; laundry. *In room:* TV, hair dryer, safe.

Hotel St-Merry *(Finds)*

The rebirth of this once-notorious brothel as a charming, upscale hotel is yet another example of how the Marais has been gentrified. It contains only a dozen rooms, each of them relatively small, but charmingly accented with exposed stone, 18th-century ceiling beams, and lots of quirky architectural details, all carefully preserved by a team of architects and decorators. Expect a clientele here that's estimated by the staff as about 50% gay and male, the other half straight and involved in the arts scene that flourishes in the surrounding neighborhood. Before it became a bordello, incidentally, this place was conceived as the presbytery of the nearby Church of St-Merry.

78 rue de la Verrerie. 75004 Paris. ✆ **01-42-78-14-15.** Fax 01-40-29-06-82. 12 units. 900F–1,300F (136.80€–197.60€, $130.50–$188.50) double; 1,900F (288.80€, $275.50) suite. Metro: Hôtel de Ville or Châtelet. *In room:* TV.

INEXPENSIVE

Hôtel de la Place des Vosges *(★★)* *(Value)*

Built about 350 years ago, during the same era as the majestic square it's named after (which lies less than a 2-min. walk away), this is a well-managed, small-scale property with reasonable prices and lots of charm. Many of the bedrooms have beamed ceilings, relatively small dimensions, tiled bathrooms (with tub or shower), small TV sets hanging from chains in the ceiling, and a sense of cozy, well-ordered efficiency. There are patches of chiseled stone at various parts of the hotel, a decorative touch that helps evoke the era of Louis XIII.

12 rue de Birague, 75004 Paris. ✆ **01-42-72-60-46.** Fax 01-42-72-02-64. hotel. place.des.vosges@gofernet.com. 16 units. 660F–690F (100.30€–104.90€, $95.70–$100.05) double. MC, V. Métro: Bastille. *In room:* TV, hair dryer.

Hôtel du 7e Art   This hotel is one of many 17th-century build-ings in this neighborhood classified as historic monuments. Don't expect grand luxury: Rooms are cramped but clean, and outfitted with the simplest of furniture, relieved by 1950s-era posters pro-moting the glories of old Hollywood. Each has white walls, and some—including those under the sloping mansard-style roof on the uppermost floor—have exposed ceiling beams. All have small shower-only bathrooms. There's a bar in the lobby and a breakfast room, but be warned in advance that there's no elevator for access to any of this place's five stories (4 *étages*). The hotel is named after the "seventh art," a French reference to filmmaking.

20 rue St-Paul, 75004 Paris. 📞 **01-44-54-85-00.** Fax 01-42-77-69-10. 23 units. 460F–592F (69.90€–90€, $66.70–$85.85) double; 789F (119.95€, $114.40) suite. AE, DC, MC, V. Parking 100F (15.20€, $14.50). Métro: St-Paul. *In room:* TV.

9TH ARRONDISSEMENT
INEXPENSIVE
Hôtel de la Tour d'Auvergne   Here's a good, safe bet for those who want to be near the Opéra or the Gare du Nord. This building was erected before Baron Haussmann reconfigured Paris's avenues around 1870. Later, Modigliani rented a room here for 6 months, and the staff will tell you that Victor Hugo and Auguste Rodin briefly lived on this street. The interior was long ago modernized into a glossy internationalism. The guest rooms are meticulously coordinated, yet the small decorative canopies over the headboards make them feel cluttered. Though the views over the back courtyard are uninspired, even gloomy, some guests request rear rooms for the relative quiet. Every year, five rooms are renovated, so the comfort level is kept at a high standard, and all units come with a tub/shower combination.

10 rue de la Tour d'Auvergne, 75009 Paris. 📞 **01-48-78-61-60.** Fax 01-49-95-99-00. 24 units. 550F–750F (83.60€–114€, $79.75–$108.75) double. AE, DC, MC, V. Métro: Cadet or Anvers. **Amenities:** Room service; babysitting. *In room:* TV, minibar, hair dryer.

11TH ARRONDISSEMENT
INEXPENSIVE
Libertel Croix de Malte   A member of a nationwide chain of mostly government-rated two-star hotels, this is a well-maintained choice. Business increased thanks to a radical 1992 overhaul and its proximity to the Opéra Bastille and the Marais. The hotel consists of buildings of two and three floors, one of which is accessible through a shared breakfast room. There's a landscaped courtyard in

back with access to a lobby bar. The cozy guest rooms contain brightly painted modern furniture accented with vivid green, blue, and pink patterns that flash back to the 1960s. About half of the units contain tubs; the rest are equipped with showers.

5 rue de Malte, 75011 Paris. ✆ **01-48-05-09-36.** Fax 01-43-57-02-54. www. all-hotels-in-paris.com. 29 units. 685F (104.10€, $99.35) double. AE, MC, V. Métro: Oberkampf. **Amenities:** Room service (breakfast); babysitting. *In room:* TV, hair dryer.

12TH ARRONDISSEMENT
MODERATE
Hôtel Pavillon Bastille   Hardly your cozy little backstreet dig, this is a bold, brassy, innovative hotel in a 1991 town house across from the Opéra Bastille and a block south of place de la Bastille. A 17th-century fountain graces the courtyard between the hotel and the street. The guest rooms have twin or double beds, partially mirrored walls, and contemporary built-in furniture. If you're looking for a bargain, note that the cheapest rooms have the same size and configuration as the more expensive *chambres privilegées* (the extra cost gets you amenities like slippers, better cosmetics, fruit baskets, and a complimentary bottle of wine—not worth it). Each unit comes with a tub/shower combination.

65 rue de Lyon, 75012 Paris. ✆ **01-43-43-65-65.** Fax 01-43-43-96-52. www. france-paris.com. 25 units. 840F–955F (127.70€–145.15€, $121.80–$138.50) double; 1,375F (209€, $199.40) suite. AE, DC, MC, V. Parking 75F (11.40€, $10.90). Métro: Bastille. **Amenities:** Laundry/dry cleaning. *In room:* A/C, TV, minibar, hair dryer, iron/ironing board, safe.

INEXPENSIVE
Nouvel Hôtel   This hotel evokes the French provinces far more than urban Paris. Surrounded by greenery in a neighborhood rarely visited by tourists, the Nouvel conjures a calmer day, when parts of Paris still seemed like small country towns. The beauty of the place is most visible from the inside courtyard, site of warm-weather breakfasts, the only meal served. Winding halls lead to small guest rooms overlooking either the courtyard or, less appealingly, the street. Each contains flowered fabrics and old-fashioned furniture, but only three have tub baths; the rest are equipped with showers.

24 av. du Bel-Air, 75012 Paris. ✆ **01-43-43-01-81.** Fax 01-43-44-64-13. www. nouvel-hotel-paris.com. 28 units. 436F–594F (66.25€–90.30€, $63.20–$86.15) double. Rates include breakfast. AE, DC, MC, V. Métro: Nation. *In room:* TV.

18TH ARRONDISSEMENT
EXPENSIVE

Terrass Hôtel ⭐⭐ *Finds*   Built in 1913 and richly renovated into a plush but traditional style in 1991, this is the only government-rated four-star hotel on the Butte Montmartre. In an area filled with some of Paris's seediest hotels, this place is easily in a class of its own. Its main advantage is its location amid Montmartre's bohemian atmosphere (or what's left of it). Staffed by English-speaking employees, it has a large, marble-floored lobby ringed with blond oak paneling and accented with 18th-century antiques and even older tapestries. The guest rooms have high ceilings, and are nicely upholstered and often feature views. All the bathrooms are well maintained, each with a shower and about half with both a shower and tub.

12–14 rue Joseph-de-Maistre, 75018 Paris. ℂ **01-46-06-72-85.** Fax 01-42-52-29-11. www.terrass-hotel.com. 100 units. 1,430F–1,580F (217.35€–240.15€, $207.35–$229.10) double; 1,920F (291.85€, $278.40) suite. Rates include breakfast. AE, DC, MC, V. Parking 100F (15.20€, $14.50). Métro: Place de Clichy or Blanche. **Amenities:** 2 restaurants (both French); bar; laundry/dry cleaning; room service; babysitting. *In room:* A/C, TV, minibar, hair dryer.

INEXPENSIVE

Hôtel Ermitage   Built in 1870 of chiseled limestone in the Napoléon III style, this hotel's facade evokes a perfectly proportioned small villa. It's set in a calm area, a brief uphill stroll from Sacré-Coeur. Views extend out over Paris, and there's a verdant garden in the back courtyard. The small guest rooms are like those in a countryside auberge with exposed ceiling beams, flowered wallpaper, and casement windows opening onto the garden or a street seemingly airlifted from the provinces. Half of the bedrooms come with tubs, the rest with showers.

24 rue Lamarck, 75018 Paris. ℂ **01-42-64-79-22.** Fax 01-42-64-10-33. 12 units. 530F (80.55€, $76.85) double. No credit cards. Parking 60F (9.10€, $8.70). Métro: Lamarck-Caulaincourt. **Amenities:** Garden; babysitting. *In room:* Hair dryer.

8TH ARRONDISSEMENT
VERY EXPENSIVE

Four Seasons Hôtel George V ⭐⭐⭐   Even in its latest reincarnation, with all its glitz and glamour, this hotel is for the merely rich. Both the Bristol and Plaza Athénée accurately claim they have more class. Its history is as gilt-edged as they come: Opened in 1928 in honor of George V (father of Queen Elizabeth II of England) and noted for grandeur that managed to stylishly survive the Depression and two world wars, it was soon-after designated as an official branch of the now-defunct League of Nations. During the liberation of Paris, it housed Dwight D. Eisenhower and his war machine. After its acquisition by Saudi Prince Al Waleed, and a 2-year shutdown for renovations, it was re-opened late in 1999 under the banner of Toronto-based Four Seasons. Rooms are about as close as you'll come to residency within a supremely well-upholstered private home. The renovation reduced the number of units from 300 to 245, which now come in three sizes. The largest are supremely magnificent, the smallest are, in the words of a spokesperson, *"très agreáble."* Security is tight here—a fact appreciated by sometimes notorious guests.

31 Ave. George V, 75008 Paris. © **800/332-3442** in the U.S. or Canada, or © **01-53-53-28-00.** Fax 01-49-52-70-20. www.fourseasons.com. 245 units. 4,264F–5,706F (648.15€–867.30€, $618.30–$827.35) double; from 8,200F (1,246.40€, $1,189) suite. Parking 263F (40€, $38.15). AE, DC, MC, V. Métro: George V. **Amenities:** 2 restaurants (both French); bar; indoor pool; health club; room service. *In room:* A/C, TV, minibar, hair dryer, safe.

Hôtel de Crillon ✦✦✦   One of Europe's grand hotels, the Crillon sits across from the U.S. Embassy. Although some international CEOs and diplomats treat it as a shrine, those seeking less pomposity might prefer the Plaza Athénée or the Ritz. The 200-plus-year-old building, once the palace of the duc de Crillon, has been a hotel since the early 1900s and is now owned by Jean Taittinger of the champagne family. The public salons boast 17th- and 18th-century tapestries, gilt-and-brocade furniture, chandeliers, fine sculpture, and Louis XVI chests and chairs. The guest rooms are large and luxurious. Some are spectacular, like the Leonard Bernstein Suite, which has one of the maestro's pianos and one of the grandest views of any hotel room in Paris. The marble bathrooms are sumptuous as well, with deluxe toiletries, dual sinks, robes, and (in some) thermal taps.

10 place de la Concorde, 75008 Paris. © **800/223-6800** in the U.S. and Canada, or © **01-44-71-15-00.** Fax 01-44-71-15-02. www.crillon.com. 160 units. 3,950F–4,650F (600.40€–706.80€, $572.75–$674.25) double; from 6,800F (1,033.60€, $986) suite. AE, DC, MC, V. Free parking. Métro: Concorde. **Amenities:** 2 restaurants (both French); bar; tearoom; exercise room; room service; laundry/dry cleaning. *In room:* A/C, TV, minibar, hair dryer, safe.

Hôtel Meurice ✦✦✦   After a spectacular 2-year renovation, the landmark Meurice, which reopened in mid-2000, is better than ever. The hotel is now more media-hip and style-conscious, in addition to being better located than the also-restored George V, its closest rival.

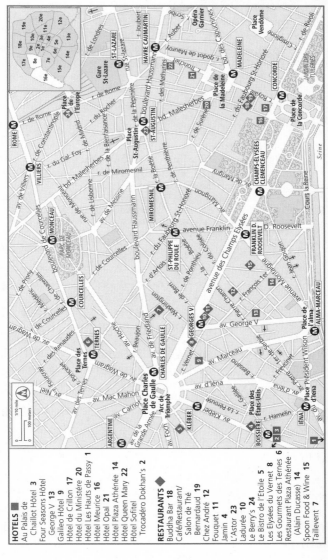

HOTELS ■

Au Palais de
Chaillot Hôtel **3**
Four Seasons Hôtel
George V **13**
Galileo Hôtel **9**
Hôtel de Crillon **17**
Hôtel du Ministère **20**
Hôtel Les Hauts de Passy **1**
Hôtel Meurice **16**
Hôtel Opal **21**
Hôtel Plaza Athénée **14**
Hôtel Queen Mary **22**
Hôtel Sofitel
Trocadéro Dokhan's **2**

RESTAURANTS ◆

Buddha Bar **18**
Café/Restaurant/
Salon de Thé
Bernardaud **19**
Chez André **12**
Fouquet **11**
Jamin **4**
L'Astor **23**
Ladurée **10**
Le Berry's **24**
Le Bistro de l'Etoile **5**
Les Elysées du Vernet **8**
Les Gourmets des Ternes **6**
Restaurant Plaza Athénée
(Alain Ducasse) **14**
Spoon Food & Wine **15**
Taillevent **7**

Since the early 1800s it has been welcoming the royal, the rich, and even the radical: The deposed king of Spain, Alfonso XIII, once occupied suite 108; and the mad genius Salvador Dalí made the Meurice his headquarters, as did General von Cholritz, the Nazi who ruled Paris during the occupation. The mosaic floors, elaborate plaster ceilings, hand-carved moldings, and Art-Nouveau glass roof atop the Winter Garden look like new. Each guest room is individually decorated with period pieces, fine carpets, Italian and French fabrics, rare marbles, and modern features such as fax and Internet access. Louis XVI and Empire styles predominate. Our favorites and the least expensive are the sixth-floor dormer rooms. Some rooms have painted ceilings of puffy clouds and blue skies along with canopied beds. Each unit comes with a full state-of-the-art bathroom.

228 rue de Rivoli, Paris 75001. ℂ **01-44-58-10-10.** Fax 01-44-58-10-15. www. meuricehotel.com. 160 units. 4,300F–4,600F (653.60€–699.20€, $623.50–$667) double; from 5,900F (896.80€, $855.50) suite. Parking 120F (18.25€, $17.40). Métro: Tuileries or Concorde. **Amenities:** 2 restaurants (both French); bar; exercise room; full-service spa; room service; babysitting; laundry/dry cleaning. *In room:* A/C, TV, minibar, hair dryer, safe.

Hôtel Plaza Athénée 🏵🏵🏵   The Plaza Athénée, an 1889 Art-Nouveau marvel, is a landmark of discretion and style. In the 8th, only the Bristol can tackle it. Its nearest competitor is George V. (What's the difference? An international CEO tells us that he goes to George V for discreet visits and here for more public ones.) About half the celebrities visiting Paris have been pampered here; in the old days, Mata Hari used to frequent the place. The finest public room is the Montaigne Salon, paneled in grained wood and dominated by a marble fireplace. The quietest guest rooms overlook a courtyard with awnings and parasol-shaded tables; they have ample closet space, and their large, tiled bathrooms contain double basins. Some rooms overlooking avenue Montaigne have views of the Eiffel Tower. In 1999, the hotel completed a radical overhaul, creating larger rooms out of some of the smaller, less desirable ones.

25 av. Montaigne, 75008 Paris. ℂ **866/732-1106** in the U.S. and Canada, or ℂ **01-53-67-66-65.** Fax 01-53-67-66-66. www.plaza-athenee-paris.com. 185 units. 3,850F–4,400F (585.20€–668.80€, $558.25–$638) double; from 4,950F (752.40€, $717.75) suite. AE, DC, MC, V. Parking 120F (18.25€, $17.40). Métro: F D. Roosevelt or Alma-Marceau. **Amenities:** 2 restaurants (both French); bar; health club; salon; room service; massage; babysitting; laundry/dry cleaning. *In room:* A/C, TV, minibar, hair dryer, safe.

MODERATE

Galileo Hôtel 🏵 *Finds*   This is one of the 8th's most charming boutique hotels. A short walk from the Champs-Elysées, the town-house hotel is the epitome of French elegance and charm. The guest rooms are medium in size for the most part and a study in understated taste, decorated in various shades of cocoa and beige. The most spacious are nos. 501 and 502, with a glass-covered veranda you can use even in winter. For such a tiny neighborhood, the prices are moderate.

54 rue Galilée, 75008 Paris. (②) **01-47-20-66-06.** Fax 01-47-20-67-17. 27 units. 950F (144.40€, $137.75) double. AE, DC, MC, V. Parking 150F (22.80€, $21.75). Métro: Charles de Gaulle–Etoile or George V. **Amenities:** Room service (drinks and snacks); babysitting; laundry/dry cleaning. *In room:* A/C, TV, minibar, hair dryer, safe.

Hôtel Queen Mary ⟨⟨✹⟩⟩ Meticulously renovated inside and out, this early-1900s hotel is graced with an iron-and-glass canopy, ornate wrought iron, and the kind of detailing normally reserved for more expensive hotels. The public rooms have touches of greenery and reproductions of mid-19th-century antiques; each guest room has an upholstered headboard, comfortable beds, and mahogany furnishings, plus a carafe of sherry. All the rooms, ranging from small to medium, were fully renovated in 1998, and 31 come with a tub/shower combination, except for 5 shower-only accommodations.

9 rue Greffulhe, 75008 Paris. (②) **01-42-66-40-50.** Fax 01-42-66-94-92. www.hotelqueenmary.com. 36 units. 780F–995F (118.55€–151.25€, $113.10–$144.30) double; 1,400F (212.80€, $203) suite. AE, DC, MC, V. Parking 100F (15.20€, $14.50). Métro: Madeleine or Havre-Caumartin. **Amenities:** Bar; business center; room service; babysitting. *In room:* A/C, TV, minibar, hair dryer, safe.

INEXPENSIVE

Hôtel du Ministère ⟨⟨✹⟩⟩ ⟨⟨*Kids*⟩⟩ The Ministère is a winning choice near the Champs-Elysées and the American Embassy, though it's far from Paris's cheapest budget hotel. In 1999 this hotel, which has long been a family hotel thanks to its affordable rates and welcoming atmosphere, received new owners, who began a program of refurbishing that made the hotel better than ever. The guest rooms are on the small side, but each is comfortably appointed and well maintained; many have oak beams and furnishings that, though worn, are still serviceable. Try to avoid a room on the very top floor, as you'll be too cramped. Each accommodation is equipped with a tub/shower combination.

31 rue de Surène, 75008 Paris. (②) **01-42-66-21-43.** Fax 01-42-66-96-04. www.argia.fr/hotel-ministere. 28 units. 890F–990F (135.30€–150.50€, $129.05–$143.55) double; from 1,090F (165.70€, $158.05) junior suite. AE, MC, V. Parking 110F (16.70€, $15.95). Métro: Madeleine or Miromesnil. **Amenities:** Bar; room service; laundry/dry cleaning. *In room:* A/C, TV, minibar, hair dryer, safe.

Hôtel Opal *(Finds)*   This rejuvenated hotel, located behind La Madeleine church and near the Opéra Garnier, is a real find. The guest rooms are somewhat tight but very clean and comfortable, and many of them are air-conditioned. Those on the top floor are reached by a narrow staircase; some have skylights. Most rooms have twin brass beds, and all of them come with a tub/shower combination. Reception will make arrangements for parking at a nearby garage.

19 rue Tronchet, 75008 Paris. (€) 01-42-65-77-97. Fax 01-49-24-06-58. www. hotels.fr/opal. 36 units. 950F–1,100F (144.40€–167.20€, $137.75–$159.50) double. Extra bed 100F (15.20€, $14.50). AE, DC, V. Parking 130F ($20.80) nearby. Métro: Madeleine. **Amenities:** Room service (breakfast); babysitting; laundry/ dry cleaning. *In room:* A/C, TV, minibar, hair dryer, safe.

16TH ARRONDISSEMENT
VERY EXPENSIVE

Hotel Sofitel Trocadéro Dokhan's *(★★)*   Except for the fact that porters tend to walk through its public areas carrying luggage, you might suspect that this well-accessorized hotel was a private home. It's housed within a stately looking 19th-century building that was vaguely inspired by Palladio, and it contains the kind of accessories that would look appropriate on the set of a Viennese operetta. These include antique paneling, lacquered Regency-era armchairs, gilded bronze chandeliers, and a pervasive sense of good, upper-bourgeois taste. Like many a large private home, the bedrooms come in a wide range of sizes from small to spacious, as do the beautifully maintained bathrooms. Bedrooms each benefit from a different decorative style, and each has antiques or good reproductions, ornamental swags and curtains above the headboards, lots of personalized touches, and triple-glazed windows to seal away noises from the neighborhood outside. Each contains a CD player and a personal fax machine. Well-respected decorator Frédéric Méchiche designed all aspects of this decor.

117 rue Lauriston, 75116 Paris. (€) 01-53-65-66-99. hotel.trocadero.dokhans@ wanadoo.fr. 45 units. 2,300F–2,700F (349.60€–410.40€, $333.50–$391.50) double; 5,000F (760€, $725) suite. AE, DC, MC, V. Parking 90F (13.70€, $13.05). Metro: Trocadéro. **Amenities:** Restaurant (French; lunch only); champagne bar. *In room:* A/C, TV, minibar, hair dryer.

INEXPENSIVE

Au Palais de Chaillot Hôtel   When Thierry and Cyrille Pien, brothers trained in the States, opened this excellent hotel in 1997, budgeters came running. Between the Champ-Elysées and Trocadéro, the town house was restored from top to bottom and the result is a contemporary yet informal style of Parisian chic. The guest rooms come in various shapes and sizes and are furnished with a light touch, with bright colors and wicker. Nos. 61, 62, and 63 afford partial views of the Eiffel Tower. Each unit comes with a neatly tiled, shower-only bathroom.

35 av. Raymond-Poincaré, 75016 Paris. ✆ **01-53-70-09-09.** Fax 01-53-70-09-08. www.chaillotel.com. 28 units. 625F (95€, $90.65) double; 755F (114.75€, $109.50) triple. AE, DC, MC, V. Parking 90F (13.70€, $13.05). Métro: Victor Hugo or Trocadéro. **Amenities:** Room service (breakfast and drinks); laundry/dry cleaning. *In room:* TV, hair dryer.

Hôtel Les Hauts de Passy   Across the river from the Eiffel Tower in a chic residential neighborhood, this hotel sits on a pedestrian-only street where an outdoor market takes place every day except Monday. All the rooms were recently renovated and are inviting, with new mattresses, large pillows, and double-glazed windows. The baths, though small, are squeaky clean, with a tub in only a few units. Just outside the front door is a wonderful *boulangerie* where you can have breakfast while watching the market bustle. Be patient with the hotel staff, as their English is minimal.

37 rue de l'Annonciation, 75016 Paris. ✆ **01-42-88-47-28.** Fax 01-42-88-99-09. 31 units. 550F–600F (83.60€–91.20€, $79.75–$87) double. MC, V. Parking 95F (14.45€, $13.80). Métro: La Muette or Passy. *In room:* TV, minibar, hair dryer.

2 On the Left Bank

We'll begin with the most centrally located arrondissements on the Left Bank, then work our way through the more outlying neighborhoods and to the area near the Eiffel Tower.

5TH ARRONDISSEMENT
MODERATE
Hôtel Abbatial St-Germain   The origins of this hotel run deep: Interior renovations have revealed such 17th-century touches as dovecotes and massive oak beams. In the early 1990s, a radical restoration made the public areas especially appealing and brought the small rooms, furnished in faux Louis XVI, up to modern standards. All windows are double-glazed, and the fifth- and sixth-floor rooms enjoy views over Notre-Dame. The small bathrooms are neatly kept and equipped with showers, or else a tub/shower combination.

46 bd. St-Germain, 75005 Paris. ✆ **01-46-34-02-12.** Fax 01-43-25-47-73. www.abbatial.com. 43 units. 780F–920F (118.70€–140.05€, $113.20–$113.50) double. AE, MC, V. Parking 110F (16.70€, $15.95). Métro: Maubert-Mutualité. **Amenities:** Babysitting; laundry/dry cleaning. *In room:* A/C, TV, minibar, hair dryer, safe.

Hotels in the Heart of the Left Bank
(Arrondissements 5 & 6)

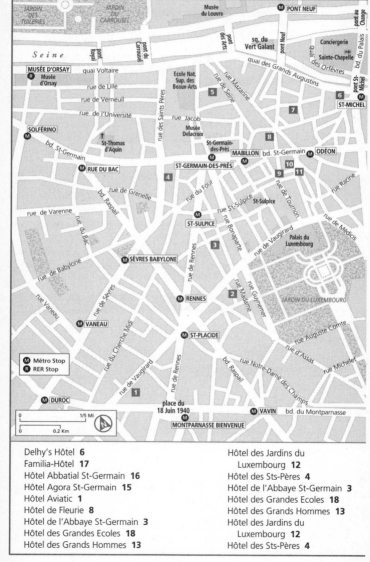

Delhy's Hôtel **6**
Familia-Hôtel **17**
Hôtel Abbatial St-Germain **16**
Hôtel Agora St-Germain **15**
Hôtel Aviatic **1**
Hôtel de Fleurie **8**
Hôtel de l'Abbaye St-Germain **3**
Hôtel des Grandes Ecoles **18**
Hôtel des Grands Hommes **13**

Hôtel des Jardins du
  Luxembourg **12**
Hôtel des Sts-Pères **4**
Hôtel de l'Abbaye St-Germain **3**
Hôtel des Grandes Ecoles **18**
Hôtel des Grands Hommes **13**
Hôtel des Jardins du
  Luxembourg **12**
Hôtel des Sts-Pères **4**

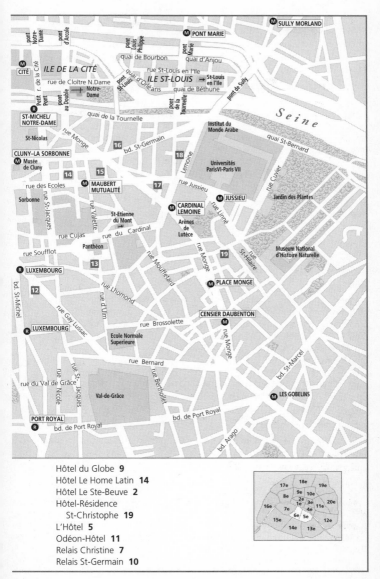

Hôtel du Globe **9**
Hôtel Le Home Latin **14**
Hôtel Le Ste-Beuve **2**
Hôtel-Résidence
  St-Christophe **19**
L'Hôtel **5**
Odéon-Hôtel **11**
Relais Christine **7**
Relais St-Germain **10**

Hôtel Agora St-Germain One of the best of the neighborhood's moderately priced choices, this hotel occupies a building constructed in the early 1600s, probably to house a group of guardsmen protecting the brother of the king at his lodgings nearby. It's in the heart of the artistic/historic Paris and offers compact soundproof guest rooms, each not particularly fashionably furnished. All but seven of the bedrooms have a tub/shower combination, the rest only a shower.

42 rue des Bernardins, 75005 Paris. © **01-46-34-13-00.** Fax 01-46-34-75-05. agorastg@hotellerie.net. 39 units. 800F–880F (121.60€–133.75€, $116–$127.60) double. AE, DC, MC, V. Parking 130F (19.75€, $18.85). Métro: Maubert-Mutualité. *In room:* A/C, TV, minibar, hair dryer, safe.

Hôtel des Grands Hommes Built in the 18th century and renovated in the early 1990s, this hotel offers direct profile views (from many rooms) of the Panthéon. All but a handful of the accommodations have exposed ceiling beams and pleasantly old-fashioned furnishings that sometimes include brass beds. Fifth- and sixth-floor rooms have small balconies and also the best views. Those with the most space are on the ground floor. In 2000, the bedrooms were renovated, and now each comes with a complete tub/shower combination.

17 place du Panthéon, 75005 Paris. © **01-46-34-19-60.** Fax 01-43-26-67-32. 32 units. 850F–1,100F (129.20€–167.20€, $123.25–$159.50) double; 1,200F–2,000F (182.40€–304€, $174–$290) suite. AE, DC, MC, V. Parking 90F (13.70€, $13.05). Métro: Cardinal Lemoine or Luxembourg. **Amenities:** Babysitting; laundry/dry cleaning. *In room:* A/C, TV, minibar, hair dryer.

Hôtel des Jardins du Luxembourg Built during Baron Haussmann's 19th-century overhaul of Paris, this hotel boasts an imposing facade of honey-colored stone accented with ornate iron balconies. The interior is outfitted in strong, clean lines, often with groupings of Art-Deco furnishings. The high-ceilinged guest rooms, some with Provençal tiles and ornate moldings, are well maintained, the size ranging from small to medium. Best of all, they overlook a quiet dead-end alley, ensuring relatively peaceful nights. Some have balconies overlooking the rooftops. In 2000, all the carpeting was replaced in all the bedrooms. Each unit comes with a tidily arranged bathroom with a tub/shower combination.

5 impasse Royer-Collard, 75005 Paris. © **01-40-46-08-88.** Fax 01-40-46-02-28. www.travel-in-paris.com. 26 units. 825F–890F (125.40€–135.30€, $119.65–$129.05) double. AE, DC, MC, V. Parking 100F (15.20€, $14.50). Métro: Cluny–La Sorbonne. RER: Luxembourg. **Amenities:** Babysitting; laundry/dry cleaning. *In room:* A/C, TV, minibar, hair dryer, safe.

Hôtel-Résidence St-Christophe   This hotel, in one of the Latin Quarter's undiscovered but charming areas, offers a gracious English-speaking staff. It was created in 1987 when a derelict hotel was connected to a butcher shop. All the small- to medium-size rooms were successfully renovated in 1998, with Louis XV–style furniture, wall-to-wall carpeting, and firm mattresses. All the bedrooms have private showers, and half the units also have a tub.

17 rue Lacépède, 75005 Paris. ℂ **01-43-31-81-54.** Fax 01-43-31-12-54. hotelst christophe@compuserve.com. 31 units. 700F (106.40€, $101.50) double. AE, DC, MC, V. Parking 100F (15.20€, $14.50). Métro: Place Monge. **Amenities:** Laundry/dry cleaning. *In room:* TV, minibar, hair dryer.

INEXPENSIVE

Familia-Hôtel   As the name implies, this is a hotel that has been family-run for decades. Many personal touches make the place unique, and it was lavishly renovated in 1998. As in many Paris hotels, rooms are quite small and cozy but still comfortable. The walls of 14 rooms are graced with finely executed, sepia-toned frescoes of Parisian scenes. Eight rooms have restored stone walls, and seven have balconies with delightful views over the Latin Quarter. All units have showers, and half the rooms also come with tubs.

11 rue des Ecoles, 75005 Paris. ℂ **01-43-54-55-27.** Fax 01-43-29-61-77. 30 units. 550F–665F (83.60€–101.10€, $79.75–$96.45) double. Rates include breakfast. AE, DC, MC, V. Métro: Jussieu or Maubert-Mutualité. *In room:* TV, minibar, hair dryer.

Hôtel des Grandes Ecoles *(Value*   Few other hotels in the neighborhood offer so much low-key charm at such reasonable prices. It's composed of a trio of high-ceilinged buildings, interconnected via a sheltered courtyard where, in warm weather, singing birds provide a worthy substitute for the TVs deliberately missing from the rooms. Accommodations, as reflected by the price, range from snug, cozy doubles to more spacious chambers. Each is comfortable, but with a lot of luggage, the very smallest would be cramped. The room decor is artfully old-fashioned, with feminine touches such as Laura Ashley–inspired flowered upholsteries and ruffles. Many offer views of a garden whose trellises and flowerbeds evoke the countryside.

75 rue de Cardinal-Lemoine, 75005 Paris. ℂ **01-43-26-79-23.** Fax 01-43-25-28-15. www.hotel-grandes-ecoles.com. 51 units. 550F–720F (83.60€–109.45€, $79.75–$104.40) double. MC, V. Parking 100F (15.20€, $14.50). Métro: Cardinal Lemoine or Monge. *In room:* Hair dryer.

Hôtel Le Home Latin *(Value*   This is one of Paris's most famous budget hotels, known since the 1970s for its simple lodgings. The blandly functional rooms were renovated in 1999; some have small balconies overlooking the street. Those facing the courtyard are quieter than those fronting the street. The elevator doesn't reach beyond the fifth floor, but to make up for the stair climb, the sixth floor's *chambres mansardées* offer a romantic location under the eaves and panoramic rooftop views. Forty-seven units come only with a shower; the rest contain a tub/shower combination.

15–17 rue du Sommerard, 75005 Paris. ℭ **01-43-26-25-21.** Fax 01-43-29-87-04. www.homelatinhotel.com. 54 units. 595F–650F (90.45€–98.80€, $86.30–$94.25) double; 750F (114€, $108.75) triple; 860F (130.70€, $124.70) quad. AE, DC, MC, V. Parking 85F (12.90€, $12.35). Métro: St-Michel or Maubert-Mutualité. *In room:* Hair dryers; no phone.

6TH ARRONDISSEMENT
VERY EXPENSIVE

Relais Christine ⟨★★⟩   The Relais Christine welcomes you into what was once a 16th-century Augustinian cloister. You enter from a narrow cobblestone street into first a symmetrical courtyard and then an elegant reception area with baroque sculpture and Renaissance antiques. Each guest room is uniquely decorated with wooden beams and Louis XIII–style furnishings; the rooms come in a wide range of styles and shapes, and some are among the Left Bank's largest, with extras like mirrored closets, plush carpets, thermostats, and even balconies facing the outer courtyard. The least attractive, smallest, and dimmest rooms are those in the interior. Each comes with a complete tub and shower bathroom.

3 rue Christine, 75006 Paris. ℭ **800/525-5800** in the U.S., or ℭ **01-40-51-60-80.** Fax 01-40-51-60-81. www.relais-christine.com. 51 units. 2,000F–2,600F (304€–395.20€, $290–$377) double; 3,200F–4,500F (486.40€–684€, $464–$652.50) duplex or suite. AE, DC, MC, V. Free parking. Métro: Odéon. **Amenities:** Honor bar in lobby; room service; babysitting; laundry/dry cleaning. *In room:* A/C, TV, minibar, hair dryer, safe.

EXPENSIVE

Hôtel de Fleurie ⟨★★⟩ *(Kids)*   Off boulevard St-Germain on a colorful little street, the Fleurie is one of the best of the "new" old hotels, with its statuary-studded facade recapturing a 17th-century elegance. The stone walls have been exposed in the reception salon, where you check in at a refectory desk. About half the guest rooms and tub and shower bathrooms were renovated in 1999, and many have elaborate curtains and antique reproductions. This hotel has long been a family favorite—interconnecting doors in certain pairs of rooms create safe havens the hotel refers to as *chambres familiales.*

32–34 rue Grégoire-de-Tours, 75006 Paris. ℭ **01-53-73-70-00.** Fax 01-53-73-70-20. www.hotel-de-fleurie.tm.fr. 29 units. 1,700F–1,800F (258.40€–273.60€,

$246.50–$261) double; 1,700F–1,800F (258.40€–273.60€, $246.50–$261) family room. Children 12 and under stay free in parent's room. AE, DC, MC, V. Métro: Odéon or St-Germain-des-Prés. **Amenities:** Bar; car-rental desk; room service; babysitting; laundry/dry cleaning. *In room:* A/C, TV, minibar, hair dryer, trouser press.

Hôtel de l'Abbaye St-Germain 🌲

This is one of the district's most charming boutique hotels, having been a convent in the early 18th century. Its brightly colored rooms have traditional furniture like you'd find in a private club, plus touches of sophisticated flair. The more expensive units are quite spacious; the cheaper ones are small but efficiently organized and still quite comfortable. In front is a small garden, and in back are a verdant courtyard with a fountain, raised flowerbeds, and masses of ivy and climbing vines. If you don't mind the expense, one of the most charming rooms has a terrace that overlooks the upper floors of neighboring buildings. Bedrooms come with neatly tiled and complete bathrooms.

10 rue Cassette, 75006 Paris. ℰ **01-45-44-38-11.** Fax 01-45-48-07-86. www. Hotel-Abbaye.com. 46 units. 1,260F–1,860F (191.50€–282.70€, $182.70–$269.70) double; 2,440F–2,540F (370.90€–386.10€, $353.80–$368.30) suite. Rates include breakfast. AE, MC, V. Métro: St-Sulpice. **Amenities:** Garden; room service; babysitting; laundry/dry cleaning. *In room:* A/C, TV, hair dryer, safe.

L'Hôtel 🌲🌲

Ranking just a notch below the Relais Christine, this is one of the Left Bank's most charming boutique hotels. It was once a 19th-century fleabag called the Alsace, whose major distinction was that Oscar Wilde died there, broke and in despair. But today's guests aren't anywhere near poverty row: This was the sophisticated creation of late French actor Guy-Louis Duboucheron, and show business and fashion celebrities love it. The guest rooms vary in size, style, and price, from quite small to deluxe, but all have non-working fireplaces and fabric-covered walls. An eclectic collection of antiques pops up here and there: One spacious room contains the original furnishings and memorabilia of stage star Mistinguette, a frequent performer with Maurice Chevalier and his on-again/off-again lover. Her pedestal bed is set in the middle of the room, surrounded by mirrors, as she liked to see how she looked or "performed" at all times. About half the bathrooms are small, tubless nooks.

13 rue des Beaux-Arts, 75006 Paris. ℰ **01-44-41-99-00.** Fax 01-43-25-64-81. www.l-hotel.com. 27 units. 2,500F–4,800F (380€–729.60€, $362.50–$696) double; from 5,000F (760€, $725) suite. AE, DC, MC, V. Métro: St-Germain-des-Prés or Mabillon. **Amenities:** Room service; babysitting; laundry/dry cleaning. *In room:* A/C, TV, minibar, hair dryer.

Odéon-Hôtel 🌲🌲

Reminiscent of a modernized Norman country inn, the Odéon offers charming rustic touches such as exposed beams, rough stone walls, high crooked ceilings, and tapestries mixed with contemporary fabrics, mirrored ceilings, and black leather furnishings. Conveniently located near both the Théâtre de l'Odéon and boulevard St-Germain, the Odéon stands on the first street in Paris to have pavements (1779) and gutters. By the turn of the 20th century, this area, which had drawn the original Shakespeare & Co. bookshop to no. 12 rue de l'Odéon, began attracting such writers as Gertrude Stein and her coterie. The guest rooms are small to medium in size but charming, and each comes with a tub/shower combination.

3 rue de l'Odéon, 75006 Paris. ✆ **01-43-25-90-67.** Fax 01-43-25-55-98. www. odeonhotel.fr. 33 units. 950F–1,400F (144.40€–212.80€, $137.75–$203) double; 1,500F (228€, $217.50) suite. AE, DC, MC, V. Parking 100F (15.20€, $14.50). Métro: Odéon. **Amenities:** Room service (drinks); babysitting. *In room:* A/C, TV, hair dryer, safe.

Relais St-Germain ☆   Adapted from a 17th-century building, the St-Germain is an oasis of charm and comfort. It's comparable to the Relais Christine, its nearest competitor, but with a more accommodating staff. The decor is a medley of traditional and modern, evoking a charming provincial house. All the necessary amenities have been tucked in under the beams, including soundproofing and full bathrooms. Bathrooms range from mid-size to roomy, each with a tub/shower combination. Four rooms feature kitchenettes, and two of the suites come with terraces.

9 carrefour de l'Odéon, 75006 Paris. ✆ **01-43-29-12-05.** Fax 01-46-33-45-30. 22 units. 1,600F–1,850F (243.20€–281.20€, $232–$268.25) double; 2,100F (319.20€, $304.50) suite. Rates include breakfast. AE, DC, MC, V. Métro: Odéon. **Amenities:** Restaurant (French); room service; massage; babysitting; laundry/ dry cleaning. *In room:* A/C, TV, minibar, hair dryer, safe.

MODERATE

Hôtel Aviatic   Completely remodeled, this is a bit of old Paris in an interesting section of Montparnasse, with a modest inner courtyard and a vine-covered wall lattice, surrounded by cafes popular with artists, writers, and jazz musicians. It has been a family-run hotel for a century and has an English-speaking staff. The reception lounge boasts marble columns, brass chandeliers, antiques, and a petite salon. The guest rooms, which are midsize and fairly standard throughout, were renovated in stages throughout the 1990s, and each comes with a shower or a tub/shower combination.

105 rue de Vaugirard, 75006 Paris. ✆ **01-53-63-25-50.** Fax 01-53-63-25-55. www. aviatic.fr. 43 units. 950F (144.40€, $137.75) double. AE, DC, MC, V. Parking 120F

(18.25€, $17.40). Métro: Montparnasse-Bienvenue or Saint-Placide. **Amenities:** Room service; babysitting; laundry/dry cleaning. *In room:* A/C, TV, minibar, hair dryer.

Hôtel des Sts-Pères This hotel off boulevard St-Germain is comparable to the Odéon, and there's no better recommendation than the long list of guests who return again and again (the late Edna St. Vincent Millay loved the camellia-trimmed garden). The hotel, designed by Louis XIV's architect, Jacques-Ange Gabriel, is decorated in part with antique paintings, tapestries, and mirrors. Many of the guest rooms face a quiet courtyard. Most sought after is the *chambre à la fresque,* with a 17th-century painted ceiling. The hotel has installed new plumbing and replastered and repainted the rooms.

65 rue des Sts-Pères, 75006 Paris. ⓒ **01-45-44-50-00.** Fax 01-45-44-90-83. www.hotelsts.peres@wanadoo.fr. 39 units. 850F–1,250F (129.20€–190€, $123.25–$181.25) double; 1,750F (266€, $253.75) suite. AE, MC, V. Métro: St-Germain-des-Prés or Sèvres-Babylone. **Amenities:** Garden. *In room:* TV, minibar.

Hôtel Le Ste-Beuve ⓡ *Finds* The location of this discreet hideaway adds to its charms, on a street that's tucked into a narrow and quiet neighborhood, reeking of bourgeois respectability, near the Luxembourg Garden. The public areas are outfitted with deep leather armchairs and a midwinter fire that blazes merrily in an open hearth. Bedrooms each contain at least one antique, and each comes in a different color scheme. None is overly large, but all of them (four to a floor) face the quiet street, noises from which are muffled by double-glazing. Full bathrooms are sheathed in dark-brown marble. Overall, the aura is one of well-managed comfort and respectability.

9 rue Ste-Beuve, 75006 Paris. ⓒ **01-45-48-30-07.** Fax 01-45-48-33-95. www. paris-hotel-charme.com. 22 units. 780F–1,440F (118.55€–218.90€, $113.10– $208.80) double; 1,700F (258.40€, $246.50) suite. Parking 90F (13.70€, $13.05). Metro: Notre-Dame-des-Champs. **Amenities:** Room service (drinks). *In room:* TV, minibar.

INEXPENSIVE

Delhy's Hôtel It's an oldie but a goodie. On a narrow, crooked alley in the Latin Quarter's densest part, this building (ca. 1400) was acquired by François I as a home for one of his mistresses. Don't expect luxury, but look for charming touches that help compensate for the lack of an elevator. The staircase is listed as a national relic, and most of the compact guest rooms still have the original, almost fossilized, timbers and beams. The rooms were for the most part renovated in the late 1990s. If you get a room without a bathroom, you'll have to go down to the ground floor for access to the public facilities.

22 rue de l'Hirondelle, 75006 Paris. ℂ **01-43-26-58-25.** Fax 01-43-26-51-06. 21 units, 7 with bathroom. 376F (57.15€, $54.50) double without bathroom, 466F (70.85€, $67.55) double with bathroom; 636F (96.65€, $92.20) triple with bathroom. Rates include breakfast. AE, DC, MC, V. Métro: St-Michel. *In room:* TV.

Hôtel du Globe Located on an evocative street, this 17th-century building has most of its original stonework and dozens of original timbers and beams. There's no elevator (you have to lug your suitcases up a very narrow antique staircase) and no breakfast area (trays are brought to your room). Each guest room is decorated with individual old-fashioned flair. *A tip:* The rooms with tubs are almost twice as large as those with shower stalls. The largest and most desirable rooms are nos. 1, 12 (with a baldachin-style bed), 14, 15, and 16. The room without a bathroom is a single at 330F (50.15€, $47.85).

15 rue des Quatre-Vents, 75006 Paris. ℂ **01-46-33-62-69.** Fax 01-46-33-62-69. hotelglobe@post.club-internet.fr. 15 units, 5 with bathroom. 430F–655F (65.35€–99.55€, $62.35–$95) double. MC, V. Closed 3 weeks in Aug. Métro: Mabillon, Odéon, or St-Sulpice. **Amenities:** Room service (drinks); laundry/dry cleaning. *In room:* TV.

7TH ARRONDISSEMENT
VERY EXPENSIVE
Hôtel Montalembert 𝕲𝕲 Unusually elegant for the Left Bank, the Montalembert dates from 1926 when it was built in the beaux-arts style. It was restored between 1989 and 1992 and again in 2001 and hailed as a smashing success, borrowing sophisticated elements of Bauhaus and postmodern design in honey beiges, creams, and golds. The guest rooms are spacious, except for some standard doubles, which are quite small unless you're a very thin model. The full bathrooms are luxurious with deep tubs, chrome fixtures, Cascais marble, and tall pivoting mirrors.

3 rue de Montalembert, 75007 Paris. ℂ **800/786-6397** in the U.S. and Canada, or ℂ **01-45-49-68-68.** Fax 01-45-49-69-49. www.montalembert.com. 56 units. 2,200F–2,700F (334.40€–410.40€, $319–$391.50) double; 3,500F (532€, $507.50) junior suite; 4,400F (668.80€, $638) suite. AE, DC, MC, V. Parking 120F (18.25€, $17.40). Métro: Rue du Bac. **Amenities:** Restaurant (French); bar; access to nearby health club; room service; babysitting; laundry/dry cleaning. *In room:* A/C, TV, minibar, hair dryer, safe.

EXPENSIVE
Hôtel de l'Université 𝕲 Long favored by well-heeled parents of North American students studying in Paris, this 300-year-old town house filled with antiques enjoys a location in a discreetly upscale neighborhood. No. 54 is a favorite room, containing a rattan bed and

Hotels & Restaurants near the Eiffel Tower & Invalides (7th Arrondissement)

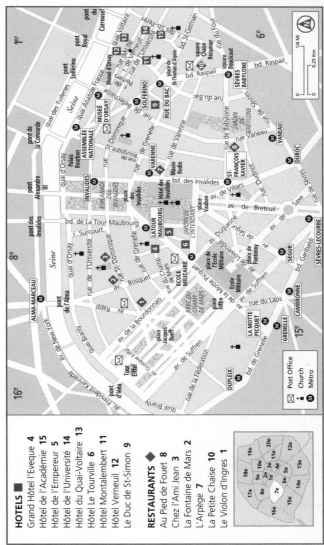

HOTELS ■

Grand Hôtel l'Eveque **4**
Hôtel de l'Académie **15**
Hôtel de l'Empereur **5**
Hôtel de l'Université **14**
Hôtel du Quai-Voltaire **13**
Hôtel Le Tourville **6**
Hôtel Montalembert **11**
Hôtel Verneuil **12**
Le Duc de St-Simon **9**

RESTAURANTS ◆

Au Pied de Fouet **8**
Chez l'Ami Jean **3**
La Fontaine de Mars **2**
L'Arpège **7**
La Petite Chaise **10**
Le Violon d'Ingres **1**

period pieces. Another charmer is no. 35 with a fireplace, opening onto a courtyard with a fountain. The most expensive accommodation has a small terrace overlooking the surrounding rooftops. Most of the bedrooms are midsize or even small, as are the bathrooms. But a few rented at the higher price tag have generous space.

22 rue de l'Université, 75007 Paris. ② **01-42-61-09-39.** Fax 01-42-60-40-84. www.hoteluniversite.com. 28 units. 850F–1,300F (129.20€–197.60€, $123.25–$188.50) double. AE, MC, V. Métro: St-Germain-des-Prés. **Amenities:** Babysitting; laundry/dry cleaning. *In room:* A/C, TV, hair dryer, safe.

Le Duc de St-Simon ⌘   On a quiet residential street, this is the only hotel in the area to pose a serious challenge to the Montalembert. Two immortal cafes, Les Deux Magots and Le Flore, are a few steps away. The small villa has a landscaped courtyard, a rear garden, and a Napoléon III (mid-18th-century) decor with trompe l'oeil panels. Climbing wisteria graces the courtyard. Each guest room is unique and sure to include at least one antique; a few are somewhat cramped, but most offer adequate space. Each room has a beautifully kept private bathroom with a tub/shower combination.

14 rue de St-Simon, 75007 Paris. ② **01-44-39-20-20.** Fax 01-45-48-68-25. 34 units. 1,275F–1,650F (193.80€–250.80€, $184.90–$239.25) double; 2,000F–2,250F (304€–342€, $290–$326.25) suite. AE, MC, V. Métro: Rue du Bac. **Amenities:** Garden; bar; room service; babysitting; laundry/dry cleaning. *In room:* Hair dryer, safe.

MODERATE

Hôtel de l'Académie ⌘⌘   The exterior walls and old ceiling beams are all that remain of this 17th-century residence of the duc de Rohan's private guards. In 1999, the hotel was completely renovated to include an elegant reception area. The up-to-date guest rooms have a lush Ile-de-France decor and views over the neighborhood's 18th- and 19th-century buildings. By American standards the rooms are small, but they're average for Paris. All but eight bathrooms have a full tub/shower combination.

32 rue des Sts-Pères, 75007 Paris. ② **800/246-0041** in the U.S. and Canada, or ② **01-45-49-80-00.** Fax 01-45-44-75-24. www.academiehotel.com. 34 units. 990F–1,290F (150.50€–196.10€, $143.55–$187.05) double; from 1,590F (241.70€, $230.55) suite. AE, DC, MC, V. Parking 150F (22.80€, $21.75). Métro: St-Germain-des-Prés. **Amenities:** Exercise room; massage; babysitting. *In room:* A/C, TV, minibar, hair dryer, safe.

Hôtel du Quai-Voltaire ⌘⌘   Built in the 1600s as an abbey, then transformed into a hotel in 1856, the Quai-Voltaire is best-known for its illustrious guests, such as Wilde, Wagner, and

Baudelaire, who occupied rooms 47, 55, and 56, respectively. Camille Pissarro painted Le Pont Royal from the window of his fourth-floor room. Many guest rooms in this modest inn have been renovated, and most overlook the bookstalls and boats of the Seine. Doubles tend to be small, the triples midsize but not spacious. Each unit comes with a small, shower-only bathroom. *Warning:* This hotel is not for everyone, although it has its diehard devotees. The front rooms enjoy one of the greatest views of Paris, but are exposed to the roar of traffic. It's also a long walk from any Métro stop.

19 quai Voltaire, 75007 Paris. ℂ **01-42-61-50-91.** Fax 01-42-61-62-26. 33 units. 750F–800F (114€–121.60€, $108.75–$116) double; 870F (132.25€, $126.15) triple. AE, DC, MC, V. Parking 110F (16.70€, $15.95) nearby. Métro: Musée d'Orsay or Rue du Bac. **Amenities:** Bar; room service; laundry. *In room:* TV, hair dryer.

Hotel Le Tourville ℛ   This is a well-managed, relatively personal-ized *hotel de charme* that occupies a desirable town house midway between the Eiffel Tower and Les Invalides. It originated in the 1930s as a hotel, and was revitalized and reconfigured during the 1990s into the stylish charmer you see today. Bedrooms each contain original artworks, an antique or an antique reproduction, and some kind of traditional wooden furniture covered in modern, sometimes bold, upholsteries. Four of the rooms, including the suite, have private ter-races for soaking up the Parisian sunshine. Rooms 16 and 18 are the most desirable. About half the bathrooms are small with shower stalls, the others are more generously endowed with a tub/shower combination. Staff is particularly well trained. Breakfast is the only meal served, but you can get a drink in the lobby.

16 av. de Tourville, 75007 Paris. ℂ **01-47-05-43-90.** Fax 01-47-05-43-90. www.hoteltourville.com. 30 units. 890F–1,390F (135.30€–211.30€, $129.05–$201.55) double; 1,990F (302.50€, $288.55) suite. AE, DC, MC, V. Métro: Ecole Militaire. **Amenities:** Bar. *In room:* A/C, TV, hair dryer.

Hôtel Verneuil ℛ *Finds*   Small-scale and personalized, this hotel, in the words of a recent critic, "combines modernist sympathies with nostalgia for *la vieille France.*" Within what was built in the 1600s as a town house, it offers a creative and intimate jumble of charm and coziness. Expect a mixture of antique and contemporary furniture, lots of books, and in the bedrooms, trompe l'oeil ceilings, antique beams that in some cases have been painted white, quilts, and walls covered in fabric in a rainbow of colors. Bathrooms come with a tub/shower combination or a shower only.

8 rue de Verneuil, 75007 Paris. ℂ **01-42-60-82-14.** Fax 01-42-61-40-38. verneuil@cybercable.fr. 26 units. 850F–1,100F (129.20€–167.20€, $123.25–$159.50) double. AE, DC, MC, V. Parking 120F (18.25€, $17.40). Métro: St Germain-des-Prés. **Amenities:** Bar; room service (drinks); babysitting; laundry/ dry cleaning. *In room:* TV, minibar, hair dryer.

INEXPENSIVE

Grand Hôtel L'Eveque   Built in the 1930s, this hotel draws lots of English-speaking guests, many of whom appreciate its proximity to the Eiffel Tower. In 2000, the interior was completely renovated and repainted with all the carpets changed. The pastel-colored guest rooms retain an Art-Deco inspiration, just enough space to be comfortable, and double-insulated windows overlooking a courtyard in back or the street in front. The small bathrooms contain showers.

29 rue Cler, 75007 Paris. ℂ **01-47-05-49-15.** Fax 01-45-50-49-36. www.hotel-leveque.com. 50 units. 400–500F (60.80–76€, $58–$72.50) double; 600F (91.20€, $87) triple. AE, MC, V. Métro: Ecole Militaire. *In room:* TV, hair dryer, safe.

Hôtel de l'Empereur   This convenient hotel was built in the early 1700s and enjoys a loyal group of repeat visitors. There's an elevator to haul you and your luggage to one of the smallish but attractively decorated guest rooms, with mostly shower-only bathrooms. In 1998, the two top floors were renovated. There's no restaurant or bar, but a nearby restaurant will send up platters of food on request.

2 rue Chevert, 75007 Paris. ℂ **01-45-55-88-02.** Fax 01-45-51-88-54. www.hotel empereur.com. 38 units. 475F–535F (72.20€–81.43€, $68.90–$77.65) double; 660F (100.30€, $95.70) triple; 760F (115.50€, $110.20) quad. AE, DC, MC, V. Parking 110–150F (16.70–22.80€, $15.95–$21.75) across the street. Métro: Latour-Maubourg. **Amenities:** Room service; laundry/dry cleaning. *In room:* TV, fridge, hair dryer.

Where to Dine

4

Welcome to the city that prides itself on being the world's culinary capital. Only in Paris can you turn onto the nearest little crooked side street, enter the first nondescript bistro you see, sit down at a bare wobbly table, order from an illegibly hand-scrawled menu, and get a truly memorable meal.

1 On the Right Bank

We'll begin with the most centrally located arrondissements on the Right Bank, then work our way through the more outlying neighborhoods and to the area around the Arc de Triomphe.

1ST ARRONDISSEMENT
VERY EXPENSIVE

Carré des Feuillants ✿✿✿ FRENCH (MODERN) This is a bastion of perfection, an elegant enclave of haute gastronomy between the place Vendôme and the Tuileries. When leading chef Alain Dutournier turned this 17th-century convent into a restaurant, it was an overnight success. The interior is like an early-1900s bourgeois house with several small salons opening onto a sky-lit courtyard, across from which is a glass-enclosed kitchen. You'll find a sophisticated reinterpretation of cuisine from France's southwest, using seasonally fresh ingredients and lots of know-how. Examples are roasted veal kidneys cooked in their own fat; grilled wood pigeon served with chutney and polenta; rabbit filet in bitter-chocolate sauce with quince; and roasted leg of suckling lamb from the Pyrénées with autumn vegetables. Lighter dishes are scallops wrapped in parsley-infused puff pastry served with cabbage and truffles, and mullet-studded risotto with lettuce. For dessert, try a slice of pistachio cream cake with candied tangerines.

14 rue de Castiglione (near place Vendôme and the Tuileries), 1st arr. ☎ **01-42-86-82-82.** Fax 01-42-86-07-71. Reservations required far in advance. Main courses 260F–340F (39.50€–51.70€, $37.70–$49.30); fixed-price lunch 360F (54.70€, $52.20); fixed-price dinner 900F (136.80€, $130.50). AE, DC, MC, V. Mon–Fri noon–2:30pm; Mon–Sat 7:30–10pm. Closed 1st 3 weeks in Aug. Métro: Tuileries, Concorde, Opéra, or Madeleine.

Restaurants in the Heart of the Right Bank
(Arrondissements 1–4, 9–12 & 19)

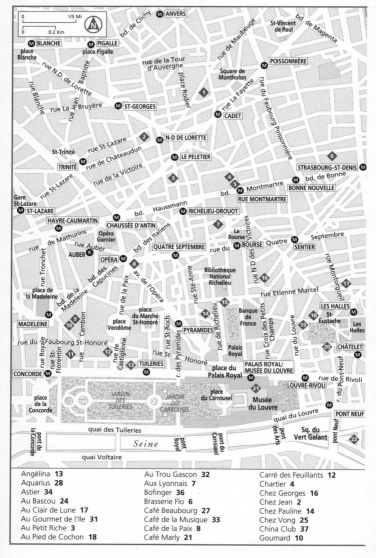

Angélina **13**	Au Trou Gascon **32**	Carré des Feuillants **12**
Aquarius **28**	Aux Lyonnais **7**	Chartier **4**
Astier **34**	Bofinger **36**	Chez Georges **16**
Au Bascou **24**	Brasserie Flo **6**	Chez Jean **2**
Au Clair de Lune **17**	Café Beaubourg **27**	Chez Pauline **14**
Au Gourmet de l'Île **31**	Café de la Musique **33**	Chez Vong **25**
Au Petit Riche **3**	Café de la Paix **8**	China Club **37**
Au Pied de Cochon **18**	Café Marly **21**	Goumard **10**

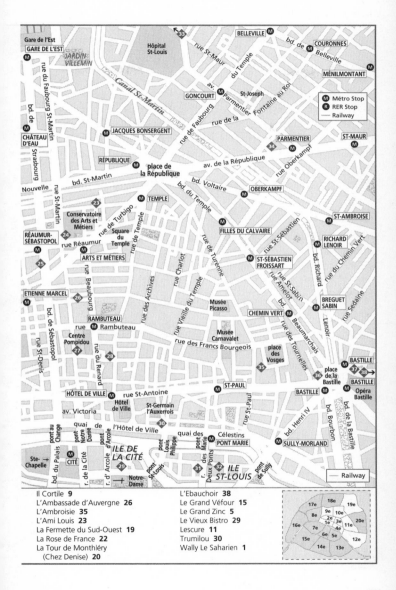

Gare de l'Est
GARE DE L'EST Ⓜ
JARDIN
VILLEMIN
Ⓜ
rue du Faubourg St-Martin
bd. de
CHÂTEAU
D'EAU Ⓜ
Strasbourg
Nouvelle
bd. St-Martin
rue St-Martin

Hôpital
St-Louis
Canal St-Martin
rue St-Maur
du Temple
GONCOURT Ⓜ
av. Parmentier
St-Joseph
rue de Faubourg
rue de la
RÉPUBLIQUE Ⓜ
place de
la République
bd. Voltaire
JACQUES BONSERGENT Ⓜ
BELLEVILLE Ⓜ
bd. de
Belleville
COURONNES
MÉNILMONTANT Ⓜ
rue Fontaine au Roi
PARMENTIER Ⓜ
ST-MAUR Ⓜ
av. de la République
rue Oberkampf
OBERKAMPF Ⓜ

bd. du Temple
Conservatoire
des Arts et
Métiers Ⓜ23
rue de Turbigo
Square
du
Temple
TEMPLE Ⓜ
rue Réaumur
RÉAUMUR-
SÉBASTOPOL Ⓜ24
ARTS ET MÉTIERS Ⓜ
Ⓜ25
ETIENNE MARCEL Ⓜ
Ⓜ26
rue Beaubourg
RAMBUTEAU Ⓜ
rue Ⓜ Rambuteau
Centre
Pompidou
Ⓜ27
Ⓜ28
rue du Renard
HÔTEL DE VILLE Ⓜ
rue St-Antoine
FILLES DU CALVAIRE Ⓜ
rue de Temple
rue Charlot
rue des Archives
rue Vieille du Temple
rue de Turenne
Musée
Picasso
Musée
Carnavalet
rue des Francs Bourgeois
ST-SÉBASTIEN
FROISSART Ⓜ
CHEMIN VERT Ⓜ
ST-AMBROISE Ⓜ
RICHARD
LENOIR Ⓜ
rue du Chemin Vert
BREGUET
SABIN Ⓜ
rue St-Sébastien
rue St-Sabin
rue Amelot
bd. Richard
Lenoir
bd. Beaumarchais
place
des
Vosges
Ⓜ35
place
de la
Bastille
Ⓜ36
BASTILLE Ⓜ37 Ⓜ38
BASTILLE Ⓜ
Opéra
Bastille

bd. de Sébastopol
rue St-Denis
bd. St-Denis
Hôtel
de Ville
av. Victoria
quai de
l'Hôtel de Ville
HÔTEL DE VILLE Ⓜ
St-Germain
l'Auxerrois
Ⓜ30
quai des
Célestins
St-PAUL Ⓜ
rue St-Paul
PONT MARIE Ⓜ
SULLY-MORLAND Ⓜ
BASTILLE Ⓜ
bd. Henri IV
bd. Bourbon
bd. de la Bastille

pont au
Change
pont Notre Dame
pont d'Arcole
Ste-
Chapelle
CITÉ Ⓜ
bd. du Palais
r. de la Cité
r. d'Arcole
ILE DE
LA CITÉ
Ⓜ29
Notre-
Dame
pont St-Louis
pont Louis Philippe
pont de la Tournelle
pont
des
Deux Ponts
ILE
ST-LOUIS
pont de Sully

Ⓜ Métro Stop
Ⓡ RER Stop
— Railway

Railway

Goumard ★★★ SEAFOOD   Opened in 1872, this landmark is one of Paris's leading seafood restaurants. It's so devoted to the fine art of preparing fish that other food is strictly banned from the menu (if you happen to dislike fish, the staff will orally present a limited roster of meat dishes). Much of the seafood is flown in directly from Brittany daily. Examples are a *craquant* (crispy) of crayfish in its own herb salad, lobster soup with coconut, grilled sea-wolf filet with a fricassée of artichokes and Provençal pistou, a grilled turbot salad on a bed of artichokes with tarragon, and poached turbot with hollandaise sauce, served with leeks in vinai-grette. In all these dishes nothing (no excess butter, spices, or salt) is allowed to interfere with the natural flavor of the sea. Be prepared for some unusual food—the staff will help translate the menu items for you. The decor consists of an unusual collection of Lalique crys-tal fish displayed in aquariums. Even more unusual are the men's and women's restrooms, now classified as historic monuments; the commodes were designed by the Art-Nouveau master cabinetmaker Majorelle in the early 1900s.

9 rue Duphot, 1st arr. ✆ 01-42-60-36-07. Fax 01-42-60-04-54. Reservations required far in advance. Main courses 190F–390F (28.90€–59.35€, $27.55–$56.55); fixed-price lunch 250F (38€, $36.25). AE, DC, MC, V. Mon–Sat 12:30–2:30pm and 7:30–10:30pm. Closed 3 weeks in Aug. Métro: Madeleine or Concorde.

Le Grand Véfour ★★★ FRENCH (TRADITIONAL)   This is the all-time winner: a great, great chef; the most beautiful restaurant decor in Paris, and a gastronomic, history-infused citadel of classic French cuisine. This restaurant has been around since the reign of Louis XV, though not under the same name. Napoléon, Danton, Hugo, Colette, and Cocteau have dined here—as the brass plaques on the tables testify—and it's still a great gastronomic experience. Guy Martin, chef here for the past decade, bases many dishes on recipes from the French Alps. His best dish is roast lamb in a juice of herbs. Other specialties are noisettes of lamb with star anise and Breton lobster and the unusual cabbage sorbet in dark-chocolate sauce. The desserts are often grand, like the *gourmandises au choco-lat,* a richness of chocolate served with chocolate sorbet.

17 rue de Beaujolais, 1st arr. ✆ 01-42-96-56-27. Fax 01-42-86-80-71. Reservations required far in advance. Main courses 310F–390F (47.10€–59.30€, $44.95–$56.55); fixed-price menu 430F (65.35€, $62.35) at lunch, 1,050F (159.60€, $152.25) at dinner. AE, DC, MC, V. Mon–Fri 12:30–2pm and Mon–Thurs 8–10pm. Métro: Louvre–Palais Royal.

MODERATE

Au Pied de Cochon *(Finds)* FRENCH (TRADITIONAL)/ LATE-NIGHT Au Pied de Cochon's famous onion soup and namesake house specialty (grilled pig's feet with béarnaise sauce) still lure visitors, and where else in Paris can you be assured of getting a good meal at 3am? Two other specialties are the *tentation* (temptation) platter, including grilled pig's tail, pig's snout, and half a pig's foot with béarnaise and *frites,* and *andouillette* (chitterling sausages) with béarnaise. Two particularly flavorful but less unusual dishes are a *jarret* (shin) of pork, caramelized in honey and served on a bed of sauerkraut, and grilled pork ribs with sage sauce. On the street outside, you can buy some of the freshest oysters in town. The attendants will give you slices of lemon to accompany them, and you can down them on the spot.

6 rue Coquillière, 1st arr. ⓒ **01-40-13-77-00.** Reservations recommended for lunch and dinner hours. Main courses 80F–150F (12.15€–22.80€, $11.60– $21.75). AE, DC, MC, V. Daily 24 hr. Métro: Les Halles.

Chez Pauline *(Finds)* BURGUNDIAN/FRENCH (TRADITIONAL) Fans say this *bistrot de luxe* is a less expensive, less majestic version of Le Grand Véfour. The early-1900s setting is grand enough to impress a business client and lighthearted enough to attract an impressive roster of VIPs. You'll be ushered to a table on one of two levels, amid polished mirrors, red leather banquettes, and memorabilia of long-ago Paris. The emphasis is on the cuisine of central France, especially Burgundy, as shown by the liberal use of wines in favorites like cassoulet of Burgundian snails with bacon and tomatoes, *boeuf bourguignonne* (braised beef in red-wine sauce) with tagliatelle, terrine of parslied ham, wild duckling filet with seasonal berries, salmon steak with green peppercorns, and ragout of wild hare in Pouilly aspic. Also wonderful is the roasted Bresse chicken with dauphinois potatoes. Dessert may include a *clafoutis* (pastry) of apricots and raspberries lightly sautéed in sugar or caramelized rice pudding. Owner/chef André Genin is an author of children's books, some on the value and techniques of French cuisine.

5 rue Villedo, 1st arr. ⓒ **01-42-96-20-70.** Reservations recommended. Main courses 190F–400F (28.90€–60.80€, $27.55–$58); fixed-price menu 220F (33.45€, $31.90). AE, DC, V. Mon–Fri 12:15–2:30pm and 7:30–10:30pm; Sat 7:30–10:30pm. Closed Sat–Sun May–early Sept. Métro: Palais Royal.

Il Cortile *(Finds)* ITALIAN/MEDITERRANEAN Flanking the verdant courtyard of a discreet small hotel, this much-talked-about restaurant serves the best Italian food in Paris. During warm weather, tables are set up in an enclosed patio—a welcome luxury in this congested neighborhood. The cuisine is fresh, inventive, and seasonal. Dishes are from throughout Italy, with emphasis on the north, as shown by a special promotion of wines of Tuscany and the Piedmont. Look for items like *farfalle* pasta with squid ink and fresh shellfish, fettuccine with *pistou* (pasta in a soup made from various vegetables), and an award-winning version of guinea fowl (spit-roasted and served with artfully-shaped slices of the bird's gizzard, heart, and liver, it comes with polenta). The service is virtually flaw-less: The Italian-speaking staff is diplomatic and good-humored. If you want to see what's cooking, ask for a seat with a view of the open rotisserie, where spit-roasted hens and guinea fowl slowly spin.

In the Hôtel Castille, 37 rue Cambon, 1st arr. (01-44-58-45-67. Reservations rec-ommended. Main courses 100F–150F (15.20€–22.80€, $14.50–$21.75); fixed-price menu 270F (41.05€, $39.15). AE, DC, DISC, MC, V. Mon–Fri noon–2:30pm and 7:30–10:30pm. Métro: Concorde or Madeleine.

INEXPENSIVE

Angélina 🕊🕊 FRENCH (TRADITIONAL)/TEA   In the high-rent area near the Inter-Continental (though on a section of rue de Rivoli that's getting scuzzy), this *salon de thé* combines fashion-industry glitter and bourgeois respectability. The carpets are plush, the ceilings are high, and the gilded accessories have the right amount of patina. This place has no equal when it comes to view-ing the lionesses of haute couture over tea and delicate sandwiches. The overwrought and slightly snooty waitresses bear silver trays with light platters, pastries, drinks, and tea or coffee to tiny, marble-topped tables. Lunch usually offers a salad and a *plat du jour* like chicken salad, steak tartare, *sole meunière*, or poached salmon. The house specialty, designed to go well with tea, is a Mont Blanc, a combination of chestnut cream and meringue.

226 rue de Rivoli, 1st arr. (01-42-60-82-00. Reservations accepted for lunch, not for teatime. Pot of tea for 1, 35F–36F (5.30€–5.45€, $5.10–$5.20); sandwiches and salads 58F–98F (8.80€–14.90€, $8.40–$14.20); main courses 68F–150F (10.35€–22.80€, $9.85–$21.75). AE, V. Mon–Fri 9am–7pm; Sat–Sun 9am–7:30pm (lunch daily 11:45am–3pm). Métro: Tuileries or Concorde.

Chez Vong 🕊 CANTONESE   This is the kind of Les Halles restaurant you head for when you've had your fill of grand French cuisine and grander culinary pretensions. The decor is a soothing mix of green and browns, steeped in a Chinese colonial ambience that evokes early-1900s Shanghai. Menu items feature shrimp and scallops served as spicy as you like, including a super-hot version with garlic and red peppers; "joyous beef" that mingles sliced filet with pepper sauce; chicken in puff pastry with ginger; and a tempting array of fresh fish dishes.

10 rue de la Grande-Truanderie, 1st arr. ✆ **01-40-26-09-36.** Reservations recommended. Main courses 88F–200F (13.40€–30.40€, $12.75–$29); fixed-price lunch Mon–Fri only, 150F (22.80€, $21.75). AE, DC, MC, V. Mon–Sat noon–2:30pm and 7pm–midnight. Métro: Etienne-Marcel or Les Halles.

La Fermette du Sud-Ouest ✿ SOUTHWESTERN FRENCH
In the heart of one of Paris's most ancient neighborhoods, a stone's throw from Ste-Eustache church, this restaurant occupies the site of a 1500s convent. After the Revolution, the convent was converted into a coaching inn that preserved the original stonework and massive beams. La Fermette prepares rich, savory stews and confits celebrating agrarian France, serving them on the ground floor and on a mezzanine resembling a medieval choir loft. Menu items include an age-old but ever-popular magret of duckling with flap mushrooms, *andouillette* (chitterling sausages), and a sometimes startling array of *cochonailles* (pork products and byproducts) that you probably need to be French to appreciate. Cassoulet and *pot-au-feu* (beef simmered with vegetables) are enduring specialties.

31 rue Coquillière, 1st arr. ✆ **01-42-36-73-55.** Reservations recommended. Main courses 85F–130F (12.90€–19.75€, $12.35–$18.85); fixed-price menus (at lunch and before 9pm at dinner) 120F–145F (18.25€–22.05€, $17.40–$21.05). MC, V. Mon–Sat noon–2pm and 7:30–10pm. Métro: Les Halles.

La Rose de France ✿ *Value* FRENCH (TRADITIONAL)   At this restaurant on Ile de la Cité near Notre-Dame, around the corner from the Pont Neuf, you'll dine with a crowd of young Parisians who know they can expect a good meal at reasonable prices. Founded more than 30 years ago by its present owner, M. Cointepas, it can be relied on for fresh food served in a friendly atmosphere. In warm weather, the sidewalk tables overlooking the Palais de Justice are most popular. Main dishes include sweetbreads, veal chop flambéed with Calvados and served with apples, beef filet en croûte, and lamb chops seasoned with Provençal herbs and served with gratin of potatoes. For dessert, try the fruit tart of the day or the sorbet of the month.

24 place Dauphine, 1st arr. ✆ **01-43-54-10-12.** Reservations recommended. Main courses 100F–110F (15.20€–16.70€, $14.50–$15.95); *menu du jour* 140F (21.30€, $20.30) without wine, 180F (27.35€, $26.10) with wine. AE, V. Mon–Fri noon–2pm and 7–10pm. Closed last 3 weeks in Aug and 15 days at end of Dec. Métro: Cité or Pont Neuf.

La Tour de Monthléry (Chez Denise) FRENCH (TRADITIONAL)/LATE-NIGHT   This restaurant is both

workaday and stylish—no small feat considering its gregarious owner, Denise Bénariac, has maintained her reign here for more than 30 years. Amid a decor that has changed little since 1900 (note the long nickel-plated bar near the entrance), you can order hearty, unfussy cuisine. The food tastes best late after a long night of carousing. Menu items include grilled pig's trotters, mutton stew, steak with peppercorns, stuffed cabbage, *pot-au-feu,* and a golden-velvety paté of chicken livers. Wine goes with this kind of food beautifully, and the restaurant complies by recommending several worthy but unpretentious vintages.

5 rue des Prouvaires, 1st arr. ✆ **01-42-36-21-82.** Main courses 95F–130F (14.45€–19.75€, $13.80–$18.85). V. Open continuously Mon 7am–Sat 7am. Métro: Louvre or Les Halles.

Lescure ⟨ℛ ⟨*Finds*⟩ FRENCH (TRADITIONAL)   This animated and appealing minibistro is a major find—one of the few reasonably priced restaurants near place de la Concorde. You'll get a lot for your franc. The tables on the sidewalk are tiny, and there isn't much room inside, but what this place does have is rustic charm. The kitchen is wide open, and the aroma of drying bay leaves, salami, and garlic pigtails hanging from the ceiling fills the room. Expect *cuisine bourgeoise*—nothing innovative, just substantial hearty fare. Perhaps begin with *paté en croûte* (paté in puff pastry). Main-course house specialties include *confit de canard* (duckling), beef bourguignonne, and cabbage stuffed with salmon. The chef's fruit tarts are a favorite dessert. In autumn and winter, expect a savory repertoire of game dishes like venison and pheasant.

7 rue de Mondovi, 1st arr. ✆ **01-42-60-18-91.** Main courses 50F–90F (7.60€– 13.70€, $7.25–$13.05); 4-course fixed-price menu 115F (17.50€, $16.70). MC, V. Mon–Fri noon–2:15pm and 7–10:30pm. Closed 3 weeks in Aug. Métro: Concorde.

2ND ARRONDISSEMENT
MODERATE

Chez Georges FRENCH (TRADITIONAL)   This bistro is something of a local landmark, opened in 1964 near La Bourse (stock exchange) and run by three generations of the same family. Naturally, at lunch it's packed with stock-exchange members. The owners serve what they call *la cuisine bourgeoise* (comfort food). Waiters bring around bowls of appetizers, like celery rémoulade, to get you started. You can follow with sweetbreads with morels, duck breast with cêpe mushrooms, classic cassoulet, or *pot-au-feu.* A delight is sole filet with a sauce made from Pouilly wine and crème fraîche. Beaujolais goes great with this hearty food.

1 rue du Mail, 2nd arr. ✆ **01-42-60-07-11**. Reservations required. Main courses 130F–160F (19.75€–24.30€, $18.85–$23.20). AE, MC, V. Mon–Sat noon–2:15pm and 7–9:45pm. Closed 3 weeks in Aug. Métro: Bourse.

INEXPENSIVE

Au Clair de Lune ALGERIAN/FRENCH (TRADITIONAL) This is a pocket of a long-gone French colonial ambition. This neighborhood staple has flourished in the heart of Paris's wholesale garment district since the 1930s, when Algeria was a distinct part of the French-speaking world. Today you'll dine in a long, narrow room whose walls are hung with colorful Berber carpets and whose patrons are likely to include shop workers from the nearby wholesale clothiers. On the menu is always the Algerian staple of couscous, as well as an array of oft-changing daily specials such as veal stew, shoulder or rack of lamb, grilled fish, and roast chicken. The portions are so large you should take along a ravenous appetite. The wines are from throughout France and North Africa.

13 rue Française, 2nd arr. ✆ **01-42-33-59-10**. Main courses 58F–80F (8.80€–12.15€, $8.40–$11.60); fixed-price menu 70F (10.65€, $10.15). MC, V. Daily noon–2:30pm and 7:30–11pm. Métro: Etienne-Marcel or Les Halles.

Aux Lyonnais ⋆⋆ FRENCH (TRADITIONAL)/LYONNAIS A LYON LE COCHON EST ROI! proclaims the sign. Pig may be king at this fin-de-siècle bistro (with walls molded with roses and garlands, brass globe lamps, potted palms, and etched glass) just behind La Bourse, but the competent kitchen staff does everything well. After a meal here, you'll know why Lyon is called the gastronomic capital of France. Everything is washed down with Beaujolais. Launch your repast with one of the large Lyonnais sausages, though a favorite opener remains a chicory salad with bacon and slices of hot sausages. Poached eggs in red-wine sauce and grilled pig's feet still appear on the menu. Pike dumplings are always prepared to perfection and served classically in white-butter sauce. The upside-down apple pie with crème fraîche is the dessert of choice.

32 rue St-Marc, 2nd arr. ✆ **01-42-96-65-04**. Reservations required. Main courses 90F–200F (13.70€–30.40€, $13.05–$29). AE, DC, MC, V. Mon–Sat 11:30am–3pm and 6:30–11:30pm. Métro: Bourse or Richelieu-Drouot.

3RD ARRONDISSEMENT
EXPENSIVE

L'Ami Louis ⋆ FRENCH (TRADITIONAL)   L'Ami Louis is in one of central Paris's least fashionable neighborhoods, far removed from the part of the Marais that has become chic, and its facade has seen better days. It was one of Paris's most famous brasseries in the

1930s, thanks to its excellent food served in copious portions and its old-fashioned decor. Its traditions are fervently maintained today. Amid a "brown gravy" decor (the walls retain a smoky patina), dishes like roasted suckling lamb, pheasant, venison, confit of duckling, and endless slices of foie gras may commune on your marble-topped table. Though some whisper that the ingredients aren't as select as they were in the restaurant's heyday, its sauces are as thick as they were between the wars. Don't save room for dessert, which isn't very good.

32 rue du Vertbois, 3rd arr. ℂ 01-48-87-77-48. Reservations required far in advance. Main courses 250F–350F (38€–53.20€, $36.25–$50.75). MC, V. Wed–Sun noon–2pm and 8–11pm. Closed July 19–Aug 25. Métro: Temple.

INEXPENSIVE

Au Bascou ⊛ *Finds* BASQUE   The succulent cuisine of France's "deep southwest" is the specialty within this restaurant, where art objects and oil paintings celebrate the beauty of the region, and hanging clusters of pimentos add spice to the air. This restaurant serves Basque food that's as good as it gets. For a ray of sunshine in your life, try the *piperade basquaise,* a spicy omelet loaded with peppers and onions; pimentos stuffed with a purée of cod; and an *axoa* of veal (shoulder of calf served with a pimento-and-pepper-based green sauce). Because all starters are priced at 55F (8.35€, $8.05), and all desserts at 40F (6.10€, $5.80), a three-course meal at this place, without wine, sells for 180F (27.35€, $26.10).

38 rue Réaumur, 3rd arr. ℂ 01-42-72-69-25. Reservations recommended. All main courses 85F (12.90€, $12.35). AE, DC, MC, V. Tues–Fri noon–3pm, Mon–Sat 8–11pm. Closed 1 week in Aug. Métro: Arts-et-Métiers.

L'Ambassade d'Auvergne ⊛ AUVERGNAT/FRENCH (TRADITIONAL)

You enter this rustic tavern through a busy bar with heavy oak beams, hanging hams, and ceramic plates. This favorite showcases the culinary generosity of France's most isolated region, the Auvergne, whose pork products are widely celebrated. The best examples are a chicory salad with apples and pieces of country ham; pork braised with cabbage, turnips, and white beans; grilled tripe sausages with mashed potatoes and cantal cheese (a strong, hard cheese) with garlic; and pork jowls with green lentils. The cholesterol is intense, but devotees love this type of food. Non-pork specialties are pan-fried duck liver with gingerbread, perch filets steamed in verbena tea, and roasted rack of lamb with wild mushrooms. Dessert might be a poached pear with crispy almonds and caramel sauce or a wine-flavored sorbet.

22 rue de Grenier St-Lazare, 3rd arr. ✆ **01-42-782-31-22.** Reservations recommended. Main courses 86F–120F (13.05€–18.25€, $12.45–$17.40); fixed-price menu 170F (25.85€, $24.65). AE, MC, V. Daily noon–2pm and 7:30–11pm. Closed 2 weeks in Aug. Métro: Rambuteau.

4TH ARRONDISSEMENT
VERY EXPENSIVE

L'Ambroisie 🍷🍷🍷 FRENCH (MODERN & TRADITIONAL) One of Paris's most talented chefs, Bernard Pacaud draws world attention with his vivid flavors and expert culinary skill. Expect perfection at this early-17th-century town house in Le Marais, with two high-ceilinged salons whose decor vaguely recalls an Italian palazzo. In summer, there's outdoor seating as well. Pacaud's tables are nearly always filled with satisfied diners who come back again and again to see where his imagination will take him next. The dishes change seasonally and may include fricassée of Breton lobster with a civet/red-wine sauce, served with a purée of peas; turbot filet braised with celery, served with a julienne of black truffles; or one of our favorite dishes in all Paris, *poulard de Bresse demi-deuil homage à la Mère Brazier* (chicken roasted with black truffles and truffled vegetables in a style invented by a Lyonnais matron after World War II). An award-winning dessert is the *tarte fine sablée* served with bitter chocolate and vanilla-flavored ice cream.

9 place des Vosges, 4th arr. ✆ **01-42-78-51-45.** Reservations required far in advance. Main courses 370F–610F (56.25€–92.70€, $53.65–$88.45). AE, MC, V. Tues–Sat noon–1:30pm and 8–9:30pm. Métro: St-Paul or Chèmin Vert.

MODERATE

Bofinger 🍷 ALSATIAN/FRENCH (MODERN & TRADITIONAL) Opened in the 1860s, Bofinger is the oldest Alsatian brasserie in town and certainly one of the best. It's a Belle-Epoque dining palace, resplendent with shiny brass and stained glass. Weather permitting, you can dine on an outdoor terrace. Affiliated today with La Coupole and Brasserie Flo, the restaurant has updated its menu, retaining only the most popular of its traditional dishes, like sauerkraut and a well-prepared *sole meunière.* Recent additions have included roasted leg of lamb with a fondant of artichoke hearts and a purée of parsley, grilled turbot with a *brandade* of fennel, and stingray filet with chives and burnt-butter sauce. Shellfish, including an abundance of fresh oysters and lobster, is almost always available in season.

5–7 rue de la Bastille, 4th arr. ✆ **01-42-72-87-82.** Reservations recommended. Main courses 90F–160F (13.70€–24.30€, $13.05–$23.20). AE, DC, MC, V. Mon–Fri noon–3pm and 6:30pm–1am; Sat–Sun noon–1am. Métro: Bastille.

Le Vieux Bistro ❀ *(finds* FRENCH (TRADITIONAL)   This is one of the last old-fashioned bistros still left in the heart of Paris. Few other restaurants offer so close-up, and so forbidding, a view of the massive walls of Paris's largest cathedral, visible through lacy curtains from the windows of the front dining room. To reach it, you'll bypass a dozen souvenir stands, then settle into one of the two old-time dining rooms for a flavorful meal of French staples. The cuisine evokes the kind you're served along a little back road deep in the heart of France—a bit heavy perhaps, but evocative of food of long ago. You can order snails with garlic butter, filet mignon roasted in a bag and served with marrow sauce, veal filets, and a classic dessert, *tarte tatin* (studded with apples and sugar, drenched with Calvados, and capped with fresh cream).

14 rue du Cloître-Notre-Dame, 4th arr. ✆ **01-43-54-18-95.** Main courses 90F–330F (13.70€–50.15€, $13.05–$47.85). MC, V. Daily noon–2pm and 7:30–11pm. Métro: Cité.

INEXPENSIVE

Aquarius ❀❀ VEGETARIAN   In a 17th-century building whose original stonework forms part of the earthy decor, this is one of the best-known vegetarian restaurants in Le Marais. The owners serve only a limited array of (strictly organic) wine, and smoking is expressly forbidden. Their flavorful meals are healthfully prepared. Choose from an array of soups and salads; a galette of wheat served with crudités and mushroom tarts; or a country plate composed of fried mushrooms and potatoes, garlic, and goat cheese, served with a salad.

54 rue Ste-Croix-de-la-Bretonnerie, 4th arr. ✆ **01-48-87-48-71.** Main courses 45F–64F (6.85€–9.75€, $6.55–$9.30); fixed-price menu 95F (14.45€, $13.85). MC, V. Mon–Sat noon–10:15pm. Métro: Hôtel de Ville. RER: Châtelet–Les Halles.

Au Gourmet de l'Ile ❀ *(Value* FRENCH (TRADITIONAL) Locals swear by the cuisine at Au Gourmet de l'Ile, whose fixed-price meals are among Paris's best bargains. The setting is beautiful, with a beamed ceiling, walls from the 1400s, and candlelit tables. In the window is a sign emblazoned with AAAAA, which, roughly translated, stands for the Amiable Association of Amateurs of the Authentic Andouillette. These chitterling sausages are soul food to the French. Popular and tasty too are *la charbonnée de l'Ile,* a savory pork with onions, and stuffed mussels in shallot butter. The fixed-price menu includes a choice of 15 appetizers, 15 main courses, salad or cheese, and 15 desserts.

42 rue St-Louis-en-l'Ile, 4th arr. ℰ **01-43-26-79-27**. Reservations required. Main courses 75F–120F (11.40€–18.25€, $10.40–$17.40); fixed-price menus 155F–195F (23.55€–29.65€, $22.50–$28.30). AE, MC, V. Wed–Sun noon–2pm and daily 7–10:30pm. Métro: Pont Marie.

Trumilou ⚑ FRENCH (TRADITIONAL)   This is one of the most popular of the restaurants surrounding Paris's Hôtel de Ville and has welcomed most of France's politicians, including George Pompidou, who came here frequently before he was elected president. ("As soon as they become president, they opt for grander restaurants," say the good-natured owners, the Drumonds.) The countrified decor includes a collection of farm implements and family memorabilia, amid a clutch of tables. Most diners remain on the street level, though additional seating is in the cellar. The menu rarely changes and doesn't need to, with chicken Provençal, sweetbreads "in the style of our grandmother," duckling with plums, stuffed cabbage, and *blanquette de veau* (veal in white sauce).

84 quai de l'Hôtel-de-Ville, 4th arr. ℰ **01-42-77-63-98**. Reservations recommended Sat–Sun. Main courses 75F–100F (11.40€–15.20€, $10.95–$14.50); fixed-price menu 98F (14.90€, $14.20). MC, V. Daily noon–3pm and 7–11pm. Métro: Hôtel de Ville.

9TH ARRONDISSEMENT
EXPENSIVE

Chez Jean ⚑ FRENCH (MODERN & TRADITIONAL)   The crowd is young, the food is good, and the vintage brassiere aura of the 1950s makes you think that the Parisian expat novelist, James Baldwin, will arrive for his table at any minute. There has been a brasserie of some sort on this site since around 1900. Amid well-oiled pinewood panels and carefully polished copper, you can choose from some of grandmother's favorites as well as more modern dishes like risotto with lobster and squid ink, scallops with endive fricassée, lamb roasted with basil, "nougat" of oxtails with balsamic vinaigrette, and pavé of duckling with honey sauce and exotic mushroom fricassée. The changing menu attracts fans who consider the food a lot more sophisticated than that served at other brasseries (the chefs gained their experience in upscale restaurants).

8 rue St-Lazare, 9th arr. ℰ **01-48-78-62-73**. Reservations recommended far in advance. Main courses 130F–245F (19.75€–37.25€, $18.85–$35.55); fixed-price menu 195F (29.65€, $28.30). MC, V. Mon–Fri noon–2:30pm and 7–11pm; Sat–Sun 7–11pm. Métro: Notre-Dame de Lorette, Opéra, or Cadet.

MODERATE
Au Petit Riche LOIRE VALLEY (ANJOU)   No, that's not Flaubert or Balzac walking through the door. But should they

miraculously come back, the decor of old Paris with the original gas lamps and time-mellowed paneling would make them feel right at home. When it opened in 1865, this bistro was the food outlet for the Café Riche next door; today it offers yesterday's grandeur and simple well-prepared food. You'll be ushered to one of five areas crafted for maximum intimacy, with red velour banquettes, ceilings painted with allegorical themes, and accents of brass and frosted glass. The wine list favors Loire Valley vintages that go well with such dishes as *rillettes* and *rillons* (potted fish or meat, especially pork) in Vouvray wine aspic, poached fish with buttery white-wine sauce, old-fashioned blanquette of chicken, and seasonal game dishes like civet of rabbit.

25 rue Le Peletier, 9th arr. ℭ **01-47-70-68-68.** Reservations recommended. Main courses 88F–160F (13.40€–24.30€, $12.75–$23.20); fixed-price menus 165F (25.15€, $23.95) at lunch, 140F–180F (21.35€–27.35€, $20.30–$26.10) at dinner. AE, DC, MC, V. Mon–Sat noon–2:15pm and 7pm–midnight. Métro: Le Peletier or Richelieu-Drouot.

Wally Le Saharien ALGERIAN   Head to this dining room—lined with desert photos and tribal artifacts crafted from ceramics, wood, and weavings—for an insight into the spicy, slow-cooked cuisine that fueled the colonial expansion of France into North Africa. The fixed-price dinner menu begins with a trio of starters: a spicy soup, stuffed and grilled sardines, and a savory *pastilla* of pigeon in puff pastry. This can be followed by any of several kinds of couscous or a *méchouia* (slow-cooked tart) of lamb dusted with an optional coating of sugar, according to your taste. *Merguez,* the cumin-laden spicy sausage of the North African world, factors importantly into any meal, as does homemade (usually honey-infused) pastries. End your meal with traditional mint-flavored tea.

36 rue Rodier, 9th arr. ℭ **01-42-85-51-90.** Reservations recommended. A la carte main courses (available only at lunch) 85F–138F (12.90€–21.05€, $12.35–$20); fixed-price dinner 250F (38€, $36.25). MC, V. Tues–Sat noon–2pm; Mon–Sat 7–10pm. Métro: Anvers.

INEXPENSIVE

Chartier FRENCH (TRADITIONAL)   Opened in 1896, this unpretentious fin-de-siècle restaurant, long a budget favorite, is now an official monument featuring a whimsical mural with trees, a flowering staircase, and an early depiction of an airplane; it was painted in 1929 by a penniless artist who executed his work in exchange for food. The menu follows brasserie-style traditions, including items you might not dare to eat—boiled veal's head, tripe, tongue, sweetbreads, lamb's brains, chitterling sausages—as well as some old-time tempters. The waiter will steer you through dishes like *boeuf bourguignonne, pot-au-feu* (a bestseller, combining beef, turnips, cabbage, and carrots), pavé of rump steak, and at least five kinds of fish. The prices are low, even for a three-course meal, a fact that as many as 320 diners appreciate at a time.

7 rue de faubourg Montmartre, 9th arr. ℂ 01-47-70-86-29. Main courses 40F–68F (6.10€–10.35€, $5.80–$9.85). MC, V. Daily 11:30am–3pm and 6–10pm. Métro: Grands Boulevards or Rue Montmartre.

Le Grand Zinc FRENCH (TRADITIONAL)   The Paris of the 1880s lives on here. You make your way into the restaurant past baskets of *bélons* (brown-fleshed oysters) from Brittany, a year-round favorite. The specialties of the house are *coq au vin* (chicken in white wine) and old-fashioned savory staples like rack of lamb, rump steak, veal chops with morels, and even a simple form of Provençal bouillabaisse. Nothing ever changes—certainly not the time-tested recipes.

5 rue de faubourg Montmartre, 9th arr. ℂ **01-47-70-88-64.** Main courses 110F–300F (16.70€–45.60€, $15.95–$43.50); fixed-price menu 120F (18.25€, $17.40). AE, DC, MC, V. Mon–Sat noon–midnight. Closed Aug. Métro: Grands Boulevards.

10TH ARRONDISSEMENT
MODERATE
Brasserie Flo 🍴 ALSATIAN   This remote restaurant is a bit hard to find, but once you arrive (after walking through passageway after passageway), you'll see that fin-de-siècle Paris lives on. The restaurant opened in 1860 and has changed its decor very little since. The house specialty is *la formidable choucroute* (a heaping mound of sauerkraut with boiled ham, bacon, and sausage) for two. The onion soup and *sole meunière* are always good, as is the warm foie gras and guinea hen with lentils. Look for the *plats du jour,* ranging from roast pigeon to veal fricassée with sorrel.

7 cour des Petites-Ecuries, 10th arr. ℂ 01-47-70-13-59. Reservations recommended. Main courses 90F–168F (13.70€–25.55€, $13.05–$24.35); fixed-price menus 138F–179F (21.05€–27.20€, $20–$25.95) at lunch, 189F (28.75€, $27.40) at dinner; fixed-price late-night supper (after 10pm) 142F (21.65€, $20.65). AE, DC, MC, V. Daily noon–3pm and 7pm–1:30am. Métro: Château d'Eau or Strasbourg–St-Denis.

11TH ARRONDISSEMENT
MODERATE
Astier 🍴 *(Finds)* FRENCH (TRADITIONAL)   Nobody could accuse this place of being glamorous, understanding that well-prepared hearty food has its own allure. The mandatory set menu is

a good value, with at least 10 choices for each of four courses. For some real down-home cookery, French style, order the roasted rabbit with mustard sauce, *racasse* (scorpionfish) with fresh spinach, or duckling breast with foie-gras cream sauce. There's also a superbly varied cheese platter and desserts like crème caramel and chocolate mousse.

44 rue Jean-Pierre-Timbaud, 11th arr. ℂ **01-43-57-16-35.** Reservations recommended. Fixed-price menus 140F–208F (21.35€–31.60€, $20.30–$30.15). AE, DC, MC, V. Mon–Fri noon–2pm and 8–11pm. Métro: Oberkampf or Parmentier.

12TH ARRONDISSEMENT
EXPENSIVE

Au Trou Gascon ⭐⭐⭐ GASCONY   One of Paris's most acclaimed chefs, Alain Dutournier lures some of the most fashionable palates of Paris to this unchic location in the 12th. He launched his cooking career in southwest France's Gascony region. His parents mortgaged their own inn to allow him to open this early-1900s bistro. At first he got little business, but word eventually spread of a savant in the kitchen who practiced authentic *cuisine moderne.* His wife, Nicole, is the welcoming hostess, and the wine steward has distinguished himself for his exciting cave containing several little-known wines along with a fabulous collection of Armagnacs. It's estimated the wine cellar has some 800 varieties. Start with fresh duck foie gras cooked in a terrine or Gascony cured ham cut from the bone. The best main courses include fresh tuna with braised cabbage, the best cassoulet in town, and chicken from the Chalosse region of Landes, which Dutournier roasts and serves in its own drippings.

40 rue Taine, 12th arr. ℂ **01-43-44-34-26.** Reservations required far in advance. Main courses 145F–165F (22.05€–25.10€, $21.05–$23.95); fixed-price menu 200F (30.40€, $29) at lunch, 320F (48.65€, $46.40) at dinner. AE, DC, MC, V. Mon–Fri noon–2pm; Mon–Sat 7:30–10pm. Closed Aug. Métro: Daumesnil.

MODERATE

China Club ⭐ CANTONESE/CHINESE   Evoking 1930s Hong Kong, this favorite is still going strong, still laughing at upstart new Asian restaurants, and still serving some of the best Asian cuisine in Paris. It's our favorite. We always imagine we're James Bond when we dine here. The food is mainly Cantonese, prepared with flair and taste. Before dinner, you might want to enjoy a drink in the upstairs smoking lounge. Nearly everything is good, especially the sautéed shrimp and calamari, Shanghai chicken, and red rice sautéed with vegetables. The vast menu offers plenty of choices. Downstairs, the

Sing Song club has live music, including something called Sino-French jazz, but only on Friday and Saturday.

50 rue de Charenton, 12th arr. ℂ **01-43-43-82-02.** Main courses 70F–190F (10.65€–28.95€, $10.15–$27.55); fixed-price dinner 160F (24.30€, $23.20); fixed-price Sun dinner 115F (17.55€, $16.70). AE, MC, V. Sun–Thurs 7pm–2am; Fri–Sat 7pm–3am. Closed Aug. Métro: Bastille or Ledru-Rollin.

INEXPENSIVE

L'Ebauchoir 🖈 *(Finds* FRENCH (TRADITIONAL)   Tucked into a neighborhood rarely visited by foreigners and featuring a 1950s decor that has become fashionable again, this bistro attracts neighborhood carpenters, plumbers, and electricians, as well as an occasional journalist and screenwriter. With buffed aluminum trim and plaster-and-stucco walls tinted dark orange-yellow and blue, the place might remind you of a canteen in an auto factory. You can order surprisingly generous and well-prepared stuffed sardines, snapper filet with olive oil and garlic, crabmeat soup, fried calf's liver with coriander and honey, and rack of lamb combined with saddle of lamb.

43 rue de Cîteaux, 12th arr. ℂ **01-43-42-49-31.** Reservations recommended for dinner. Main courses 65F–110F (9.95€–16.70€, $9.45–$15.95); fixed-price menus 70F–90F (10.65€–13.75€, $10.15–$13.05). MC, V. Mon–Sat noon–2:30pm and 8–10:30pm. Métro: Faidherbe-Chaligny.

8TH ARRONDISSEMENT
VERY EXPENSIVE

L'Astor 🖈🖈🖈 FRENCH (MODERN)   What happens to a great French chef when he retires? If he's lucky enough—and respected enough—he takes on the title of "culinary consultant" and attaches himself to a restaurant where he can drop in several times a week to keep an eye on things. That's what happened when guru Joël Robuchon retired from his avenue Raymond-Poincaré citadel in favor of a quieter life (his replacement there was Alain Ducasse). The chef here is respected Eric Lecerf, who knows better than anyone else how to match his master's tours de force. The setting is a tawny-colored enclave beneath an etched-glass Art-Deco ceiling, with luxurious touches inspired by the 1930s. Expect an almost religious devotion to Robuchon's specialties and less emphasis on newer dishes created by Lecerf. Examples of "classic Robuchon" are caramelized sea urchins in aspic with fennel-flavored cream sauce, eggplant-stuffed cannelloni with tuna filets and olive oil, and spit-roasted Bresse chicken with flap mushrooms. Items created by Lecerf include carpaccio of Breton lobster with olive oil and tomato

---

Tips Finding Your Way

See the map "Hotels & Restaurants near the Champs-Elysées (Arrondissements 8 & 16)" in chapter 3 for the locations of restaurants in those arrondissements.

---

confit, creamy cannelloni with eggplant, roasted and braised rack of lamb, and pigeon supreme with cabbage and foie gras.

In the Hôtel Astor, 11 rue d'Astorg, 8th arr. ✆ **01-53-05-05-20.** Fax 01-53-05-05-30. Reservations required far in advance. Main courses 150F–310F (22.80€–47.10€, $21.75–$44.95); fixed-price menus 325F–590F (49.40€–89.75€, $47.15–$85.55). AE, DC, MC, V. Mon–Fri noon–2pm and 7:30–10pm. Closed Aug. Métro: St-Augustin or Madeleine.

Les Elysées du Vernet 🌶🌶🌶 PROVENÇAL   This darling of *tout Paris* is rising rapidly as a gastronomic wonder. Capping the restaurant is one of the neighborhood's most panoramic glass ceilings, a gray and green translucent dome designed by Gustav Eiffel, who also conceived Paris' famous tower. That—plus the fact that the Montpellier-born chef, Alain Solivérès, was recently awarded two Michelin stars—keeps the crowds lining up. Menu items are focused on Provençal models and change every 2 months, based on whatever is fresh at the season of your arrival. During our midwinter visit, award-winning examples included scallops with truffles, *tournedos Rossini* (a slab of beef layered with foie gras), and a *cocotte* (small stew-pot) of lobster. There's also a melt-in-your mouth version of apple charlotte, and even a newfangled take on black-truffle ice cream, a dish that traditionalists consider somewhat far-fetched. Candles help illuminate the place at night, and during the dinner hour there's either a harpist (Mon–Wed) or a pianist (Thurs–Fri), whose music reverberates pleasantly off the glass dome overhead.

In the Hotel Vernet, 25 rue Vernet, 8th arr. ✆ **01-44-31-98-98.** Reservations required. Main courses 280F–670F (42.55€–101.85€, $40.60–$97.15). AE, DC, MC, V. Mon–Sat 12:30–2pm and 7:30–9pm. Métro: George V.

Restaurant Plaza Athénée (Alain Ducasse) 🌶🌶🌶 FRENCH (MODERN & TRADITIONAL)   Few other chefs in the history of French cuisine have been catapulted to international fame as quickly as Alain Ducasse. The most recent setting for his world-renowned cuisine is an appropriately world-renowned hotel, the Plaza Athénée. There's a lot of marketing and glitter associated with this new *marriage de convenience,* but what you'll find is a lobby-level hideaway that topnotch decorator Patrick Jouin transformed with layers of pearl-gray paint and many yards of translucent organdy. By anyone's standards, the cuisine is spectacular. This five-star Michelin chef seeds his dishes with produce from every corner of France—rare local vegetables, fish from the coasts, and dishes incorporating cardoons, turnips, celery, turbot, cuttlefish, and Bresse fowl. His French cuisine is contemporary and Mediterranean, yet not new. Though many dishes are light, Ducasse isn't afraid of lard, as he proves by his thick, oozing slabs of pork grilled to a crisp. There's an occasional *homage* to the great chef, Joël Robuchon, in the form of such dishes as caviar in aspic with cauliflower cream. More individualized is crayfish drenched with caviar sauce. The wine list is superb, with some selections deriving from the best vintages of France, Germany, Switzerland, Spain, California, and Italy.

In the Hotel Plaza Athénée, 25av. Montaigne, 8th arr. ℂ **01-53-67-65-00.** Fax 01-53-67-65-12. Reservations required 8 weeks in advance. Main courses 360F–558F (54.70€–84.80€, $52.20–$80.90); fixed-price menus 985F–1,490F (149.70€–226.55€, $142.85–$216.05). AE, DC, MC, V. Thurs–Fri noon–2pm; Mon–Fri 8–10:30pm. Closed mid-July–mid-Aug and Dec. 22–30. Métro: FDR or Alma-Marceau.

Taillevent ⭐⭐⭐ FRENCH (MODERN & TRADITIONAL) This is the Parisian *ne plus ultra* of gastronomy. Taillevent opened in 1946 and has climbed steadily in excellence. Today, it ranks as Paris's most outstanding all-around restaurant, challenged only by Lucas-Carton and Pierre Gagnaire in this highly competitive area. The restaurant, named after famous 14th-century chef Guillaume Tirel Taillevent, who wrote one of the oldest known books on French cookery, is set in a grand 19th-century town house off the Champs-Elysées, with paneled rooms and crystal chandeliers. The place is small, as the owner wishes, so he can give personal attention to every facet of the operation and maintain a discreet club atmosphere. You might begin with a *boudin* (sausage) of Breton lobster à la Nage, cream of watercress soup with Sevruga caviar, or duck liver with spice bread and ginger. Main courses include red snapper with black olives, Scottish salmon cooked in sea salt with a sauce of olive oil and lemons, and cassoulet of crayfish from Brittany. Dessert might be a *nougatine glacé* with pears. The wine list is among the best in Paris. Though owner M. Vrinat likes Americans, it isn't always easy for visitors from the States and other countries to book a table, because he prefers that about 60% of his guests be French.

15 rue Lamennais, 8th arr. ℂ **01-44-95-15-01.** Fax 01-42-25-95-18. Reservations required weeks, even months, in advance for lunch and dinner. Main courses

290F–330F (44.15€–50.15€, $42.05–$47.85). AE, DC, MC, V. Mon–Fri noon–2:30pm and 7–10pm. Closed Aug. Métro: George V.

EXPENSIVE

Buddha Bar 🐀🐀 FRENCH (MODERN)/PACIFIC RIM   This place is hot, hot, hot—and still remains as Paris's "restaurant of the moment," even though it has been around a while. A location on a chic street near the Champs-Elysées and place de la Concorde and an allegiance to a fusion of French, Asian, and Californian cuisines guarantees trendy diners devoted to the whims of fashion. The vast dining room is presided over by a giant Buddha, and the cutting-edge culinary theme combines Japanese sashimi, Vietnamese spring rolls, lacquered duck, sautéed shrimp with black-bean sauce, grilled chicken skewers with orange sauce, sweet-and-sour spareribs, and crackling squab à l'orange. There are two sittings for dinner: from 7 to 9pm and from 10:30pm to 12:30am. Many come here just for a drink in the carefully lacquered and very hip bar, upstairs from the street-level dining room.

8 rue Boissy d'Anglas, 8th arr. ✆ 01-53-05-90-00. Reservations required far in advance. Main courses 115F–260F (17.55€–39.50€, $16.75–$37.70). AE, MC, V. Mon–Fri noon–3pm; daily 7pm–12:30am. Métro: Concorde.

Spoon, Food & Wine 🐀 INTERNATIONAL   This hyper-modern venture of *wunderkind* chef Alain Ducasse is hailed as a "restaurant for the millennium" and condemned by some Parisian food critics as surreal and a bit absurd. The claustrophobic dining room evokes stylish Paris and California, and the cuisine roams the world for inspiration, with such middlebrow offerings as American macaroni and cheese, a BLT, barbecued ribs, chicken wings, and pastrami. Other dishes evoke Italy, Latin America, Asia, and India. The steamed lobster with mango chutney is a winner. For a "vegetable garden," you can mix and match among 15 ingredients, including iceberg lettuce. Pasta comes with a selection of five sauces.

In the Hôtel Marignan-Elysée, 14 rue Marignan, 8th arr. ✆ 01-40-76-34-44. Reservations recommended far in advance. Main courses, vegetable side dishes 135F–185F (20.50€–28.10€, $19.60–$26.85). AE, DC, V. Mon–Fri noon–2pm and 7–11pm. Métro: F. D. Roosevelt.

MODERATE

Chez André FRENCH (TRADITIONAL)   Chez André is one of the neighborhood's favorite bistros. Its major drawback is that you'll feel a bit left out in the cold if you're not a regular. Outside, a discreet red awning stretches over an array of shellfish on ice; inside, an Art-Nouveau decor includes etched glass and masses of flowers. This has been a landmark on rue Marbeuf since 3 years before the invasion of France in 1940. It remains the same as it was when it was founded (an agreement was made with the original owners). The old-style cuisine on the menu includes paté of thrush, Roquefort in puff pastry, grilled veal kidneys, roast rack of lamb, and bouillabaisse, several kinds of omelets, calf's head vinaigrette, a potage du jour, and fresh shellfish, along with several reasonably priced wines. For variety, some locals opt for the *plat du jour.* The dessert choices may be rum baba, chocolate cake, or a daily pastry.

12 rue Marbeuf (at rue Clément-Marot), 8th arr. ℂ **01-47-20-59-57.** Reservations recommended. Main courses 89F–150F (13.55€–22.80€, $12.90–$21.75); fixed-price menu 180F (27.35€, $26.10). AE, DC, MC, V. Daily noon–1am. Métro: F. D. Roosevelt.

Ladurée FRENCH (TRADITIONAL)   Ladurée, acclaimed since 1862 as one of Paris's grand cafes (located near La Madeleine), is now installed on the Champs-Elysées, adding a touch of class to this neighborhood of fast-food places. This offshoot expanded in 1999 and caters to an international set wearing everything from Givenchy to GAP. The Belle-Epoque setting is ideal for sampling Ladurée's celebrated macaroons—not the sticky coconut version familiar to Americans, but two almond meringue cookies, flavored with vanilla, coffee, strawberry, pistachio, or other flavor, stuck together with butter cream. The menu of talented young chef Philippe Dandrieux is constantly adjusted to take advantage of the freshest daily ingredients and may include a crisp and tender pork filet with potato-and-parsley purée and marinated red mullet filets on a salad of cold ratatouille. If you're looking for a mid-afternoon pick-me-up to accompany your tea and macaroons, consider a *plaisir sucré,* a chocolate confection artfully decorated with spun sugar. The service isn't always efficient.

75 av. des Champs-Elysées, 8th arr. ℂ **01-40-75-08-75.** Reservations required for the restaurant, not for the cafe. Main courses 150F–250F (22.80€–38€, $21.75–$36.25); pastries from 28F (4.25€, $4.05). AE, DC, MC, V. Daily 7:30am–1am.

INEXPENSIVE

Le Berry's FRENCH (TRADITIONAL)   This inexpensive bistro, with a setting celebrating rugby, complements one of the area's grandest restaurants, Le Grenadin. Its platters emerge from the same kitchen and are infused with the same kind of zeal as those presented next door for three times the price. Don't expect cutting-edge fare, but do look for honest dishes from France's agrarian heartland and a refreshing lack of pretension. The dishes listed on a chalkboard include fricassée of chicken with olives and mashed potatoes, thin-sliced smoked ham from Sancerre, veal filet with red-wine sauce, raw pike with cabbage, and a traditional Berry pear tart.

46 rue de Naples, 8th arr. ℭ 01-40-75-01-56. Reservations recommended. Main courses 56F–92F (8.50€–14.05€, $8.10–$13.35); fixed-price menu 110F (16.70€, $15.95). MC, V. Mon–Fri noon–2:30pm; Mon–Sat 7pm–1am. Métro: Villie Tues.

Les Gourmets des Ternes *Value* FRENCH (TRADITIONAL) Les Gourmets des Ternes caters to hordes who appreciate its affordable prices and lack of pretension. Despite the brusque service, satisfied diners have included the mayor of Atlanta, who wrote the bistro a thank-you letter, as well as hundreds of ordinary folks from this neighborhood. Thriving in this spot since 1892, the place retains an early-1900s paneled decor, with some additions from the 1950s, including bordeaux-colored banquettes, mirrors, wooden panels, touches of brass, and paper tablecloths. During clement weather, there's an outdoor terrace as well. The finely grilled signature dishes include rib steak with marrow sauce and fries; country patés and sausages; sole, turbot, and monkfish; and satisfying desserts like peach Melba and *baba au Rhum* (rum cake with raisins).

87 bd. de Courcelles, 8th arr. ℭ 01-42-27-43-04. Main courses 90F–145F (13.75€–22.05€, $13.05–$21.05). AE, MC, V. Mon–Fri noon–2:30pm and 7–10pm. Métro: Ternes.

16TH ARRONDISSEMENT
VERY EXPENSIVE

Jamin *ରରର* FRENCH (TRADITIONAL)   This is where Paris's great chef of the 1980s, Joël Robuchon, made his sensational mark. Now in charge is Robuchon's longtime second in command, Benoit Guichard, who is clearly inspired by his master but is an imaginative chef in his own right. Guichard has chosen pale green panels and pink banquettes (referred to as "Italo–New Yorkaise") for a soothing backdrop to his brief but well-chosen menu. Lunches can be relatively simple, though each dish, like a beautifully seasoned salmon tartare, is done to perfection. Classic technique and an homage to tradition characterize the cuisine—John Dory with celery and fresh ginger; pigeon sausage with foie gras, pistachios, and mâche lettuce; and beef shoulder so tender it has obviously been braising for hours. A particularly earthy dish celebrates various parts of the sow that are usually rejected, blending the tail and cheeks on a platter with walnuts and fresh herbs. Finish with a *tarte tatin*.

32 rue de Longchamp, 16th arr. ℂ **01-45-53-00-07.** Fax 01-45-53-00-15. Reservations required far in advance. Main courses 230F–330F (35€–50.25€, $33.40–$47.90); fixed-price menus 310F–495F (47.20€–75.35€, $45–$71.85) at lunch, 495F (75.35€, $71.85) at dinner. AE, DC, MC, V. Mon–Fri 12:30–2pm and 7:45–10pm. Métro: Trocadéro.

INEXPENSIVE

Le Bistro de l'Etoile ✦ *Value* FRENCH (TRADITIONAL)   This is the most interesting of three baby bistros, each with the same name, clustered around place Charles de Gaulle–Etoile. They serve affordable versions of grand cuisine. The setting is a warmly contemporary dining room in shades of butterscotch and caramel. Menu items include a *mijotée* (pork and sage cooked over low heat for hours, coming out extremely tender—almost mushy), cod studded with lard and prepared with a coconut-lime sauce, and red-snapper filets with caramelized endive and exotic mushrooms. A particularly interesting sampler combines three creations on a platter—a cup of lentil cream soup, a fondant of celery, and a pan-fried slice of foie gras. Expect some odd terms on the dessert menu, which only a professional chef can fully describe: An example is spice bread baked in the fashion of *pain perdu* (lost bread) garnished with banana sorbet and pineapple sauce.

19 rue Lauriston, 16th arr. ℂ **01-40-67-11-16.** Reservations recommended. Main courses 97F–130F (14.75€–19.75€, $14.05–$18.85); fixed-price lunch 165F (25.15€, $23.95). AE, DC, MC, V. Mon–Fri noon–2:30pm, Mon–Sat 7:30pm–midnight. Métro: Kleber.

2 On the Left Bank

We'll begin with the most centrally located arrondissements on the Left Bank, then work our way through the more outlying neighborhoods and to the area near the Eiffel Tower.

5TH ARRONDISSEMENT
VERY EXPENSIVE

La Tour d'Argent ✦✦✦ FRENCH (TRADITIONAL)   This penthouse restaurant, a national institution, serves up an amazing view over the Seine and the apse of Notre-Dame. Although La Tour d'Argent's long-established reputation as "the best" in Paris has been eclipsed, dining here remains an unsurpassed theatrical event. A restaurant of some sort has stood on this site since at least 1582: Mme de Sévigné refers to a cafe here in her celebrated letters, and Dumas used it as a setting for one of his novels. The fame of La Tour d'Argent spread during its ownership by Frédéric Delair, who

Restaurants in the Heart of the Left Bank
(Arrondissements 5–6 & 14)

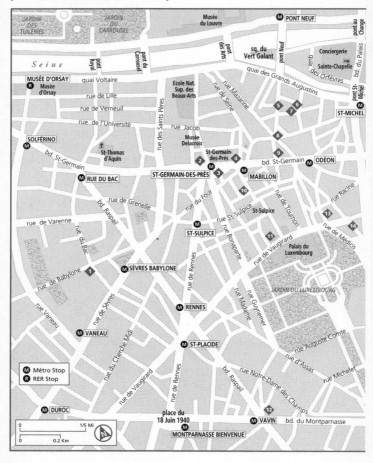

started the practice of issuing certificates to diners who ordered the house specialty—*caneton* (pressed duckling). The birds are numbered: The first was served to Edward VII in 1890, and now they're up over 1 million! Under the sharp eye of current owner Claude Terrail, the cooking is superb and the service impeccable. A good part of the menu is devoted to duck, but the kitchen does know how to prepare other dishes. We especially recommend you start with the

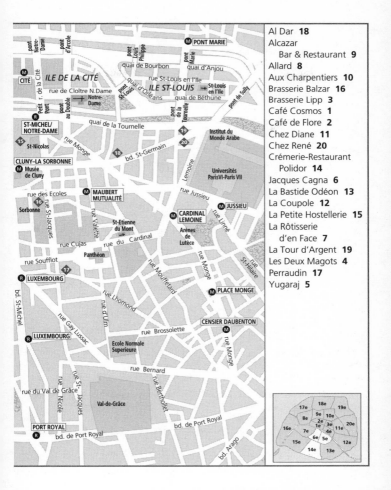

Al Dar **18**
Alcazar
  Bar & Restaurant **9**
Allard **8**
Aux Charpentiers **10**
Brasserie Balzar **16**
Brasserie Lipp **3**
Café Cosmos **1**
Café de Flore **2**
Chez Diane **11**
Chez René **20**
Crémerie-Restaurant
  Polidor **14**
Jacques Cagna **6**
La Bastide Odéon **13**
La Coupole **12**
La Petite Hostellerie **15**
La Rôtisserie
  d'en Face **7**
La Tour d'Argent **19**
Les Deux Magots **4**
Perraudin **17**
Yugaraj **5**

pheasant consommé or the pikeperch quenelles André Terrail and follow with the ravioli with foie gras or the salmon and turbot *à la Sully.*

15–17 quai de la Tournelle, 5th arr. ℂ **01-43-54-23-31.** Fax 01-44-07-12-04. Reservations required far in advance. Main courses 270F–515F (41.05€–78.35€, $39.15–$74.75); fixed-price lunch 390F (59.35€, $56.55). AE, DC, MC, V. Tues–Sun noon–2:30pm and 7:30–10:30pm. Métro: St-Michel or Pont Marie.

MODERATE

Brasserie Balzar ✿✿ FRENCH (TRADITIONAL) Opened in 1898, Brasserie Balzar is battered but cheerful, with some of Paris's friendliest waiters. The menu makes almost no concessions to nouvelle cuisine and includes pepper steak, *sole meunière,* sauerkraut with ham and sausage, pig's feet, and fried calf's liver served without garnish. Be warned that if you want just coffee or a drink, you probably won't get a table at meal hours. But, accustomed as they are to the odd hours of their many patrons, the staff will be happy to serve you if you want a full dinner in the mid-afternoon. Former patrons have included Sartre and Camus (who often got in arguments), James Thurber, countless professors from the nearby Sorbonne, and bevies of English and American journalists

49 rue des Ecoles, 5th arr. ℭ **01-43-54-13-67.** Reservations strongly recommended. Main courses 75F–125F (11.40€–19€, $10.90–$18.15). AE, MC, V. Daily noon–midnight. Métro: Odéon or Cluny–La Sorbonne.

Chez René FRENCH (TRADITIONAL) Restaurants like this used to be widespread, particularly on the Left Bank, but many became pizzerias. Opened in 1957, Chez René maintains its allegiance to the tenets of French cuisine. The staff is often overwhelmed and the seating cramped as only a bistro can be. The dining room isn't fancy, but its patrons return loyally for the steady and reliable stream of food and the frequently changing *plats du jour.* For an appetizer, try the wild mushrooms laced with butter and garlic or the platter of country-style sausages. You'll find such reliable old-time fare as *boeuf bourguignonne* and *blanquette de veau* (veal in white sauce). Enjoy it all with a bottle of Beaujolais.

14 bd. St-Germain, 5th arr. ℭ **01-43-54-30-23.** Reservations recommended. Main courses 80F–170F (12.15€–25.85€, $11.60–$24.65); fixed-price lunch 175F (26.60€, $25.45); fixed-price dinner 250F (38€, $36.25). V. Tues–Sat 12:15–2:15pm and 7:45–11pm. Closed Aug and 15 days in Dec. Métro: Maubert-Mutualité.

INEXPENSIVE

Al Dar LEBANESE This well-respected restaurant works hard to popularize the savory cuisine of Lebanon. You'll dine on dishes like *taboulé,* a refreshing combination of finely chopped parsley, mint, milk, tomatoes, onions, lemon juice, olive oil, and salt; *baba ganoush,* pulverized and seasoned eggplant; and *hummus,* pulverized chickpeas with herbs. These can be followed with savory roasted chicken; tender minced lamb prepared with mint, cumin, and Mediterranean herbs; and any of several kinds of delectable tangines and couscous.

8 rue Frédéric-Sauton, 5th arr. ✆ **01-43-25-17-15.** Reservations recommended. Main courses 88F–96F (13.45€–14.65€, $12.75–$13.90). AE, MC, V. Daily noon–midnight. Métro: Maubert-Mutualité.

La Petite Hostellerie ✦ *Value* FRENCH (TRADITIONAL) This 1902 restaurant offers a ground-floor dining room that's usually crowded and a larger one (seats 100) upstairs with attractive 18th-century woodwork. People come for the cozy ambience and decor, decent French country cooking, polite service, and excellent prices. The fixed-price dinner menu might feature favorites like coq au vin, duckling à l'orange, and steak with mustard sauce. Start with onion soup or stuffed mussels, and finish with cheese or salad and peach Melba or apple tart.

35 rue de la Harpe (just east of bd. St-Michel), 5th arr. ✆ **01-43-54-47-12.** Fixed-price menus 65F–89F (9.95€–13.55€, $9.45–$12.90). AE, DC, MC, V. Tues–Sat noon–2pm; Mon–Sat 6:30–11pm. Closed 2 weeks in Feb and 3 weeks in Aug. Métro: St-Michel or Cluny–La Sorbonne.

Perraudin ✦✦ FRENCH (TRADITIONAL) Everything about this place—decor, cuisine, price, and service—attempts to duplicate an early-1900s bistro. This one was built in 1870 as an outlet for coal and wine (sold as remedies against the cold). Eventually, it evolved into the wood-paneled bistro you see today, where little has changed since Zola was buried nearby in the Panthéon. The walls look like they've been marinated in tea; the marble-topped tables, old mirrors, and Parisian vaudeville posters have likely been here forever. Reservations aren't made in advance: Instead, diners usually drink a glass of kir at the zinc-topped bar as they wait. (Tables turn over quickly.) The menu includes roast leg of lamb with dauphinois potatoes, navarin of lamb, *boeuf bourguignonne,* and grilled salmon with sage sauce. An onion tart, pumpkin soup, or a terrine can precede the main course.

157 rue St-Jacques, 5th arr. ✆ **01-46-33-15-75.** Main courses 59F (8.95€, $8.55); fixed-price menu 65F (9.90€, $9.45) at lunch, 150F (22.80€, $21.75) at dinner. No credit cards. Tues–Fri noon–2:15pm; Mon–Sat 7:30–10:15pm. Closed 2 weeks in Aug. Métro: Cluny–La Sorbonne. RER: Luxembourg.

6TH ARRONDISSEMENT
VERY EXPENSIVE
Jacques Cagna ✦✦✦ FRENCH (MODERN & TRADITIONAL) St-Germain knows no finer dining than at Jacques Cagna, a sophisticated restaurant in a 17th-century town house with massive timbers, burnished paneling, and 17th-century Dutch paintings. Jacques Cagna is one of the best classically trained chefs in Paris,

though he has become a half-apostle to *cuisine moderne.* This is evident in his delectable carpaccio of pearly sea bream with caviar-lavished *céleric rémoulade* (celery root in mayonnaise with capers, parsley, gherkins, spring onions, chervil, chopped tarragon, and anchovy essence). Also sublime are the rack of suckling veal with ginger-and-lime sauce, Challons duckling in burgundy sauce, and fried scallops with celery and potatoes in truffle sauce. The menu is forever changing, according to the season and Cagna's inspirations, but if you're lucky, it will include his line-caught sea bass served with caviar in a potato shell.

14 rue des Grands-Augustins, 6th arr. ℂ **01-43-26-49-39.** Fax 01-43-54-54-48. Reservations required far in advance. Main courses 180F–350F (27.35€–53.20€, $26.10–$50.75); fixed-price menus 260F–490F (39.50€–74.50€, $37.70–$71.05) at lunch, 490F (74.50€, $71.05) at dinner. AE, DC, MC, V. Tues–Fri noon–2pm; Mon–Sat 7:30–10:30pm. Closed 3 weeks in Aug. Métro: St-Michel or Odéon.

MODERATE

Alcazar Bar & Restaurant ✷ FRENCH (MODERN)   Paris's most high-profile *brasserie de luxe* is this artfully high-tech place funded by British restaurateur/*wunderkind* Sir Terence Conran. (His chain of restaurants in London has succeeded in captivating a tough audience of jaded European foodies.) It features an all-white futuristic decor in a large street-level dining room and a busy bar a floor above. Menu examples are grilled entrecôte with béarnaise sauce and fried potatoes, Charolais duckling with honey and spices, sashimi and sushi with lime, monkfish filet with saffron in puff pastry, and a collection of shellfish and oysters from the waters of Brittany. The wines are as stylish and diverse as you'd expect, and the trendy crowd tends to wear a lot of black.

62 rue Mazarine, 6th arr. ℂ **01-53-10-19-99.** Reservations recommended. Main courses 90F–170F (13.75€–25.85€, $13.05–$24.65); fixed-price lunch menus 140F–160F (21.35€–24.30€, $20.30–$23.20). AE, DC, MC, V. Daily noon–3pm and 7pm–2am. Métro: Odéon.

Allard ✷✷ FRENCH (TRADITIONAL)   Long missing from this guide, this old-time bistro, opened in 1931, is back and as good as ever following a long decline. Once, it was the leading bistro, although today the competition is too great to reclaim that reputation. In the front room is a zinc bar, a haven preferred by many celebrities over the years, including Mme Pompidou and movie actor Alain Delon. All the old Allard specialties are still offered, with quality ingredients deftly handled by the kitchen. Try the snails, foie gras, veal stew, or frogs' legs. We head here on Mondays for the *boeuf à la mode* (beef braised in red wine with carrots) and on

Wednesdays for the *coq au vin*. The *cassoulet Toulousain* (casserole of white beans and goose and other meats) remains one of the Left Bank's best. For dessert, we vote for the *tarte tatin*.

41 rue St-André-des-Arts, 6th arr. ℂ **01-43-26-48-23.** Reservations required. Main courses 120F–200F (18.25€–30.40€, $17.40–$29); fixed-price menus 150F (22.80€, $21.75) at lunch, 150F–200F (22.80€–30.40€, $21.75–$29) at dinner. AE, DC, MC, V. Mon–Sat 12:30–2:30pm and 7:30–11:30pm. Métro: St-Michel or Odéon.

La Rôtisserie d'en Face ✿ *(Value* FRENCH (TRADITIONAL)
This is Paris's most frequented baby bistro, operated by Jacques Cagna, whose vastly expensive restaurant (above) is across the street. The informal place features a postmodern decor with high-tech lighting and black lacquer chairs, and the simply prepared food is very good and uses high-quality ingredients. It includes several types of ravioli, paté of duckling *en croûte* with foie gras, *friture d'éperlans* (tiny fried freshwater fish), and smoked Scottish salmon with spinach. Monsieur Cagna has added pork cheeks, based on an old family recipe. His Barbary duckling in red-wine sauce is incomparable.

2 rue Christine, 6th arr. ℂ **01-43-26-40-98.** Reservations recommended. Fixed-price menus 145F–165F (22.05€–25.10€, $21.05–$23.95) at lunch, 245F (37.25€, $35.55) at dinner. AE, MC, V. Mon–Fri noon–2:30pm; Mon–Sat 7–11:30pm. Métro: Odéon.

Yugaraj INDIAN
On two floors of an old Latin Quarter building, Yugaraj serves flavor-filled food based on the recipes of northern and (to a lesser degree) southern India. In recently renovated rooms done in vivid shades of "Indian pink," with a formally dressed staff and lots of intricately carved Kashmiri panels and statues, you can sample the spicy, aromatic tandoori dishes that are all the rage in France. Seafood specialties are usually made with warm-water fish imported from the Seychelles, including thiof, capitaine, and bourgeois, prepared as they would be in Calcutta, with tomatoes, onions, cumin, coriander, ginger, and garlic. Curried lamb with coriander is a particular favorite.

14 rue Dauphine, 6th arr. ℂ **01-43-26-44-91.** Reservations recommended. Main courses 102F–128F (15.50€–19.45€, $14.85–$18.55); fixed-price menus 99F–290F (15.05€–44.15€, $14.35–$42.05) at lunch, 180F–290F (27.35€–44.15€, $26.10–$42.05) at dinner. AE, DC, MC, V. Tues–Sun noon–2:15pm and daily 7–11pm. Métro: Pont-Neuf.

INEXPENSIVE
Aux Charpentiers FRENCH (TRADITIONAL)   This battered old veteran bistro attracts those seeking Left Bank Paris of yesterday.

This bistro, opened more than 130 years ago, was once the rendezvous of the master carpenters, whose guild was next door. Nowadays young men bring their dates here. Though the food isn't especially imaginative, it's well prepared in the best tradition of *cuisine bourgeoise*—hearty but not refined. Appetizers include paté of duck and rabbit terrine. Especially recommended as a main course is the roast duck with olives. The *plats du jour* recall French home cooking: salt pork with lentils, *pot-au-feu,* and stuffed cabbage. The wine list has a large selection of Bordeaux, including Château Gaussens.

10 rue Mabillon, 6th arr. (✆ **01-43-26-30-05**. Reservations required. Main courses 90F–130F (13.75€–19.75€, $13.05–$18.85); fixed-price menu 120F (18.25€, $17.40) at lunch, 158F (24€, $22.90) at dinner. AE, DC, MC, V. Daily noon–3pm and 7–11:30pm. Métro: St-Germain-des-Près.

Chez Diane FRENCH (MODERN & TRADITIONAL)   Come here for fashionable restaurant food at simple bistro prices. Designed to accommodate only 40 diners, this place is illuminated with Venetian glass chandeliers and paved with old-fashioned floor tiles. The deep ochres and terra cottas are redolent of Provence's landscapes and villas. Chez Diane's offerings change with the seasons and the owners' inspirations. Recently, we enjoyed sweetbreads in flap mushroom sauce, nuggets of wild boar in honey sauce, minced salmon terrine with green peppercorns, and a light-textured modern adaptation of *hachis Parmentier,* an elegant meat loaf lightened with parsley, chopped onions, and herbs. To finish with a sweet touch, we recommend the *charlotte au fromage blanc,* a tasty cheesecake with blueberry sauce.

25 rue Servandoni, 6th arr. (✆ **01-46-33-12-06**. Reservations recommended for groups of 4 or more. Main courses 100F–140F (15.20€–21.35€, $14.50–$20.30); fixed-price menu 160F (24.30€, $23.20). V. Mon–Fri noon–2pm; Mon–Sat 8–11:30pm. Métro: St-Sulpice.

Crémerie-Restaurant Polidor ★★ (Kids FRENCH (TRADI-TIONAL)   Crémerie Polidor is the most traditional bistro in the Odéon area, serving *cuisine familiale.* Its name dates from the early 1900s, when it specialized in frosted cream desserts, but the restaurant itself can trace its history back to 1845. The Crémerie was André Gide's favorite, and Joyce, Hemingway, Valéry, Artaud, and Kerouac also dined here. The place is still frequented largely by students and artists, who head for the rear. Peer beyond the lace curtains and brass hat racks to see drawers where repeat customers lock up their cloth napkins. Overworked but smiling waitresses with frilly aprons and T-shirts bearing the likeness of old mère Polidor serve the 19th-century cuisine. Try the pumpkin soup followed by *boeuf bourguignonne,* Basque-style chicken, or *blanquette de veau.* For dessert, get a chocolate, raspberry, or lemon tart—the best in all of Paris.

41 rue Monsieur-le-Prince, 6th arr. ✆ **01-43-26-95-34.** Main courses 40F–78F (6.10€–11.85€, $5.80–$11.30); fixed-price menu 55F (8.35€, $8.05) Mon–Fri only, 110F (16.70€, $15.95) at dinner. No credit cards. Daily noon–2:30pm; Mon–Sat 7pm–12:30am, Sun 7–11pm. Métro: Odéon.

La Bastide Odéon ✮ *Finds* PROVENÇAL   The sunny climes of Provence come through in the pale yellow walls, heavy oaken tables, and artfully arranged bouquets of wheat and dried roses. Chef Gilles Ajuelos, formerly employed in some grand restaurants, prepares a market-based cuisine. His simplest first courses are the most satisfying, like sardines and seared sweet peppers with olive oil and pine nuts, grilled eggplant with herbs and oil, and eggplant-stuffed roasted rabbit with olive toast and balsamic vinegar. Main courses include wild duckling with pepper sauce and exotica like lamb's feet and giblets. A winning dessert is the warm almond pie with prune and Armagnac ice cream.

7 rue Corneille, 6th arr. ✆ **01-43-26-03-65.** Reservations recommended. Fixed-price menus 159F–199F (24.15€–30.25€, $23.05–$28.85). MC, V. Tues–Sat 12:30–2pm and 7:30–11pm. Métro: Odéon. RER: Luxembourg.

7TH ARRONDISSEMENT
VERY EXPENSIVE

L'Arpège ✮✮✮ FRENCH (MODERN)   L'Arpège is best known for Alain Passard's adventurous specialties—no restaurant in the 7th serves better food. Across from the Musée Rodin in a prosperous residential neighborhood, L'Arpège has claimed the site of what for years was the world-famous L'Archestrate, where Passard worked in the kitchens. Amid a modern decor of etched glass, burnished steel, monochromatic oil paintings, and pearwood paneling, you can enjoy innovative specialties like Breton lobster in sweet-and-sour rosemary sauce, scallops prepared with cauliflower and lime-flavored grape sauce, and pan-fried duck with juniper and lime sauce. The signature dessert is a candied tomato stuffed with 12 kinds of dried and fresh fruit and served with anise-flavored ice cream.

84 rue de Varenne, 7th arr. ✆ **01-47-05-09-06.** Fax. 01-44-18-98-39. Reservations required far in advance. Main courses 320F–780F (48.65€–118.55€, $46.40–$113.10); *menu dégustation* (tasting menu) 1,400F (212.80€, $203). AE, DC, MC, V. Mon–Fri 12:30–2pm and 8–10pm. Métro: Varenne.

Tips **Finding Your Way**

See the map "Hotels & Restaurants near the Eiffel Tower & Invalides (7th Arrondissement)" in chapter 3 for the locations of restaurants in those arrondissements.

EXPENSIVE

Le Violon d'Ingres ✿✿✿ FRENCH (MODERN & TRADITIONAL) This restaurant is Paris's pièce de résistance. Chef/owner Christian Constant is "the new Robuchon." Those who are fortunate enough to dine in the Violon's warm atmosphere of rose-colored wood, soft cream walls, and elegant chintz fabrics patterned with old English tea roses always rave about the cleverly artistic dishes. They range from a starter of pan-fried foie gras with gingerbread and spinach salad to more elegant main courses like lobster ravioli with crushed vine-ripened tomatoes, roasted veal in a light and creamy milk sauce served with tender spring vegetables, and even a selection from the rotisserie, like spit-roasted leg of lamb rubbed with fresh garlic and thyme. Chef Constant keeps a well-chosen selection of wine to accompany his meals. The service is charming and discreet.

135 rue St-Dominique, 7th arr. ✆ **01-45-55-15-05**. Fax 01-45-55-48-42. Reservations required at least 3–4 days in advance. Main courses 190F–230F (28.95€–34.95€, $27.55–$33.35); fixed-price *menu dégustation* 590F (89.75€, $85.55). AE, MC, V. Mon–Sat 7–11pm. Métro: Ecole Militaire.

MODERATE

La Petite Chaise FRENCH (TRADITIONAL) This is Paris's oldest restaurant, opened as an inn in 1680 by the baron de la Chaise at the edge of what was a large hunting preserve. (According to popular lore, the baron used the upstairs bedrooms for afternoon dalliances, between fox and pheasant hunts.) Very Parisian, the "Little Chair" invites you into a world of cramped but attractive tables, old wood paneling, and ornate wall sconces. A vigorous chef has brought renewed taste and flavor to this longtime favorite, and the four-course set menu offers a large choice of dishes in each category. Examples are a salad with duck breast strips on a bed of fresh lettuce, seafood-and-scallop ragout with saffron, beef filet with green peppercorns, and poached fish with steamed vegetables served in a sauce of fish and vegetable stock and cream.

36–38 rue de Grenelle, 7th arr. ✆ **01-42-22-13-35.** Reservations recommended. Fixed-price menus 160F–195F (24.30€–29.65€, $23.20–$28.35). AE, V. Daily noon–2pm and 7–11pm. Métro: Sèvres-Babylone or Rue du Bac.

INEXPENSIVE

Au Pied de Fouet FRENCH (TRADITIONAL)   Au Pied de Fouet is one of the neighborhood's smallest, oldest, and most reasonably priced restaurants. In the 1700s, it was a stopover for carriages en route to Paris from other parts of Europe, offering wine, food, and stables. Don't expect a leisurely or attentive meal: Food and drink will disappear quickly from your table, under the gaze of others waiting their turn. The dishes are solid and unpretentious and include *blanquette de veau, petit salé* (a savory family-style stew made from pork and vegetables), and *sole meunière,* a warhorse of French cuisine but always good.

45 rue de Babylone, 7th arr. ✆ **01-47-05-12-27.** Main courses 55F–85F (8.35€–12.90€, $8.05–$12.35). No credit cards. Mon–Sat noon–2:30pm; Mon–Fri 7–9:30pm. Closed Aug. Métro: Vaneau.

Chez l'Ami Jean BASQUE/SOUTHWESTERN FRENCH   This restaurant was opened by a Basque nationalist in 1931, and ardent fans claim its Basque cuisine and setting are the most authentic on the Left Bank. Decorative details include wood panels, memorabilia from *pelote* (a Basque game like jai alai) and soccer, and red-and-white woven tablecloths like the ones sold in Bayonne. Menu items include cured Bayonne ham; herb-laden Béarn-influenced vegetable soups; a succulent omelet with peppers, tomatoes, and onions; squid stewed in its own ink and served with tomatoes and herbs; and *poulet basquaise,* cooked with spicy sausage, onions, peppers, and very strong red wine. In springtime, look for a truly esoteric specialty rarely available elsewhere: *saumon de l'Adour* (Adour salmon) with béarnaise sauce.

27 rue Malar, 7th arr. ✆ **01-47-05-86-89.** Reservations recommended. Main courses 80F–100F (12.15€–15.20€, $11.60–$14.50). MC, V. Mon–Sat noon–3pm and 7–10:30pm. Métro: Invalides.

La Fontaine de Mars PYRENEAN/SOUTHWESTERN FRENCH   The restaurant name derives not from its location near the Champ de Mars but from the historic stone fountain on its tree-lined terrace. You'll find a sometimes boisterous dining room on the street level, plus two cozier and calmer upstairs rooms whose round tables and wooden floors make you feel like you're in a private home. An additional 70 or so seats become available by the fountain whenever weather permits. Much of the cuisine derives from the Pyrénées and southwestern France, bearing rich, heady flavors that go well with robust red wines. Examples are duckling confit with parsley potatoes, a Toulouse-inspired cassoulet, veal chops with morels, and red mullet or monkfish filets with herb-flavored butter. Our favorite dessert is a thin tart filled with a sugared purée of apples, capped with more apples, and garnished with Calvados and prunes.

129 rue St-Dominique, 7th arr. ℂ **01-47-05-46-44.** Reservations recommended. Main courses 75F–165F (11.40€–25.15€, $10.95–$23.95). AE, MC, V. Daily noon–2:30pm and 7:30–11pm. Métro: Ecole Militaire.

3 The Top Cafes

As surely everyone knows, the cafe is a Parisian institution. Parisians use them as combination club/tavern/snack bars, almost as extensions of their living rooms.

Coffee, of course, is the chief drink. It comes black in a small cup, unless you specifically order it *au lait* (with milk). Tea (*thé,* pronounced "tay") is also fairly popular but is generally not of a high quality. If you prefer beer, we advise you to pay a bit more for the imported German, Dutch, or Danish brands, which are much better than the local brew. If you insist on a French beer, at least order it *à pression* (draft), which is superior. There's also a vast variety of fruit drinks, as well as Coca-Cola, which can be rather expensive. French chocolate drinks—either hot or iced—are absolutely superb and on par with the finest Dutch brands. They're made from ground chocolate, not a chemical compound.

EXPENSIVE

Brasserie Lipp 𝒜 This is a Left Bank institution. On the day of Paris's liberation in 1944, late owner Roger Cazes welcomed Hemingway as the first man to drop in for a drink. Then, as now, famous people often drop by for beer, wine, and conversation. Cazes's nephew, Michel-Jacques Perrochon, now runs this quintessential Parisian brasserie, where the food is secondary, yet quite good, providing you can get a seat (an hour and a half waiting time is customary if the management doesn't know you). The specialty is *choucroute garni,* Paris's best—you get not only sauerkraut but also a thick layer of ham and braised pork, which you can down with the house Riesling (an Alsatian white wine) or beer. Even if you don't go inside for a drink, you can sit at a sidewalk table to enjoy a cognac and people-watch.

151 bd. St-Germain, 6th arr. ℂ **01-45-48-53-91.** Full meals average 290F (44.10€, $42.05); *café au lait* 18F (2.75€, $2.60). AE, DC, MC, V. Daily 9am–2am; restaurant service 11am–1am. Métro: St-Germain-des-Prés.

Café de Flore ✸✸
It's the most famous cafe in the world, still fighting to maintain the Left Bank aura in spite of massive hordes of visitors from around the world. Sartre—the granddaddy of existentialism, a key figure in the Resistance movement, and a renowned cafe-sitter—often came here during World War II. Wearing a leather jacket and beret, he sat at his table and wrote his trilogy, *Les Chemins de la Liberté* (The Roads to Freedom). Camus, Picasso, and Apollinaire also frequented the Flore. The cafe is still going strong, though the famous patrons have moved on and tourists have taken up all the tables. The menu offers omelets, salads, pavé of beef with pepper sauce, *sole meunière,* and more. The place is especially popular on Sunday mornings.

172 bd. St-Germain, 6th arr. ℂ **01-45-48-55-26.** *Café espresso* 24F (3.65€, $3.55); glass of beer 42F (6.45€, $6.15). AE, DC, MC, V. Daily 7am–1:30am. Métro: St-Germain-des-Prés.

Café de la Paix ✸✸
This hub of the tourist world rules place de l'Opéra, and the legend goes that if you sit here long enough, you'll see someone you know passing by. Huge, grandiose, fashionable, and sometimes brusque and anonymous, it harbors not only Parisians but also, at one time or another, nearly every visiting American—a tradition dating from the end of World War I. Once Emile Zola sat on the terrace; later, Hemingway and Fitzgerald frequented it. The best news for tourists who stop in for a bite is that prices have recently been lowered because of stiff competition in the area. Menu items may include escalope of veal with mushrooms and cream sauce, seafood *bourride* (stew) in the style of Provence, and beef filet with red-wine/mushroom sauce.

Place de l'Opéra, 17 bd. des Capucines, 9th arr. ℂ **01-40-07-30-20.** *Café espresso* 19F (2.95€, $2.75); fixed-price menu 138F (21.05€, $20) for 2 courses, 178F (27.05€, $25.80) for 3 courses. Daily noon–midnight. Métro: Opéra.

Fouquet's ✸
For people-watching, this is definitely on the see-and-be-seen circuit. Fouquet's has been collecting anecdotes and a patina since it was founded in 1901. A celebrity favorite, it has attracted Chaplin, Chevalier, Dietrich, Churchill, Roosevelt, and Jackie O. The premier cafe on the Champs-Elysées sits behind a barricade of potted flowers at the edge of the sidewalk. You can choose a table in the sunshine or retreat to the glassed-in elegance of the

leather banquettes and rattan furniture of the grill room. Though this is a full-fledged restaurant, with a beautiful formal dining room on the second floor, most visitors come by just for a glass of wine, coffee, or sandwich.

99 av. des Champs-Elysées, 8th arr. ℭ 01-47-23-50-00. Glass of wine from 36F (5.45€, $5.20); sandwiches 55F (8.35€, $8.05); main courses 160F–380F (24.30€–57.75€, $23.20–$55.10); fixed-price menu 300F (45.60€, $43.50). AE, MC, V. Daily 8am–2am. Restaurant daily noon–3pm and 7pm–12:30am; bar 9am–2am. Métro: George V.

MODERATE

Café Beaubourg   Located next to the all-pedestrian plaza of the Centre Pompidou, this is a trendy avant-garde cafe with soaring concrete columns and a minimalist decor. Many of the regulars work in the neighborhood's eclectic shops and galleries. You can order salads, omelets, grilled steak, chicken Cordon Bleu, pastries, and daily platters. In warm weather, tables are set up on the sprawling outdoor terrace, providing a great place to watch the young and the restless go by.

100 rue St-Martin, 4th arr. ℭ 01-48-87-63-96. Glass of wine 23F–40F (3.50€–6.10€, $3.35–$5.80); beer 27F–40F (4.10€–6.10€, $3.90–$5.80); American breakfast 110F (16.70€, $15.95); sandwiches and platters 40F–170F (6.10€–25.85€, $5.80–$24.65). AE, DC, MC, V. Sun–Thurs 8am–1am; Fri–Sat 8am–2am. Métro: Rambuteau or Hôtel de Ville.

Café Cosmos ℱℱ   Does today's generation have a cafe to equal the Lost Generation's Coupole? Perhaps it's the ultramodern Cosmos, where you might rub elbows with a French film star or an executive ("no one writes novels anymore"). The cafe features wooden tables, black leather chairs, and black clothing in winter— the perfect backdrop for smoked salmon with toast, rump steak with Roquefort sauce, or grilled tuna steak.

101 bd. du Montparnasse, 6th arr. ℭ 01-43-26-74-36. Café espresso 25F (3.80€, $3.65); platters 42F–85F (6.40€–12.90€, $6.15–$12.35); fixed-price lunch 69F (10.55€, $10). AE, DC, MC, V. Daily 7am–2am. Métro: Vavin.

Café de la Musique   This cafe's location in one of the grandest of Mitterrand's *grands travaux* guarantees a crowd passionately devoted to music; the recorded sounds that play in the background are likely to be more diverse and more eclectic than those in any other cafe in Paris. The red-and-green velour setting might remind you of a modern opera house, with windows overlooking nearby place de la Fontaine. On the menu you'll find pasta with shellfish, roast pork in cider sauce, and braised stingray in black butter sauce.

Wednesdays from 10pm to 1am bring a program of live jazz, and Fridays from 10pm to 1am bring live music; Saturdays a DJ entertains with disco music.

In the Cité de la Musique, Place Fontaine Aux Lions, 212 av. Jean-Jaurès, 19th arr. ℭ **01-48-03-15-91**. Plats du jour 75F (11.40€, $10.95). AE, DC, MC, V. Daily 7am–2am (full menu daily 11am–midnight). Métro: Porte de Pantin.

Café Marly This is for your rendezvous at the Louvre, especially if you're meeting a modern-day La Giaconda or a guy who looks like he posed for one of those Adonis statues inside the museum. In 1994, the French government gave the green light for a cafe and restaurant to open in one of the Louvre's most historic courtyards, accessible only from a point close to the famous glass pyramid that rises above the cour Marly. It has become a favorite refuge of Parisians trying to escape the traffic roar on rue de Rivoli. Anyone is welcome to sit down for a *café au lait* daily from 8am to 2am. But more substantial fare is the norm here, served in one of three dining rooms done in tones of burgundy, black, and gilt. Menu items include club sandwiches, fresh fish, pepper steak, and an array of upscale bistro-inspired food. In summer, outdoor tables overlook the celebrated courtyard.

In the cour Napoléon du Louvre, 93 rue de Rivoli, 1st arr. ℭ **01-49-26-06-60**. Reservations recommended. Main courses 110F–150F (16.70€–22.80€, $15.95–$21.75). AE, DC, MC, V. Daily 8am–2am (meals 11:30am–1am). Métro: Palais Royal or Musée du Louvre.

Café/Restaurant/Salon de Thé Bernardaud ☆☆ Few other Paris cafes/tearooms mingle salesmanship with culinary pizzazz as effectively as this one. The venerable Limoges-based manufacturer of porcelain Bernardaud opened it in 1995, and the staggeringly beautiful stuff is on display everywhere. Occupying some of Europe's most expensive commercial real estate, the medium-green space is upscale Art Deco in style. Lunchtime is flooded with employees of the nearby offices and shoppers, and you can opt for just a salad or something more substantial, like a medley of fresh fish in herb sauce with vegetables. Afternoon tea adds a new twist: A staff member will present a choice of five porcelain patterns in which your tea will be served, and if you finish your Earl Grey with a fixation on the pattern you've chosen, you'll be directed into the adjacent showroom to place your order.

9 rue Royale, 8th arr. ℭ **01-42-66-22-55**. Reservations recommended at lunch. Continental breakfast 55F (8.35€, $8.05); lunch main courses 90F–130F (13.70€–19.75€, $13.05–$18.85); afternoon tea with pastry 75F (11.40€, $10.95). MC, V. Mon–Sat 8am–7pm. Métro: Concorde.

La Coupole ⟨ℛ⟩   Born in 1927 and once a leading center of artistic life, La Coupole is now the epitome of the grand Paris brasserie in Montparnasse. Former patrons included Josephine Baker, Henry Miller, Dalí, Calder, Hemingway, Fitzgerald, and Picasso. The sweeping outdoor terrace is among the finest in Paris. At one of its sidewalk tables, you can sit and watch the passing scene and order a coffee or a cognac VSOP. The food is quite good, despite the fact that the dining room resembles an enormous rail-station waiting room. Try main dishes like *sole meunière,* cassoulet, fresh oysters, shellfish, and some of the best pepper steak in Paris. The waiters are as rude and inattentive as ever, and aficionados of the place wouldn't have it any other way.

102 bd. du Montparnasse, 14th arr. ⓒ **01-43-20-14-20.** Breakfast buffet 90F (13.75€, $13.05); main courses 92F–195F (14.05€–29.65€, $13.35–$28.35) at lunch, 110F–210F (16.70€–31.90€, $15.95–$30.45) at dinner; fixed-price menus 138F–189F (21.05€–28.75€, $20–$27.40) at lunch, 189F (28.75€, $27.40) at dinner before 10:30pm, 138F–189F (21.05€–28.75€, $20–$27.40) after 10:30pm. AE, DC, MC, V. Daily 8:30am–1am (breakfast buffet Mon–Fri 8:30am–10:30pm). Métro: Vavin.

Les Deux Magots ⟨ℛℛ⟩   This legendary hangout for the sophisticated residents of St-Germain-des-Prés becomes a tourist favorite in summer. Visitors monopolize the few sidewalk tables as the waiters rush about, seemingly oblivious to anyone's needs. Regulars from around the neighborhood reclaim it in the off-season. Les Deux Magots was once a gathering place of the intellectual elite, like Sartre and de Beauvoir and Giraudoux. Inside are the two large statues of Confucian wise men (*magots*) that give the cafe its name. The crystal chandeliers are too brightly lit, but the regulars seem to be accustomed to the glare. After all, some of them even read their daily newspapers here. You can order salads, pastries, ice cream, or one of the daily specials; the fresh fish is usually a good bet.

6 place St-Germain-des-Prés, 6th arr. ⓒ **01-45-48-55-25.** *Café au lait* 25F (3.80€, $3.65); whiskey soda 70F (10.65€, $10.15); *plats du jour* 90F–140F (13.75€–21.35€, $13.05–$20.30). AE, DC, V. Daily 7:30am–1:30am. Métro: St-Germain-des-Prés.

5

Exploring Paris

Paris is a city where taking in the street life—shopping, strolling, and hanging out—should claim as much of your time as sightseeing in churches or museums. Watching children sail toy boats in the Jardin du Luxembourg, taking a sunrise amble along the Seine, spending an afternoon bartering at a flea market—Paris bewitches you with these kinds of experiences. For all the Louvre's beauty, you'll probably remember the Latin Quarter's crooked alleyways better than the 370th oil painting you see during your visit.

SIGHTSEEING SUGGESTIONS FOR THE FIRST-TIMER

IF YOU HAVE 1 DAY   Get up early and begin your day with some live theater by walking the streets around your hotel. Find a little cafe and order a typical Parisian breakfast of coffee and croissants. If you're a museum and monument junkie and don't dare return home without seeing the "must" sights, know that the two top museums are the **Musée du Louvre** and **Musée d'Orsay,** and the three top monuments are the **Eiffel Tower, Arc de Triomphe,** and **Notre-Dame** (which you can see later in the day). If it's a toss-up between the Louvre and the d'Orsay, we'd make it the Louvre because it holds a greater variety of works. If you need to choose among the monuments, we'd make it the Eiffel Tower just for the panoramic view of the city.

If your day is too short to visit museums or wait in line for the tower, we suggest you spend most of your time strolling the streets. The most impressive neighborhood is on **Ile St-Louis,** the most elegant place for a walk. After exploring this island and its mansions, wander at will through such Left Bank districts as **St-Germain-des-Prés** and the area around **place St-Michel,** the heart of the student quarter. As the sun sets, head for **Notre-Dame,** which stands majestically along the banks of the Seine. This is a good place to watch the shadows fall over Paris as the lights come on for the night. Afterward, walk along the Seine, where vendors sell books and souvenir prints. Promise yourself a return visit and have dinner in the Left Bank bistro of your choice.

IF YOU HAVE 2 DAYS   Follow the above for day 1, except now you can fit in on day 2 more of the top five sights we mention above. Day 1 covered a lot of the Left Bank, so if you want to explore the Right Bank, begin at the **Arc de Triomphe** and stroll down the **Champs-Elysées,** Paris's main boulevard, until you reach the Egyptian obelisk at **place de la Concorde,** where some of France's most notable figures lost their heads on the guillotine. Place de la Concorde affords terrific views of **La Madeleine,** the **Palais Bourbon,** the **Arc de Triomphe,** and the **Musée du Louvre.** Nearby **place Vendôme** is well worth a visit, as it represents the Right Bank at its most elegant, with the Hôtel Ritz and Paris's top jewelry stores. Now we suggest a rest stop in the **Jardin de Tuileries,** directly west and adjacent to the Louvre. After a bistro lunch, go for a walk in the **Marais** to get a total contrast to monumental Paris. Our favorite stroll is along narrow **rue des Rosiers,** at the heart of the Jewish community. And don't miss **place des Vosges.** After a rest at your hotel, select one of the restaurants down in **Montparnasse,** following in Hemingway's footsteps. This area is far livelier at night.

IF YOU HAVE 3 DAYS   Spend days 1 and 2 as above. As you've already gotten a look at the Left Bank and the Right Bank, this day should be about following your special interests. You might target the restored **Centre Pompidou** and the **Musée Carnavalet,** Paris's history museum. If you're a Monet fan, you might head for the **Musée Marmottan–Claude Monet.** Or perhaps you'd rather wander the sculpture garden of the **Musée Rodin.** If you select the **Musée Picasso,** you can use part of the morning to explore a few of the Marais's art galleries. After lunch, spend the afternoon on **Ile de la Cité,** where you'll get not only to see Notre-Dame again but also to visit the **Conciergerie,** where Marie Antoinette and others were held captive before they were beheaded. And you certainly can't miss the stunning stained glass of **Ste-Chapelle** in the Palais de Justice. After dinner, if your energy holds, you can sample Paris's nightlife—whatever you fancy, the dancers at the **Lido** or the **Folies-Bergère** or a smoky Left Bank jazz club or a frenzied disco. If you'd like to just sit and have a drink, Paris has some of the most elegant hotel bars in the world—try the **Hôtel de Crillon** or the **Plaza Athénée.**

IF YOU HAVE 4 DAYS   For your first 3 days, follow the above. On day 4, head to **Versailles,** 21 kilometers (13 miles) south of Paris, the greatest attraction in the Ile-de-France. When Louis XIV decided to move to the suburbs, he created a spectacle unlike anything the world had ever seen. The good news is that most of the palace remains intact, in all its opulence and glitter. A full day here almost feels like too little time. After you return to Paris for the night, take a good rest and spend the evening wandering around the Left Bank's **Latin Quarter,** enjoying the student cafes and bars and selecting your bistro of choice for the evening. Two of the livelier streets for wandering are rue de la Huchette and rue Monsieur-le-Prince.

IF YOU HAVE 5 DAYS   Spend days 1 to 4 as above. On day 5, devote at least a morning to a neglected area: **Montmartre,** the community formerly known for its artists perched atop the highest of Paris's seven hills. Though the starving artists who made it the embodiment of *la vie de bohème* have long departed, there's much to enchant you, especially if you wander the back streets and avoid place du Tertre. Away from the tacky shops and sleazy clubs, you'll see the picture-postcard lanes and staircases known to Picasso, Toulouse-Lautrec, and Utrillo. Of course, it's virtually mandatory to visit **Sacré-Coeur,** for the view if nothing else. Because it's your last night in Paris, let your own interests take over. Lovers traditionally spend it clasping hands in a walk along the Seine; less goo-goo-eyed visitors can still find a full agenda. We suggest a final evening at **Willi's Wine Bar** (see p. 173), with more than 250 vintages and good food to go along with it. For a nightcap, we always head for the **Hemingway Bar** at the Ritz, where Garbo, Coward, and Fitzgerald once lifted their glasses.

1 The Top Attractions

Arc de Triomphe ✶✶✶   At the western end of the Champs-Elysées, the Arc de Triomphe suggests one of those ancient Roman arches, only it's larger. Actually, it's the biggest triumphal arch in the world, about 163 feet high and 147 feet wide. To reach it, *don't try to cross the square;* it's Paris's busiest traffic hub. With a dozen streets radiating from the "Star," the roundabout has been called by one writer "vehicular roulette with more balls than numbers." (Death is certain!) Take the underground passage and live a little longer.

Paris Attractions

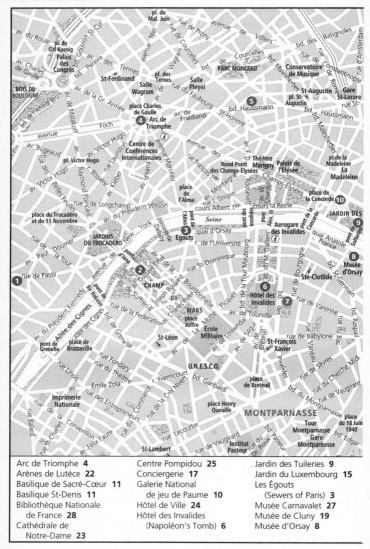

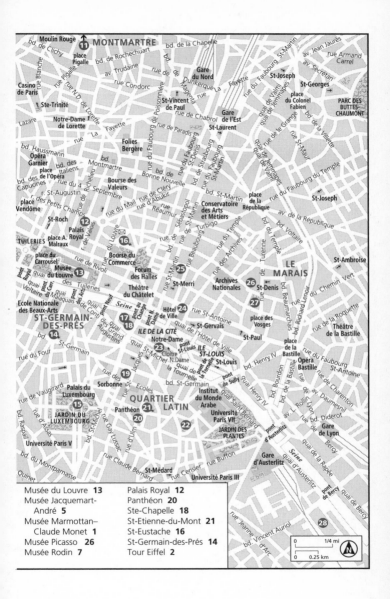

Musée du Louvre **13**	Palais Royal **12**
Musée Jacquemart-André **5**	Panthéon **20**
	Ste-Chapelle **18**
Musée Marmottan–Claude Monet **1**	St-Etienne-du-Mont **21**
Musée Picasso **26**	St-Eustache **16**
Musée Rodin **7**	St-Germain-des-Prés **14**
	Tour Eiffel **2**

Commissioned by Napoléon in 1806 to commemorate the victories of his Grand Armée, the arch wasn't ready for the entrance of his new empress, Marie-Louise, in 1810. (He'd divorced Joséphine because she couldn't provide him an heir.) It served its ceremonial purpose anyway but wasn't completed until 1836, under the reign of Louis-Philippe. Four years later, Napoléon's remains, brought from his grave on St. Helena, passed under the arch on their journey to his tomb at the Hôtel des Invalides. Since that time it has become the focal point for state funerals. It's also the site of the permanent tomb of the unknown soldier, in whose honor an eternal flame is kept burning.

The greatest state funeral was Victor Hugo's in 1885; his coffin was placed under the arch, and much of Paris turned out to pay tribute. Another notable funeral was in 1929 for Ferdinand Foch, supreme commander of the Allied forces in World War I. The arch has been the centerpiece of some of France's proudest moments and some of its most humiliating defeats, notably those of 1871 and 1940. The memory of German troops marching under the arch that had come to symbolize France's glory is still painful to the French. Who can forget the 1940 newsreel of the Frenchman standing on the Champs-Elysées weeping as the Nazi storm troopers goose-stepped through Paris? The arch's happiest moment occurred in 1944, when the liberation of Paris parade passed beneath it. That same year, Eisenhower paid a visit to the tomb of the unknown soldier, a new tradition among leaders of state and important figures. After Charles de Gaulle's death, the French government (despite protests from anti-Gaullists) voted to change the name of this site from place de l'Etoile to place Charles de Gaulle. Nowadays it's often known as place Charles de Gaulle–Etoile.

Of the sculptures on the monument, the best known is Rude's *Marseillaise,* also known as *The Departure of the Volunteers.* J. P. Cortot's *Triumph of Napoléon in 1810* and Etex's *Resistance of 1814* and *Peace of 1815* also adorn the facade. The monument is engraved with the names of hundreds of generals (those underlined died in battle) who commanded French troops in Napoleonic victories.

You can take an elevator or climb the stairway to the top, where there's an exhibition hall with lithographs and photos depicting the arch throughout its history, as well as an observation deck with a fantastic view.

Place Charles de Gaulle–Etoile, 8th arr. (℡ **01-55-37-73-77.** www.monuments.fr. Admission 42F (6.40€, $6.10) adults, 26F (3.95€, $3.75) ages 12–25, children 11 and under free. Apr–Sept daily 9:30am–11pm; Oct–Mar daily 10am–10:30pm. Métro: Charles de Gaulle–Etoile.

Basilique du Sacré-Coeur ✦✦

Sacré-Coeur is one of Paris's most characteristic landmarks and has been the subject of much controversy. One Parisian called it "a lunatic's confectionery dream." An offended Zola declared it "the basilica of the ridiculous." Sacré-Coeur has had warm supporters as well, including poet Max Jacob and artist Maurice Utrillo. Utrillo never tired of drawing and painting it, and he and Jacob came here regularly to pray. Atop the *butte* (hill) in Montmartre, its multiple gleaming white domes and *campanile* (bell tower) tower over Paris like a 12th-century Byzantine church. But it's not that old. After France's 1870 defeat by the Prussians, the basilica was planned as a votive offering to cure France's misfortunes. Rich and poor alike contributed money to build it. Construction began in 1876, and though the church wasn't consecrated until 1919, perpetual prayers of adoration have been made here day and night since 1885. The interior is brilliantly decorated with mosaics: Look for the striking depiction of Christ on the ceiling and the mural of his Passion at the back of the altar. The stained-glass windows were shattered during the struggle for Paris in 1944 but have been well replaced. The crypt contains a relic of what some of the devout believe is Christ's sacred heart—hence, the name of the church.

Insider's tip: Although the view from the Arc de Triomphe is the greatest panorama of Paris, we also want to endorse this stunning view from the gallery around the inner dome of Sacré-Coeur. On a clear day, your eyes can take in a panoramic sweep of Paris extending for 30 miles into the Ile-de-France. You can also walk around the inner dome, an attraction even better than the interior of Sacré-Coeur itself.

Place St-Pierre, 18th arr. (✆) **01-53-41-89-00.** Free admission to basilica; joint ticket to dome and crypt 30F (4.55€, $4.35) adults, 16F (2.45€, $2.30) students/children. Apr–Sept daily 9am–5:45pm; Oct–Mar daily 9am–6pm. Métro: Abbesses; then take the elevator to the surface and follow the signs to the *funiculaire,* which goes up to the church for the price of a Métro ticket.

Cathédrale de Notre-Dame ✦✦✦

Notre-Dame is the heart of Paris and even of the country itself: Distances from the city to all parts of France are calculated from a spot at the far end of place du Parvis, in front of the cathedral, where a circular bronze plaque marks **Kilomètre Zéro.**

The cathedral's setting on the banks of the Seine has always been memorable. Founded in the 12th century by Maurice de Sully, bishop of Paris, Notre-Dame has grown and grown over the years, changing as Paris has changed, often falling victim to whims of decorative taste. Its famous flying buttresses (the external side supports, giving the massive interior a sense of weightlessness) were rebuilt in 1330. Though many disagree, we feel Notre-Dame is more interesting outside than in, and you'll want to walk all around it to fully appreciate this "vast symphony of stone." Better yet, cross over the pont au Double to the Left Bank and view it from the quay.

The histories of Paris and Notre-Dame are inseparable. Many prayed here before going off to fight in the Crusades. "Our Lady of Paris" wasn't spared by the revolutionaries, who destroyed the Galerie des Rois and converted the building into a secular temple. Later, Napoléon crowned himself emperor here, yanking the crown out of Pius VII's hands and placing it on his own head before crowning his Joséphine empress (see David's *Coronation of Napoléon* in the Louvre). But carelessness, vandalism, embellishments, and wars of religion had already demolished much of the previously existing structure.

The cathedral was once scheduled for demolition, but, because of the popularity of Victor Hugo's *Hunchback of Notre-Dame* and the revival of interest in the Gothic period, a movement mushroomed to restore the cathedral to its original glory. The task was completed under Viollet-le-Duc, an architectural genius. The houses of old Paris used to crowd in on Notre-Dame, but during his redesigning of the city, Baron Haussmann ordered them torn down to show the cathedral to its best advantage from the parvis. This is the best vantage for seeing the three sculpted 13th-century portals.

On the left, the **Portal of the Virgin** depicts the signs of the zodiac and the coronation of the Virgin, an association found in dozens of medieval churches. The restored central **Portal of the Last Judgment** depicts three levels: The first shows Vices and Virtues; the second, Christ and his Apostles; and above that, Christ in triumph after the Resurrection. The portal is a close illustration of the Gospel according to Matthew. Over it is the remarkable **west rose window** 🎯🎯, 31 feet wide, forming a showcase for a statue of the Virgin and Child. On the far right is the **Portal of St. Anne,** depicting scenes like the Virgin enthroned with Child; it's Notre-Dame's best preserved and most perfect piece of sculpture. Equally interesting (though often missed) is the **Portal of the Cloisters** (around on the left), with its dour-faced 13th-century Virgin, a survivor among the figures that originally adorned the facade. (Alas, the Child she's holding has been decapitated.) Finally, on the Seine side of Notre-Dame, the **Portal of St. Stephen** traces that saint's martyrdom.

If possible, come to see Notre-Dame at sunset. Inside, of the three giant medallions warming the austere cathedral, the **north rose window** ⬥⬥ in the transept, from the mid-13th century, is best. The main body of the church is typically Gothic, with slender, graceful columns. In the **choir,** a stone-carved screen from the early 14th century depicts such biblical scenes as the Last Supper. Near the altar stands the 14th-century *Virgin and Child* ⬥, highly venerated among Paris's faithful. In the **treasury** are displayed vestments and gold objects, including crowns. Exhibited are a cross presented to Haile Selassie, former emperor of Ethiopia, and a reliquary given by Napoléon. Notre-Dame is especially proud of its relic of the True Cross and the Crown of Thorns.

Finally, to visit those grimy **gargoyles** ⬥⬥ immortalized by Hugo, you have to scale steps leading to the twin square **towers** rising to a height of 225 feet. Once there, you can closely inspect the devils (some giving you the raspberry), hobgoblins, and birds of prey. Look carefully and you may see the hunchback Quasimodo with Esmerelda.

6 place du Parvis Notre-Dame, 4th arr. ✆ **01-42-34-56-10.** www.paris.org/ Monuments/NDame. Free admission to cathedral; towers 35F (5.30€, $5.10) adults, 23F (3.50€, $3.35) ages 12–25/over 60, children under 12 free; treasury 15F (2.30€, $2.20) adults, 10F (1.50€, $1.45) ages 12–25/over 60, children under 12 free. Cathedral daily 8am–6:45pm year-round. Towers and crypt Apr–Sept daily 9:30am–6pm, Oct–Mar daily 10am–5:15pm. Museum Wed and Sat–Sun 2:30–5pm. Treasury Mon–Sat 9:30–11:30am and 1–5:45pm. Métro: Cité or St-Michel. RER: St-Michel.

Hôtel des Invalides (Napoléon's Tomb) ⬥⬥⬥   In 1670, the Sun King decided to build this "hotel" to house disabled soldiers. It wasn't an entirely benevolent gesture, however, because the men had been injured, crippled, or blinded while fighting his battles. When the building was finally completed (Louis XIV had long been dead), a gilded dome by Jules Hardouin-Mansart crowned it, and its corridors stretched for miles. The best way to approach the Invalides is by crossing over the Right Bank via the early-1900s pont Alexander-III and entering the cobblestone forecourt, where a display of massive cannons makes a formidable welcome.

Before rushing on to Napoléon's Tomb, you may want to visit the world's greatest military museum, the **Musée de l'Armée.** In 1794, a French inspector started collecting weapons, uniforms, and equipment, and with the accumulation of war material over the centuries, the museum has become a horrifying documentary of man's self-destruction. Viking swords, Burgundian battle axes, 14th-century blunderbusses, Balkan khandjars, American Browning machine guns, war pitchforks, salamander-engraved Renaissance serpentines, a 1528 Griffon, musketoons, grenadiers . . . if it can kill, it's enshrined here. As a sardonic touch, there's even the wooden leg of General Daumesnil, the governor of Vincennes who lost his leg in the battle of Wagram. Oblivious to the irony of committing a crime against a place that documents man's evil nature, the Nazis looted the museum in 1940.

Among the outstanding acquisitions are suits of armor worn by the kings and dignitaries of France, including Louis XIV, the best of which are in the new Arsenal. The most famous one, the "armor suit of the lion," was made for François I. Henri II ordered his suit engraved with the monogram of his mistress, Diane de Poitiers, and (perhaps reluctantly) that of his wife, Catherine de Médicis. Particularly fine are the showcases of swords and the World War I mementos, including those of American and Canadian soldiers—seek out the Armistice Bugle, which sounded the cease-fire on November 7, 1918, before the general cease-fire on November 11, 1918. The west wing's Salle Orientale shows arms of the Eastern world, including Asia and the Mideast Muslim countries, from the 16th to the 19th century. Turkish armor (look for Bajazet's helmet) and weaponry and Chinese and Japanese armor and swords are on display.

And then there's that little Corsican who became France's greatest soldier. Here you can see the plaster death mask Antommarchi made of him, as well as an oil by Delaroche, painted at the time of Napoléon's first banishment (Apr 1814) and depicting him as he probably looked, paunch and all. The First Empire exhibit displays Napoléon's field bed with his tent; in the room devoted to the Restoration, the 100 Days, and Waterloo, you can see his bedroom as it was at the time of his death on St. Helena. On the more personal side, you can view stuffed Vizir, a horse he owned, as well as a saddle he used mainly for state ceremonies. The Turenne Salon contains other souvenirs, like the hat Napoléon wore at Eylau, the sword from his Austerlitz victory, and his "Flag of Farewell," which he kissed before departing for Elba.

You can gain access to the **Musée des Plans-Reliefs** through the west wing. This collection shows French towns and monuments done in scale models (the model of Strasbourg fills an entire room) as well as models of military fortifications since the days of the great Vauban.

A walk across the cour d'Honneur (Court of Honor) delivers you to the **Eglise du Dôme,** designed by Hardouin-Mansart for Louis XIV. The great architect began work on the church in 1677, though he died before its completion. The dome is the second-tallest monument in Paris (the Eiffel Tower is the tallest, of course). The hearse used at the emperor's funeral on May 9, 1821, is in the Napoléon Chapel.

To accommodate **Napoléon's tomb** ✪✪✪, the architect Visconti had to redesign the church's high altar in 1842. First buried on St. Helena, Napoléon's remains were exhumed and brought to Paris in 1840 on the orders of Louis-Philippe, who demanded the English return the emperor to French soil. The triumphal funeral procession passed beneath the Arc de Triomphe, down the Champs-Elysées, and to the Invalides, as snow swirled through the air. The remains were locked inside six coffins in this tomb made of red Finnish porphyry, with a green granite base. Surrounding it are a dozen amazon-like figures representing Napoléon's victories. Almost lampooning the smallness of the man, everything is done on a gargantuan scale. In his coronation robes, the statue of Napoléon stands 8½ feet high. The grave of the "King of Rome," his son by second wife Marie-Louise, lies at his feet. Napoléon's Tomb is surrounded by those of his brother Joseph Bonaparte; the great Vauban, who built many of France's fortifications; World War I Allied commander Foch; and the vicomte de Turenne, the republic's first grenadier. (Actually, only his heart is entombed here.)

Place des Invalides, 7th arr. ☎ **01-44-42-37-72.** Admission to Musée de l'Armée, Napoléon's Tomb, and Musée des Plans-Reliefs 40F (6.10€, $5.80) adults, 30F (4.55€, $4.35) ages 12–18, children 11 and under free. Oct–Mar daily 10am–5pm; Apr–May and Sept daily 10am–6pm; June–Aug daily 10am–7pm. Closed Jan 1, May 1, Nov 1, and Dec 25. Métro: Latour-Maubourg, Varenne, or Invalides.

Musée du Louvre ✪✪✪   The Louvre is the world's largest palace and largest museum. As a palace, it leaves us cold, except for its old section, the **cour Carrée.** As a museum, it's one of the greatest art collections ever. To enter, you pass through I. M. Pei's controversial 71-foot **glass pyramid** ✪—a startling but effective contrast of ultra-modern against the palace's classical lines. Commissioned by the late president François Mitterrand and completed in 1989, it allows sunlight to shine on an underground reception area with a complex of shops and restaurants. Automatic ticket machines help relieve the long lines of yesteryear.

People on one of those "Paris-in-a-day" tours try to break track records to get a glimpse of the Louvre's two most famous ladies: the beguiling *Mona Lisa* and the armless *Venus de Milo* ⭐⭐⭐. (The scene at the *Mona Lisa* is a circus—as the staff looks idly on, viewers push and shove in front of her bulletproof glass and forbidden flashbulbs pop all over. Yet still she smiles that smile, at peace among the fracas.) The herd then dashes on a 5-minute stampede in pursuit of *Winged Victory* ⭐⭐⭐, the headless statue discovered at Samothrace and dating from about 200 B.C. In defiance of the assembly-line theory of art, we head instead for David's *Coronation of Napoléon,* showing Napoléon poised with the crown aloft as Joséphine kneels before him, just across from his *Portrait of Madame Récamier* ⭐, depicting Napoléon's opponent at age 23; she reclines on her sofa agelessly in the style of classical antiquity.

Then a big question looms: Which of the rest of the 30,000 works on display would you like to see?

Between the Seine and rue de Rivoli, the Palais du Louvre suffers from an embarrassment of riches, stretching for almost half a mile. In the days of Charles V, it was a fortress, but François I, a patron of Leonardo da Vinci, had it torn down and rebuilt as a royal residence. Less than a month after Marie Antoinette's head and body parted company, the Revolutionary Committee decided the king's collection of paintings and sculpture should be opened to the public. At the lowest point in its history, in the 18th century, the Louvre was home for anybody who wanted to set up housekeeping there. Laundry hung out the windows, corners were literally pigpens, and families built fires to cook their meals during the long winters. Napoléon ended all that, chasing out the squatters and restoring the palace. In fact, he chose the Louvre as the site of his wedding to Marie-Louise.

So where did all these paintings come from? The kings of France, notably François I and Louis XIV, acquired many of them, and others were willed to or purchased by the state. Many contributed by Napoléon were taken from reluctant donors: The Church was one especially heavy and unwilling giver. Much of Napoléon's plunder had to be returned, though France hasn't yet seen its way clear to giving back all the booty.

The collections are divided into seven departments: Egyptian Antiquities; Oriental Antiquities; Greek, Etruscan, and Roman Antiquities; Sculpture; Painting; Decorative Arts; and Graphic Arts. A number of galleries, devoted to Italian paintings, Roman glass and bronzes, Oriental antiquities, and Egyptian antiquities, were opened in 1997 and 1998. If you don't have to do Paris in a day, perhaps you can come here several times, concentrating on different collections or schools of painting. Those with little time should go on one of the guided tours in English.

Acquired by François I to hang above his bathtub, Leonardo's much-traveled *La Gioconda (Mona Lisa)* ⭐⭐⭐ has been the source of legend for centuries. Note the guard and bulletproof glass: The world's most famous painting was stolen in the summer of 1911 and found in Florence in the winter of 1913. At first, both the poet Guillaume Apollinaire and Picasso were suspected, but it was discovered in the possession of a former Louvre employee, who'd apparently carried it out under his overcoat. Less well known (but to us even more enchanting) are Leonardo's *Virgin and Child with St. Anne* ⭐ and the *Virgin of the Rocks.*

After paying your respects to the "Smiling One," allow time to see some French works stretching from the Richelieu wing through the entire **Sully wing** and even overflowing into the **Denon wing.** It's all here: Watteau's *Gilles* with the mysterious boy in a clown suit staring at you; Fragonard's and Boucher's rococo renderings of the aristocracy; and the greatest masterpieces of David, including his stellar 1785 *The Oath of the Horatii* and the vast and vivid *Coronation of Napoléon.* Only Florence's Uffizi rivals the Denon wing for its Italian Renaissance collection—everything from Raphael's *Portrait of Balthazar Castiglione* to Titian's *Man with a Glove.* Veronese's gigantic *Wedding Feast at Cana* ⭐, a romp of Viennese high society in the 1500s, occupies an entire wall (that's Paolo himself playing the cello).

Of the Greek and Roman antiquities, the most notable collections, aside from *Venus de Milo* and *Winged Victory,* are fragments of a **Parthenon frieze** (in the Denon wing). In Renaissance sculpture, you'll see Michelangelo's *Esclaves (Slaves),* originally intended for the tomb of Julius II but sold into other bondage. The Denon wing houses masterpieces like Ingres's *The Turkish Bath;* the **Botticelli frescoes** from the Villa Lemmi; Raphael's *La Belle Jardinière;* and Titian's *Open Air Concert.* The Sully wing is also filled with old masters, like Boucher's *Diana Resting After Her Bath* and Fragonard's *Bathers.*

> **Tips** **Some Louvre Tips**
>
> Long waiting lines outside the Louvre's pyramid entrance
> are notorious, but there are some tricks for avoiding them.
>
> • Order tickets by phone at ℂ **08-03-80-88-03** and have
>   them charged to your Visa or MasterCard, then pick
>   them up at any FNAC store. This gives you direct entry
>   through the Passage Richelieu, 93 rue de Rivoli.
> • Enter via the underground shopping mall, the Carrousel
>   du Louvre, at 99 rue de Rivoli.
> • Enter directly from the Palais Royal–Musée du Louvre
>   Métro station.
> • Buy Le Pass Musée et Monuments (Museum and Monu-
>   ments Pass) allowing direct entry through the priority
>   entrance at the Passage Richelieu, 93 rue de Rivoli. The
>   pass is available at any of the museums honoring it or at
>   any branch of the Paris Tourist office (see p. 15).

The **Richelieu wing** 𝕽𝕽𝕽, reopened in 1993 after decaying
empty for years, was expanded to add some 230,000 square feet
of exhibition space. It houses northern European and French
paintings, along with decorative arts, French sculpture, Oriental
antiquities (a rich collection of Islamic art), and the Napoléon III
salons. One of its galleries displays 21 works Rubens painted in a
space of only 2 years for Marie de Médicis's Palais de Luxembourg.
The masterpieces here include Dürer's *Self-Portrait,* Van Dyck's
Portrait of Charles I of England, and Holbein the Younger's
Portrait of Erasmus of Rotterdam.

When you get tired, consider a pick-me-up at **Café Marly** in the
cour Napoléon (see p. 103). This grandiose cafe overlooks the glass
pyramid and offers coffees, pastries (by Paris's most legendary
pastry-maker, Lenôtre), salads, sandwiches, and simple platters.

34–36 quai du Louvre, 1st arr. Main entrance in the glass pyramid, cour Napoléon.
ℂ 01-40-20-53-17 (01-40-20-51-51 recorded message, 08-03-80-88-03 advance
credit-card sales). www.louvre.fr. Admission 46F (7€, $6.65) before 3pm, 30F
(4.55€, $4.35) after 3pm and on Sun, free for ages 17 and under, free 1st Sun of
every month. Mon and Wed 9am–9:45pm (Mon short tour only), Thurs–Sun
9am–6pm. (Parts of the museum begin to close at 5:30pm.) 1½-hr. English-
language tours leave Mon and Wed–Sat various times of the day for 17F (2.60€,
$2.45), children 12 and under free with museum ticket. Métro: Palais Royal–Musée
du Louvre.

Musée d'Orsay ✹✹✹   Architects created one of the world's greatest museums from a defunct rail station, the neoclassical Gare d'Orsay, across the Seine from the Louvre and the Tuileries. Don't skip the Louvre, of course, but come here even if you have to miss all the other art museums in town. The Orsay boasts an astounding collection devoted to the watershed years 1848 to 1914, with a treasure trove by the big names plus all the lesser-known groups (the Symbolists, Pointillists, Nabis, Realists, and late Romanticists). The 80 galleries also include Belle-Epoque furniture, photographs, objets d'art, and architectural models. There's even a cinema showing classic films.

A monument to the Industrial Revolution, the Orsay is covered by an arching glass roof that allows the light to flood in. It displays works ranging from the creations of academic and historic painters (such as Ingres) to Romanticists (such as Delacroix) to Neorealists (such as Courbet and Daumier). The Impressionists and Post-impressionists, including Manet, Monet, Cézanne, van Gogh, and Renoir, share space with the Fauves (such as Matisse), the Cubists, and the Expressionists in a setting once used by Orson Welles to film a nightmarish scene in *The Trial,* based on Kafka's unfinished novel. You'll find Millet's sunny wheat fields, Barbizon landscapes, Corot's mists, and parti-colored Tahitian Gauguins all in the same hall.

But the Impressionists are the ones who keep the crowds lining up. When the nose-in-the-air Louvre chose not to display their works, a great rival was born. Led by Manet, Renoir, and Monet, the Impressionists shunned ecclesiastical and mythological set pieces for a light-bathed Seine, faint figures strolling in the Tuileries, pale-faced women in hazy bars, and even vulgar rail stations like the Gare St-Lazare. And the Impressionists were the first to paint that most characteristic feature of Parisian life: the sidewalk cafe, especially in the artists' quarter of Montmartre.

The most famous painting from this era is Manet's 1863 **Déjeuner sur l'herbe (Picnic on the Grass),** whose forest setting with a nude woman and two fully clothed men sent shock waves through respectable society when it was first exhibited. Two years later, Manet's **Olympia** created another scandal by depicting a woman lounging on her bed and wearing nothing but a flower in her hair and high-heeled shoes; she's attended by an African maid in the background. Zola called Manet "a man among eunuchs."

One of Renoir's most joyous paintings is also here: the *Moulin de la Galette* (1876). Degas is represented by his paintings of racehorses and dancers; his 1876 cafe scene, *Absinthe,* remains one of his most reproduced works. Paris-born Monet was fascinated by the effect changing light had on Rouen Cathedral, and its stone bubbles to life in a series of five paintings—our favorite is *Rouen Cathedral: Full Sunlight.* Another celebrated work is by an American: Whistler's *Arrangement in Grey and Black: Portrait of the Painter's Mother,* better known as *Whistler's Mother.* It's said this painting heralded modern art, though many critics denounced it at the time as "Whistler's Dead Mother" because of its funeral overtones. Whistler was content to claim he'd made "Mummy just as nice as possible."

1 rue de Bellechasse or 62 rue de Lille, 7th arr. ℂ 01-40-49-48-14. www. musee-orsay.fr. Admission 40F (6.10€, $5.80) adults, 30F (4.55€, $4.35) ages 18–24/seniors, children 17 and under free. Tues–Wed and Fri–Sat 10am–6pm, Thurs 10am–9:45pm, Sun 9am–6pm (June 20–Sept 20 opens 9am). Métro: Solférino. RER: Musée d'Orsay.

Ste-Chapelle ⟡⟡⟡ Countless writers have called this tiny chapel a jewel box. Yet that hardly suffices. Nor will it do to call it "a light show." Go when the sun is shining and you'll need no one else's words to describe the remarkable effects of natural light on Ste-Chapelle. You approach the church through the cour de la Ste-Chapelle of the Palais de Justice. If it weren't for the chapel's 247-foot spire, the law courts here would almost swallow it up.

Begun in 1246, the bi-level chapel was built to house relics of the True Cross, including the Crown of Thorns acquired by St. Louis (the Crusader king, Louis IX) from the emperor of Constantinople. (In those days, cathedrals throughout Europe were busy acquiring relics for their treasuries, regardless of their authenticity. It was a seller's, perhaps a sucker's, market.) Louis IX is said to have paid heavily for his relics, raising the money through unscrupulous means. He died of the plague on a crusade and was canonized in 1297.

You enter through the *chapelle basse* **(lower chapel),** used by the palace servants; it's supported by flying buttresses and ornamented with fleur-de-lis designs. The king and his courtiers used the *chapelle haute* **(upper chapel),** one of the greatest achievements of Gothic art; you reach it by ascending a narrow spiral staircase. Viewed on a bright day, the 15 stained-glass windows up there seem to glow with Chartres blue and with reds that have inspired the saying "wine the color of Ste-Chapelle's windows." The walls consist almost entirely of the glass (612m² of it), which had to be removed for safekeeping during the Revolution and again during both world wars. In their Old and New Testament designs are embodied the hopes and dreams (and the pretensions) of the kings who ordered their construction. The 1,134 scenes depict the Christian story from the Garden of Eden through the Apocalypse, and you read them from bottom to top and from left to right. The great rose window depicts the Apocalypse.

Ste-Chapelle stages **concerts** most nights in summer, with tickets from 120F to 150F (18.25€–22.80€, $17.40–$21.75). Call ℂ **01-42-77-65-65** for more details (daily 11am–6pm).

Palais de Justice, 4 bd. du Palais, 4th arr. ℂ **01-53-73-78-50.** www.monuments.fr. Admission 35F (5.30€, $5.10) adults, 23F (3.50€, $3.35) students/ages 18–25, ages 17 and under free. Apr–Sept daily 9:30am–6:30pm; Oct–Mar daily 10am–5pm. Métro: Cité, St-Michel, or Châtelet–Les Halles. RER: St-Michel.

Eiffel Tower ⭐⭐⭐

This is without doubt the single most recognizable structure in the world. Weighing 7,000 tons but exerting about the same pressure on the ground as an average-size person sitting in a chair, the wrought-iron tower wasn't meant to be permanent. It was built by Gustave-Alexandre Eiffel, the French engineer whose fame rested mainly on his iron bridges, to add flair to the 1889 Universal Exhibition. (Eiffel also designed the framework for the Statue of Liberty.) Praised by some and denounced by others (some called it a "giraffe," the "world's greatest lamppost," or the "iron monster"), the tower created as much controversy in the 1880s as I. M. Pei's glass pyramid at the Louvre did in the 1980s. What saved it from demolition in the early 1890s was the advent of radio—as the tallest structure in Europe at the time, it made a perfect spot to place a radio antenna (now a TV antenna).

The tower, including its 55-foot TV antenna, is 1,056 feet high. On a clear day, you can see it from some 40 miles away. An open-framework construction, the tower unlocked the almost unlimited possibilities of steel construction, paving the way for the 20th century's skyscrapers. Skeptics said it couldn't be built, and Eiffel actually wanted to make it soar higher. For years it remained the tallest man-made structure on earth, until skyscrapers like the Empire State Building surpassed it.

We could fill an entire page with tower statistics. (Its plans spanned 6,000 sq. yd. of paper, and it contains 2½ million rivets.) But forget the numbers. Just stand beneath the tower and look straight up. It's like a rocket of steel lacework shooting into the sky.

Champ de Mars, 7th arr. ✆ **01-44-11-23-23.** www.tour-eiffel.fr. Admission to 1st landing 24F (3.65€, $3.50), 2nd landing 45F (6.85€, $6.55), 3rd landing 62F (9.40€, $9). Stairs to 2nd floor 18F (2.75€, $2.60). Sept–May daily 9:30am–11pm; June–Aug daily 9am–midnight. Fall and winter, stairs open only to 6:30pm. Métro: Trocadéro, Ecole Militaire, or Bir-Hakeim. RER: Champ de Mars–Tour Eiffel.

2 The Major Museums

Turn to "The Top Attractions," above, for a comprehensive look at the **Musée du Louvre** and the **Musée d'Orsay.**

You can buy **Le Pass Musée et Monuments (Museum and Monuments Pass)** at any of the museums honoring it or at any branch of the Paris Tourist office (see p. 15). It offers free entrance to the permanent collections of 65 monuments and museums in Paris and the Ile-de-France. A 1-day pass is 80F (12.15€, $11.60), a 3-day pass 160F (24.30€, $23.20), and a 5-day pass 240F (36.50€, $34.80). See p. 26 for details on the **Paris Visite** pass, valid for 1 to 5 days on the public transport system, including the Métro, the city buses, the RER (regional express) trains within Paris city limits, and even the funicular to the top of Montmartre.

Centre Pompidou 𝒜𝒜𝒜   Reopened in January 2000 in what was called in the 1970s "the most avant-garde building in the world," the restored Centre Pompidou is packing in the art-loving crowds again. The dream of former president Georges Pompidou, this center for 20th- and 21st-century art, designed by Richard Rogers and Renzo Piano, opened in 1977 and quickly became the focus of controversy. Its bold exoskeletal architecture and the brightly painted pipes and ducts crisscrossing its transparent facade (green for water, red for heat, blue for air, yellow for electricity) were jarring in the old Beaubourg neighborhood. Perhaps the detractors were right all along—within 20 years the building began to deteriorate so badly a major restoration was called for. The renovation added 5,000 square feet of exhibit space and a rooftop restaurant, a cafe, and a boutique; in addition, a series of auditoriums were created for film screenings and dance, theater, and musical performances. Access for visitors with disabilities has also been improved.

⟨Tips⟩ Museum Closing Days

Generally, all museums are closed on January 1, May 1, Bastille Day (July 14), and December 25.

The Centre Pompidou encompasses five attractions:

The **Musée National d'Art Moderne (National Museum of Modern Art)** 𝕽𝕽𝕽 offers a large collection of 20th- and 21st-century art. With some 40,000 works, this is the big attraction, though only some 850 works can be displayed at one time. If you want to view some real charmers, seek out Calder's 1926 *Josephine Baker,* one of his earlier versions of the mobile, an art form he invented. You'll also find two examples of Duchamps' series of dada-style sculptures he invented in 1936: *Boîte en Valise* (1941) and *Boîte en Valise* (1968). And every time we visit we have to see Dalí's *Hallucination partielle: Six images de Lénine sur un piano* (1931), with Lenin dancing on a piano.

In the **Bibliothèque Information Publique (Public Information Library),** people have free access to a million French and foreign books, periodicals, films, records, slides, and microfilms in nearly every area of knowledge. The **Centre de Création Industriel (Center for Industrial Design)** emphasizes the contributions made in the fields of architecture, visual communications, publishing, and community planning; and the **Institut de Recherche et de Coordination Acoustique-Musique (Institute for Research and Coordination of Acoustics/Music)** brings together musicians and composers interested in furthering the cause of contemporary and traditional music. Finally, you can visit a re-creation of the jazz-age studio of Romanian sculptor Brancusi, the **Atelier Brancusi** 𝕽, a mini-museum slightly separate from the rest of the action.

The museum's **forecourt** is a free "entertainment center" featuring mimes, fire-eaters, would-be circus performers, and sometimes first-rate musicians. Don't miss the nearby **Stravinsky fountain,** containing mobile sculptures by Tinguely and Saint Phalle.

Place Georges-Pompidou, 4th arr. ℭ **01-44-78-12-33.** www.centrepompidou.fr. Admission 30F (4.55€, $4.35) adults, 20F (3.05€, $2.90) students, under age 13 free. Special exhibits 40F (6.10€, $5.80) adults, 30F (4.55€, $4.35) students, under age 13 free. Wed–Mon 11am–9pm. Métro: Rambuteau or Hôtel de Ville. RER: Châtelet–Les Halles.

Galerie Nationale du Jeu de Paume   For years, the Jeu de Paume was one of Paris's treasures, displaying some of the finest works of the Impressionists. To the regret of many, that collection was hauled off to the Musée d'Orsay in 1986. After a $12.6-million face-lift, the Second Empire building was transformed into a state-of-the-art gallery with a video screening room. There's no permanent collection—a new show is mounted every 2 or 3 months. Sometimes the works of little-known contemporary artists are displayed;

other times, exhibits feature unexplored aspects of established artists. Originally, Napoléon III built in this part of the gardens a ball court on which *jeu de paume,* an antecedent of tennis, was played—hence, the museum's name. The most infamous period in the gallery's history came during the Nazi occupation, when it served as an "evaluation center" for modern artworks: Paintings from all over France were shipped to the Jeu de Paume, and any condemned by the Nazis as "degenerate" were burned.

In the northeast corner of the Jardin des Tuileries/1 place de la Concorde, 1st arr. ℂ 01-47-03-12-50. Admission 45F (6.85€, $6.55) adults, 35F (5.30€, $5.10) students, age 13 and under free. Tues noon–9:30pm; Wed–Fri noon–7pm; Sat–Sun 10am–7pm. Métro: Concorde.

Musée Carnavalet 🗭 If you enjoy history, but history tomes bore you, spend an hour or two here for some insight into Paris's past, which comes alive in intimate detail, right down to the chess-men Louis XVI used to distract his mind while waiting to go to the guillotine. The comprehensive and lifelike exhibits are great for kids, too. The building, a renowned Renaissance palace, was built in 1544 by Pierre Lescot and Jean Goujon and later acquired by Mme de Carnavalet. The great François Mansart transformed it between 1655 and 1661.

The palace is best known because one of history's most famous letter writers, Mme de Sévigné, moved here in 1677. Fanatically devoted to her daughter (she ended up moving in with her because she couldn't bear their separation), she poured out nearly every detail of her life in her letters, virtually ignoring her son. A native of the Marais district, she died at her daughter's château in 1696. It wasn't until 1866 that the city of Paris acquired the mansion and turned it into a museum. Several salons cover the Revolution, with a bust of Marat, a portrait of Danton, and a model of the Bastille (one painting shows its demolition). Another salon tells the story of the captivity of the royal family at the Conciergerie, including the bed in which Mme Elisabeth (the sister of Louis XVI) slept and the exercise book of the dauphin.

Exhibits continue at the **Hôtel le Pelletier de St-Fargeau,** across the courtyard. On display is furniture from the Louis XIV period to the early 20th century, including a replica of Marcel Proust's cork-lined bedroom with his actual furniture, including his brass bed.

23 rue de Sévigné, 3rd arr. ℂ 01-44-59-58-58. Admission 35F (5.30€, $5.10) adults, 18F (2.75€, $2.60) ages 7–26, under 7 free. Tues–Sun 10am–5:40pm. Métro: St-Paul or Chemin-Vert.

Musée Jacquemart-André ✰✰   This is the finest museum of its type in Paris, the treasure trove of a couple devoted to 18th-century French paintings and furnishings, 17th-century Dutch and Flemish paintings, and Italian Renaissance works. Edouard André, the last scion of a family of Protestants who made a fortune in banking and industry in the 19th century, spent most of his life as an army officer stationed abroad; he eventually returned to marry a well-known portraitist of government figures and the aristocracy, Nélie Jacquemart, and they went on to compile a collection of rare decorative art and paintings in this 1850s town house.

In 1912, Mme Jacquemart willed the house and its contents to the Institut de France, which paid for an extensive renovation and enlargement. The salons drip with gilt and are the ultimate in fin-de-siècle style. Works by Bellini, Carpaccio, Uccelo, Van Dyck, Rembrandt (*The Pilgrim of Emmaus*), Tiepolo, Rubens, Watteau, Boucher, Fragonard, and Mantegna are complemented by Houdon busts, Savonnerie carpets, Gobelin tapestries, della Robbia terra cottas, and an awesome collection of antiques. Outstanding are the three 18th-century Tiepolo frescoes depicting spectators on balconies viewing Henri III's 1574 arrival in Venice.

Take a break from the gilded age with a cup of tea in Mme Jacquemart's high-ceilinged dining room, adorned with 18th-century tapestries. Salads, tarts, *tourtes* (round pastries filled with meat or fruit), and Viennese pastries are served during the museum's hours.

158 bd. Haussmann, 8th arr. © 01-45-62-11-59. www.musee-jacquemart-andre. com. Admission 50F (7.60€, $7.25) adults, 38F (5.80€, $5.50) ages 7–17, age 6 and under free. Daily 10am–6pm. Métro: Miromesnil or St-Philippe-du-Roule.

Musée Marmottan–Claude Monet ✰✰   In the past, an art historian or two would sometimes venture here to the edge of the Bois de Boulogne to see what Paul Marmottan had donated to the Académie des Beaux-Arts. Hardly anyone else did until 1966, when Claude Monet's son Michel died in a car crash, leaving a then-$10-million bequest of his father's art to the little museum. The Académie suddenly found itself with 130-plus paintings, watercolors, pastels, and drawings . . . and a passel of Monet lovers, who can now trace the evolution of the great man's work in a single museum. The collection includes more than 30 paintings of Monet's house at Giverny and many of waterlilies, his everlasting fancy, plus **Willow** (1918), **House of Parliament** (1905), and a **Renoir portrait** of the 32-year-old Monet. Ironically, the museum had always owned Monet's *Impression: Sunrise* (1872), from which the Impressionist movement got its name. Paul Marmottan's original collection includes fig-leafed nudes, First Empire antiques, assorted objets d'art, Renaissance tapestries, bucolic paintings, and crystal chandeliers. You can also see countless miniatures donated by Daniel Waldenstein.

2 rue Louis-Boilly, 16th arr. ℂ **01-42-24-07-02.** Admission 40F (6.10€, $5.80) adults, 25F (3.80€, $3.65) ages 8–24, ages 7 and under free. Tues–Sun 10am–5pm. Métro: La Muette.

Musée National du Moyen Age/Thermes de Cluny (Musée de Cluny) 🏛🏛

Along with the Hôtel de Sens in the Marais, the Hôtel de Cluny is all that remains of domestic medieval architecture in Paris. You enter through the cobblestoned cour d'Honneur (Court of Honor), where you can admire the Flamboyant Gothic building with its clinging vines, turreted walls, gargoyles, and dormers with seashell motifs. First, the Cluny was the mansion of a rich 15th-century abbot, built on top of/next to the ruins of a Roman bath (see below). By 1515, it was the residence of Mary Tudor, teenage widow of Louis XII and daughter of Henry VII and Elizabeth of York. Seized during the Revolution, the Cluny was rented in 1833 to Alexandre du Sommerard, who adorned it with his collection of medieval artworks; on his 1842 death, the building and the collection were bought back by the government.

This collection of medieval arts and crafts is superb. Most people come primarily to see the *Unicorn Tapestries,* the most acclaimed tapestries of their kind. A beautiful princess and her handmaiden, beasts of prey, and just plain pets—all the romance of the age of chivalry lives on in these remarkable yet mysterious tapestries only a century ago in Limousin's Château de Boussac. Five seem to deal with the senses (one, for example, depicts a unicorn looking into a mirror held by a dour-faced maiden). The sixth shows a woman under an elaborate tent with jewels, her pet dog resting on an embroidered cushion beside her, with the lovable unicorn and his friendly companion, a lion, holding back the flaps. The background in red and green forms a rich carpet of spring flowers, fruit-laden trees, birds, rabbits, donkeys, dogs, goats, lambs, and monkeys.

The other exhibits range widely: Flemish retables; a 14th-century Sienese John the Baptist and other Italian sculptures; statues from Ste-Chapelle (1243–48); gem-studded 12th- and 13th-century crosses; golden chalices, manuscripts, ivory carvings, vestments, leatherwork, jewelry, coins; a 13th-century Adam; and recently discovered heads and fragments of statues from Notre-Dame de Paris. In the fan-vaulted medieval chapel hang tapestries depicting scenes from the life of St. Stephen.

Downstairs are the ruins of the **Roman baths,** from around A.D. 200. Of these once-flourishing baths, the best-preserved section is seen in room X, the frigidarium (where one bathed in cold water). Once, it measured 70 by 36 feet, rising to a height of 50 feet, with stone walls nearly 7 feet thick. The ribbed vaulting here rests on consoles evoking ships' prows. Credit for this unusual motif goes to the builders of the baths, Paris's boatmen. During Tiberius's reign, a column to Jupiter was found beneath Notre-Dame's chancel and is now on view in the court—called the "Column of the Boatmen," it's believed to be the oldest sculpture created in Paris.

In the Hôtel de Cluny, 6 place Paul-Painlevé, 5th arr. ℂ **01-53-73-78-00.** www. musee-moyenage.fr. Admission 30F (4.55€, $4.35) adults, 20F (3.05€, $2.90) ages 18–25, age 17 and under free. Wed–Mon 9:15am–5:45pm. Métro: Cluny–La Sorbonne.

Musée Picasso ✦✦✦ When it opened at the beautifully restored Hôtel Salé (Salt Mansion, built by a man who made his fortune by controlling the salt distribution in 17th-century France) in the Marais, the press hailed it as a "museum for Picasso's Picassos." And that's what it is. The state acquired the world's greatest Picasso collection in lieu of $50-million in inheritance taxes: 203 paintings, 158 sculptures, 16 collages, 19 bas-reliefs, 88 ceramics, and more than 1,500 sketches and 1,600 engravings, along with 30 notebooks. These works span some 75 years of the artist's life and ever-changing style.

The range of paintings includes a remarkable 1901 self-portrait; *The Crucifixion* and *Nude in a Red Armchair;* and *Le Baiser (The Kiss), Reclining Nude,* and *Man with a Guitar,* all painted at Mougins on the Riviera in 1969 and 1970. Stroll through the handsome museum seeking your own favorite—perhaps a wicked one: *Jeune garçon à la langouste (Young Man with a Lobster),* painted in Paris in 1941. There are also several intriguing studies for *Les Demoiselles d'Avignon,* which shocked the establishment and launched Cubism in 1907. Because the collection is so vast, temporary exhibits featuring items like his **studies of the Minotaur** are held twice per year. Also here is Picasso's own treasure trove of art, with works by Cézanne, Rousseau, Braque, Derain, and Miró. Picasso was fascinated with African masks, many of which are on view.

In the Hôtel Salé, 5 rue de Thorigny, 3rd arr. ℂ 01-42-71-25-21. www.paris.org/
Musees/Picasso. Admission 30F (4.55€, $4.35) adults, 20F (3.05€, $2.90) ages
18–25/over 60, age 17 and under free. Apr–Sept Wed–Mon 9:30am–6pm; Oct–Mar
Wed–Mon 9:30am–5:30pm. Métro: St-Paul, Filles du Calvaire, or Chemin Vert.

Musée Rodin 🐸🐸   Today Rodin is acclaimed as the father of
modern sculpture, but in a different era his work was labeled
obscene. The world's artistic taste changed, and in due course in
1911, the French government purchased Rodin's studio in this
gray stone 18th-century mansion in the faubourg St-Germain. The
government restored the rose gardens to their 18th-century splendor,
making them a perfect setting for Rodin's most memorable works.

In the courtyard are three world-famous creations. Rodin's first
major public commission, *The Burghers of Calais* commemorated
the heroism of six citizens of Calais who in 1347 offered themselves
as a ransom to Edward III in return for ending his siege of their
port. Perhaps the single best-known work, *The Thinker,* in Rodin's
own words, "thinks with every muscle of his arms, back, and legs,
with his clenched fist and gripping toes." Not completed when
Rodin died, *The Gate of Hell,* as he put it, is "where I lived for a
whole year in Dante's *Inferno.*"

Inside the building, the sculpture, plaster casts, reproductions,
originals, and sketches reveal the freshness and vitality of a remarkable artist. You can practically see many of his works emerging from
marble into life. Everybody is attracted to *Le Baiser (The Kiss),* of
which one critic wrote, "the passion is timeless." Upstairs are two
versions of the celebrated and condemned **nude of Balzac,** his
bulky torso rising from a tree trunk (Albert E. Elsen commented on
the "glorious bulging" stomach). Included are many versions of his
Monument to Balzac (a large one stands in the garden), Rodin's last
major work. Other significant sculptures are the soaring *Prodigal
Son, The Crouching Woman* (the "embodiment of despair"), and
The Age of Bronze, an 1876 study of a nude man modeled after
a Belgian soldier. (Rodin was falsely accused of making a cast
from a living model.) Generally overlooked is a room devoted
to Rodin's mistress, Camille Claudel, a towering artist in her
own right. She was his pupil, model, and lover, and created such
works as *Maturity, Clotho,* and the recently donated *The Waltz*
and *The Gossips.*

In the Hôtel Biron, 77 rue de Varenne, 7th arr. ℂ 01-44-18-61-10. www.musee-
rodin.fr. Admission 28F (4.25€, $4.05) adults, 18F (2.75€, $2.60) ages 18–25, age
17 and under free. Apr–Sept Tues–Sun 9:30am–5:45pm; Oct–Mar Tues–Sun
9:30am–4:45pm. Métro: Varenne.

3 The Important Churches

Turn to "The Top Attractions," earlier in this chapter, for a full look at the **Cathédrale de Notre-Dame, Basilique du Sacré-Coeur,** and **Ste-Chapelle.**

Basilique St-Denis ✦✦ In the 12th century, Abbot Suger placed an inscription on the bronze doors here: "Marvel not at the gold and expense, but at the craftsmanship of the work." France's first Gothic building that can be dated precisely, St-Denis was the "spiritual defender of the State" during the reign of Louis VI ("the Fat"). The massive facade has a rose window and a crenellated parapet on the top similar to the fortifications of a castle. The stained-glass windows—in stunning mauve, purple, blue, and rose—were restored in the 19th century.

The first bishop of Paris, St. Denis became the patron saint of the monarchy, and royal burials began here in the 6th century and continued until the Revolution. The sculpture designed for the **tombs**—some two stories high—span French artistic development from the Middle Ages to the Renaissance. (There are guided tours of the crypt, but in French only.) François I was entombed at St-Denis, and his funeral statue is nude, though he demurely covers himself with his hand. Other kings and queens here include Louis XII and Anne de Bretagne, as well as Henri II and Catherine de Médicis. Revolutionaries stormed through the basilica during the Reign of Terror, smashing many marble faces and dumping royal remains in a lime-filled ditch in the garden. (These remains were reburied under the main altar during the 19th century.) Free organ concerts are given Sundays at 11:15am.

Place de l'Hôtel-de-Ville, 2 rue de Strasbourg, St-Denis. ✆ **01-48-09-83-54.** Admission 32F (4.85€, $4.65) adults, 21F (3.20€, $3.05) seniors/students, age 11 and under free. Apr–Sept Mon–Sat 10am–7:30pm, Sun noon–6:30pm; Oct–Mar Mon–Sat 10am–5pm, Sun noon–5pm. Métro: St-Denis.

St-Germain-des-Prés ✦✦ Outside, it's a handsome early-17th-century town house. Inside, it's one of Paris's oldest churches, from the 6th century, when a Benedictine abbey was founded here by Childebert, son of Clovis. Alas, the marble columns in the triforium are all that remain from that time. The Normans nearly destroyed the abbey at least four times. The present building has a Romanesque nave and a Gothic choir with fine capitals. At one time, the abbey was a pantheon for Merovingian kings. Restoration of the site of their tombs, **Chapelle de St-Symphorien,** began in 1981, and unknown Romanesque paintings were discovered on the triumphal arch. Among the others interred here are Descartes heart at least) and Jean-Casimir, the king of Poland who abdicated his throne. The Romanesque tower, topped by a 19th-century spire, is the most enduring landmark in St-Germain-des-Prés. Its church bells, however, are hardly noticed by the patrons of Les Deux Magots across the way.

When you leave the church, turn right on rue de l'Abbaye and have a look at the 17th-century pink **Palais Abbatial.**

3 place St-Germain-des-Prés, 6th arr. (☎) 01-43-25-41-71. Free admission. Daily 8am–8pm. Métro: St-Germain-des-Prés.

St-Etienne-du-Mont ⭐⭐ Once, there was an abbey here, founded by Clovis and later dedicated to St. Geneviève, the patroness of Paris. Such was the fame of this popular saint that the abbey proved too small to accommodate the pilgrimage crowds. Now part of the Lycée Henri IV, the Tour de Clovis (Tower of Clovis) is all that remains of the ancient abbey—you can see the tower from rue Clovis. Today the task of keeping St. Geneviève's cult alive has fallen on this church, practically adjoining the Panthéon. The interior is Gothic, an unusual style for a 16th-century church. Building began in 1492 and was plagued by delays until the church was finally finished in 1626.

Besides the patroness of Paris, such men as Pascal and Racine were entombed here. Though St. Geneviève's tomb was destroyed during the Revolution, the stone on which her coffin rested was discovered later, and her relics were gathered for a place of honor at St-Etienne. The church possesses a remarkable early-16th-century **rood screen:** Crossing the nave, it's unique in Paris—called spurious by some and a masterpiece by others. Another treasure is a wood-carved **pulpit,** held up by Samson, clutching a bone in one hand, with a slain lion at his feet. The fourth chapel on the right when you enter contains impressive 16th-century stained glass.

Place Ste-Geneviève, 5th arr. (☎) 01-43-54-11-79. Free admission. Sept–June Mon–Sat 8:30am–noon and 2–7pm, Sun 8:30am–noon and 3–7:30pm; July–Aug Tues–Sun 10am–noon and 4–7pm. Métro: Cardinal Lemoine or Luxembourg.

St-Eustache ⭐⭐ This mixed Gothic and Renaissance church completed in 1637 is rivaled only by Notre-Dame. Madame de Pompadour and Richelieu were baptized here, and Molière's funeral was held here in 1673. The church has been known for organ recitals ever since Liszt played here in 1866. Inside rests the **black-marble tomb** of Jean-Baptiste Colbert, the minister of state under Louis XIV; atop the tomb is his marble effigy flanked by statues of

Abundance by Coysevox and *Fidelity* by Tuby. The church's most famous painting is Rembrandt's ***The Pilgrimage to Emmaus.*** There's a side entrance on rue Rambuteau.

2 rue du Jour, 1st arr. 🕐 **01-42-36-31-05.** www.st-eustache.org. Free admission. Apr–Sept daily 9am–8pm; Oct–Mar daily 9am–7pm. Sun mass 9:30am, 11am, and 6pm; Sun organ recitals 5:30pm. Métro: Les Halles.

4 Architectural & Historic Highlights

Arènes de Lutéce   Discovered and partially destroyed in 1869, this amphitheater is Paris's second most important Roman ruin after the baths in the Musée de Cluny (see p. 126). Today the site is home to a small arena, not as grand as the original, and pleasant gardens. You may feel as if you've discovered a private spot in the heart of the city, but don't be fooled. Your solitude is sure to be interrupted, if not by groups of students playing soccer then at least by parents pushing strollers down the walking paths. This is an ideal spot for a picnic—bring a bottle of wine and fresh baguettes to enjoy in this vestige of the ancient city of Lutétia.

At rues Monge and Navarre, 5th arr. No phone. Free admission. May–Sept daily 10am–10pm; Oct–Apr daily 10am–5:30pm. Métro: Jussieu.

Bibliothèque Nationale de France, Site Tolbiac/François Mitterrand (French National Library)   Opened in 1996 with a dramatic futuristic design by Dominique Perrault (a quartet of 24-story towers evoking the look of open books), this is the last of the *grand projets* of the late François Mitterrand. It houses the nation's literary and historic archives; it's regarded as a repository of the French soul, replacing outmoded facilities on rue des Archives. The library incorporates space for 3,600 readers at a time, many of whom may enjoy views over two levels of a garden-style courtyard that seems far removed from the urban congestion of Paris.

This is one of Europe's most user-friendly academic facilities, emphasizing computerized documentation and microfiche—a role model that'll set academic and literary priorities well into the future. The public has access to as many as 750,000 books and periodicals, with an additional 10 million historic (including medieval) documents shown only to qualified experts. Though the appeal of this place extends mainly to serious scholars researching French history and culture, there's a handful of special exhibits that might interest you, as well as concerts and lectures. Concert tickets rarely exceed 100F (15.20€, $14.50) adults and 65F (9.90€, $9.45) students, seniors, and children; a schedule is available at the library.

Quai François-Mauriac, 13th arr. ✆ **01-53-79-59-59**. Admission 20F (3.05€, $2.90). No one under 16 admitted Tues–Sat 10am–8pm, Sun noon–7pm. Métro: Bibliothèque François-Mitterrand.

Conciergerie 🏛🏛 London has its Bloody Tower and Paris has its Conciergerie. Even though the Conciergerie had a long regal history before the Revolution, it was forever stained by the Reign of Terror and lives as an infamous symbol of the time when carts pulled up constantly to haul off fresh supplies of victims for Dr. Guillotin's wonderful little invention.

Much of the Conciergerie was built in the 14th century as an extension of the Capetian royal Palais de la Cité. You approach through its landmark twin towers, the **Tour d'Argent** (where the crown jewels were stored at one time) and **Tour de César,** but the vaulted **Salle des Gardes (Guard Room)** is the actual entrance. Even more interesting is the vast, dark, and foreboding Gothic **Salle des Gens d'Armes (Room of People at Arms),** utterly changed from the days when the king used it as a banquet hall. However, architecture plays a secondary role to the list of prisoners who spent their last miserable days here. Few in its history endured tortures as severe as those imposed on Ravaillac, who assassinated Henry IV in 1610. In the Tour de César, he received pincers in the flesh and had hot lead and boiling oil poured on him like bath water before being executed (see the Hôtel de Ville entry, below). During the Revolution, the Conciergerie became a symbol of terror to the nobility and enemies of the State. A short walk away, the Revolutionary Tribunal dispensed a skewed, hurried justice—if it's any consolation, the jurists didn't believe in torturing their victims, only in decapitating them.

After being seized by a crowd of peasants who stormed Versailles, Louis XVI and Marie Antoinette were brought here to await their trials. In failing health and shocked beyond grief, *l'Autrichienne* ("the Austrian," as she was called with malice) had only a small screen (sometimes not even that) to protect her modesty from the gaze of guards stationed in her cell. By accounts of the day, she was shy and stupid though the evidence is that on her death she displayed the nobility of a true queen. (What's more, the famous "Let them eat cake" she supposedly uttered when told the peasants had no bread, is probably apocryphal—besides, at the time, cake flour was less expensive than bread flour, so even if she really said this, it wasn't meant in a coldblooded manner.) It was shortly before noon on the morning of October 16, 1793, when her executioners came for her, grabbing her and cutting her hair, as was the custom for victims marked for the guillotine.

Later, the Conciergerie housed other noted prisoners, including Mme Elisabeth; Mme du Barry, mistress of Louis XV; Mme Roland ("O Liberty! Liberty! What crimes are committed in thy name!"); and Charlotte Corday, who killed Marat with a kitchen knife while he was taking a sulphur bath. In time, the Revolution consumed its own leaders, such as Danton and Robespierre. Finally, even one of Paris's most hated men, public prosecutor Fouquier-Tinville, faced the guillotine to which he'd sent so many others. Among the few interned here who lived to tell the tale was America's Thomas Paine, who reminisced about his chats in English with Danton.

1 quai de l'Horloge, 4th arr. ℂ **01-53-73-78-50.** www.paris.org/Monuments/ Conciergerie. Admission 35F (5.30€, $5.10) adults, 23F (3.50€, $3.35) ages 13–25/ over 60, children under 12 free. Apr–Sept daily 9:30am–6:30pm; Oct–Mar daily 10am–5pm. Métro: Cité, Châtelet, or St-Michel. RER: St-Michel.

Hôtel de Ville 𝒜   On a large square with fountains and early-1900s lampposts, the 19th-century Hôtel de Ville isn't a hotel but Paris's grandiose City Hall. The medieval structure it replaced had witnessed countless municipally ordered executions. Henry IV's assassin, Ravaillac, was quartered alive on the square in 1610, his body tied to four horses that bolted in opposite directions. On May 24, 1871, the communards doused the City Hall with petrol, creating a blaze that lasted for 8 days. The Third Republic ordered the structure rebuilt, with many changes, even creating a Hall of Mirrors evocative of that at Versailles. For security reasons, the major splendor of this building is closed to the public. However, the information center sponsors exhibits on Paris in the main lobby.

29 rue de Rivoli, 4th arr. ℂ **01-42-76-43-43.** Free admission. Information center, Mon–Sat 9am–6:30pm. Métro: Hôtel de Ville.

La Grande Arche de La Défense 𝒜   Designed as the architectural centerpiece of the sprawling satellite suburb of La Défense, this massive steel-and-masonry arch rises 35 stories. It was built with the blessing of the late François Mitterrand and extends the magnificently engineered straight line linking the Louvre, Arc du Triomphe du Carrousel, Champs-Elysées, Arc de Triomphe, avenue de la Grande Armée, and place du Porte Maillot. The arch is ringed with a circular avenue patterned after the one winding around the Arc de Triomphe. The monument is tall enough to shelter Notre-Dame beneath its heavily trussed canopy. An elevator carries you up to an observation platform, where you get a view of the carefully planned geometry of the surrounding streets.

You'll notice nets rigged along the Grande Arche. When pieces of Mitterrand's *grand projet* started falling to the ground, a mesh was erected to catch fragments before they hit people on the head. If only such protection existed from all politicians' follies.

1 place du parvis de La Défense, Puteaux, 15th arr. ℂ **01-49-07-27-57.** Admission 46F (7€, $6.65) adults, 35F (5.30€, $5.10) ages 15–17, 30F (4.55€, $4.35) ages 6–14, ages 5 and under free. Daily Apr–Oct 10am–7pm; off-season 10am–8pm. RER: La Défense.

Palais Royal ⋆⋆

The Palais Royal was originally known as the Palais Cardinal, for it was the residence of Cardinal Richelieu, Louis XIII's prime minister. Richelieu had it built, and after his death it was inherited by the king, who died soon after. Louis XIV spent part of his childhood here with his mother, Anne of Austria, but later resided at the Louvre and Versailles. The palace was later owned by the duc de Chartres et Orléans, who encouraged the opening of cafes, gambling dens, and other public entertainments. Though government offices occupy the Palais Royal and are not open to the public, do visit the **Jardin du Palais Royal,** an enclosure bordered by arcades. Don't miss the main courtyard, with the controversial 1986 Buren sculpture—280 prison-striped columns, oddly placed.

Rue St-Honoré, 1st arr. No phone. Free admission. Daily 8am–7pm. Métro: Palais Royal–Musée du Louvre.

Panthéon ⋆⋆

Some of the most famous men in French history (Victor Hugo, for one) are buried here in austere grandeur, on the crest of the mount of St. Geneviève. In 1744, Louis XV vowed that if he recovered from a mysterious illness, he'd build a church to replace the decayed Abbaye de Ste-Geneviève. He recovered but took his time in fulfilling his promise. It wasn't until 1764 that Mme de Pompadour's brother hired Soufflot to design a church in the form of a Greek cross with a dome reminiscent of St. Paul's in London. When Soufflot died, his pupil Rondelet carried out the work, completing the structure 9 years after his master's death.

After the Revolution, the church was converted into a "Temple of Fame" and became a pantheon for the great men of France. Mirabeau was buried here, though his remains were later removed. Likewise, Marat was only a temporary tenant. Voltaire's body was exhumed and placed here—and allowed to remain. In the 19th century, the building changed roles so many times—a church, a pantheon, a church—that it was hard to keep its function straight. After Hugo was buried here, it became a pantheon once again. Other notable men entombed within are Rousseau, Soufflot, Zola, and Braille. Only one woman has so far been deemed worthy of placement here, Marie Curie, who joined her husband, Pierre. Most recently, the ashes of André Malraux were transferred to the Panthéon because, according to President Jacques Chirac, he "lived [his] dreams and made them live in us." As Charles de Gaulle's culture minister, Malraux decreed that the arts should be part of the lives of all French people, not just Paris's elite.

Before entering the crypt, note the striking frescoes: On the right wall are scenes from Geneviève's life and on the left are the saint with a white-draped head looking out over medieval Paris, the city whose patron she became, as well as Geneviève relieving victims of famine with supplies.

Place du Panthéon, 5th arr. (C) 01-44-32-18-00. Admission 42F (6.40€, $6.10) adults, 23F (3.50€, $3.35) ages 12–25, age 11 and under free. Apr–Sept daily 9:30am–6:30pm; Oct–Mar daily 10am–6:15pm (last entrance 45 min. before closing). Métro: Cardinal Lemoine or Maubert-Mutualité.

5 Famous Parks

Jardin des Tuileries ★★ The spectacular statue-studded Jardin des Tuileries is as much a part of Paris as the Seine. Le Nôtre, Louis XIV's gardener and planner of the Versailles grounds, designed them. About 100 years before that, Catherine de Médicis ordered a palace built here, the **Palais des Tuileries,** connected to the Louvre; other occupants have included Louis XVI (after he left Versailles) and Napoléon. Twice attacked by enraged Parisians, it was finally burned to the ground in 1871 and never rebuilt. The gardens, however, remain. In orderly French manner, the trees are arranged according to designs and even the paths are arrow-straight. Breaking the sense of order and formality are bubbling fountains.

Borders place de la Concorde, 1st arr. (C) 01-44-50-75-01. Free admission. Métro: Tuileries or Concorde.

Jardin du Luxembourg ★★ (Kids) Hemingway once told a friend that the Jardin du Luxembourg "kept us from starvation." He related that in his poverty-stricken days in Paris, he wheeled a baby carriage (the vehicle was considered luxurious) through the garden because it was known "for the classiness of its pigeons." When the gendarme went across the street for a glass of wine, the writer would eye his victim, preferably a plump one, then lure him with corn and "snatch him, wring his neck," and hide him under the blanket. "We got a little tired of pigeon that year," he confessed, "but they filled many a void."

The Luxembourg has always been associated with artists, though children, Sorbonne students, and tourists predominate nowadays. Watteau came this way, as did Verlaine. Balzac, however, didn't like the gardens at all. In 1905, Gertrude Stein would cross them to catch the Batignolles/Clichy/Odéon omnibus, pulled by three gray mares, to meet Picasso in his studio at Montmartre, where he painted her portrait.

Marie de Médicis, the neglected wife of the roving Henri IV, ordered the **Palais du Luxembourg** built on this site in 1612, shortly after she was widowed. A Florentine by birth, the regent wanted to create another Pitti Palace, where she could live with her "witch" friend, Leonora Galigal. Architect Salomon de Brossee wasn't entirely successful, though the overall effect is Italianate. Alas, the queen didn't get to enjoy the palace, as she was forced into exile by her son, Louis XIII, when he discovered she was plotting to overthrow him. She died in poverty in Cologne. For her palace, she'd commissioned from Rubens 21 paintings that glorified her life, but they're now in the Louvre. You can visit the palace only the first Sunday of each month at 10:30am, for 50F (7.60€, $7.25) adults or 40F (6.10€, $5.80) 25 years or under, and you must call ℰ **01-44-61-21-66** to make a reservation.

However, you don't come to the Luxembourg to visit the palace—not really. The gardens are the attraction. For the most part, they're in the classic French tradition: well-groomed and formally laid out, the trees planted in patterns. A large central water basin is encircled by urns and statuary on pedestals, one honoring Paris's patroness, St. Geneviève, with pigtails reaching to her thighs. Another memorial is dedicated to Stendhal. It's a good place for kids: They can sail a toy boat, ride a pony, or attend an occasional Grand Guignol puppet show. And you can play *boules* with a group of elderly men who aren't ashamed to wear black berets and have Gauloises dangling from their mouths.

Bordered by rue de Vaugirard, rue Gay Lussac, bd. St-Michel, and rue d'Assas; 6th arr. Free admission. Métro: Odéon; RER: Luxembourg.

6 A Celebrity Cemetery

Cimetière du Père-Lachaise ⟨★★★⟩   When it comes to name dropping, this cemetery knows no peer; it has been called the "grandest address in Paris." A free map of Père-Lachaise is available at the newsstand across from the main entrance.

Everybody from Sarah Bernhardt to Oscar Wilde to Richard Wright is here, along with Honoré de Balzac, Jacques-Louis David, Eugène Delacroix, Maria Callas, Max Ernst, and Georges Bizet. Colette was taken here in 1954; her black granite slab always sports flowers, and legend has it that cats replenish the roses. In time, the little sparrow, Edith Piaf, followed. The lover of George Sand, poet Alfred de Musset, was buried under a weeping willow. Napoléon's marshals, Ney and Masséna, lie here, as do Frédéric Chopin and Molière. Marcel Proust's black tombstone rarely lacks a tiny bunch of violets. (He wanted to be buried beside his friend/lover, composer Maurice Ravel, but their families wouldn't allow it.)

Some tombs are sentimental favorites: Lovelorn graffiti radiates half a mile from the tomb of Doors singer **Jim Morrison.** The great dancer **Isadora Duncan** came to rest in the Columbarium, where bodies have been cremated and "filed" away. If you search hard enough, you can find the tombs of that star-crossed pair **Abélard** and **Héloïse,** the ill-fated lovers of the 12th century—at Père-Lachaise they've found peace at last. Other famous lovers also rest here: A stone is marked **"Alice B. Toklas"** on one side and **"Gertrude Stein"** on the other, and eventually France's First Couple of film were reunited when **Yves Montand** joined his wife, **Simone Signoret.** (Montand's gravesite attracted much attention in 1998: His corpse was exhumed in the middle of the night for DNA testing in a paternity lawsuit—he wasn't the father.)

Covering more than 110 acres, Père-Lachaise was acquired by the city in 1804. Nineteenth-century sculpture abounds, as each family tried to outdo the other in ornamentation and cherubic ostentation. Frenchmen who died in the Resistance or in Nazi concentration camps are also honored by monuments. Some French Socialists still pay tribute at the **Mur des Fédérés,** the anonymous gravesite of the Communards who were executed in the cemetery on May 28, 1871. When these last-ditch fighters of the Commune, the world's first anarchist republic, made their final desperate stand against the troops of the French government, they were overwhelmed, lined up against the wall, and shot in groups. A handful survived and lived hidden in the cemetery for years like wild animals, venturing into Paris at night to forage for food.

16 rue du Repos, 20th arr. ℂ **01-43-70-70-33.** Free admission. Mon–Fri 8am–6pm, Sat 8:30am–6pm, Sun 9am–6pm (to 5:30pm early Nov–early Mar). Métro: Père-Lachaise.

7 Paris Underground

Les Catacombes ⚐ Every year an estimated 50,000 visitors explore some 1,000 yards of tunnel in these dank catacombs to look at 6 million ghoulishly arranged skull-and-crossbones skeletons. First opened to the public in 1810, this "empire of the dead" is now illuminated with overhead electric lights over its entire length. In the Middle Ages, the catacombs were quarries, but by the end of the 18th century, overcrowded cemeteries were becoming a menace to the public health. City officials decided to use the catacombs as a burial ground, and the bones of several million persons were transferred here. In 1830, the prefect of Paris closed the catacombs to the public, considering them obscene and indecent. During World War II, the catacombs were the headquarters of the French Resistance.

1 place Denfert-Rochereau, 14th arr. ⓒ **01-43-22-47-63**. www.multimania.com/houze. Admission 33F (5€, $4.80) adults, 23F (3.50€, $3.35) seniors, 17F (2.60€, $2.45) ages 7–25/students, age 6 and under free. Tues–Fri 2–4pm, Sat–Sun 9–11am and 2–4pm. Métro: Denfert-Rochereau.

Les Egouts (Sewers of Paris) ⚐ Some sociologists assert that the sophistication of a society can be judged by the way it disposes of waste. If so, Paris receives good marks for its mostly invisible sewer network. Victor Hugo is credited with making them famous in *Les Misérables:* Jean Valjean takes flight through them, "all dripping with slime, his soul filled with a strange light." Hugo also wrote, "Paris has beneath it another Paris, a Paris of sewers, which has its own streets, squares, lanes, arteries, and circulation."

In the early Middle Ages, drinking water was taken directly from the Seine and wastewater poured onto fields or thrown onto the then-unpaved streets, transforming the urban landscape into a sea of rather smelly mud. Around 1200, the streets were paved with cobblestones, and open sewers ran down the center of each. These open sewers helped spread the Black Death, which devastated the city. In 1370, a vaulted sewer was built on rue Montmartre, draining effluents into a Seine tributary. During Louis XIV's reign, improvements were made, but the state of waste disposal in Paris remained deplorable.

During Napoléon's reign, 18½ miles of sewer were constructed beneath the Parisian landscape. By 1850, as the Industrial Revolution made the manufacture of iron pipe and steam-digging equipment more practical, Baron Haussmann developed a system that used separate underground channels for drinking water and sewage. By 1878, it was 360 miles long. Beginning in 1894, the network was enlarged, and new laws required that discharge of all waste and storm-water runoff be funneled into the sewers. Between 1914 and 1977, an additional 600 miles were added beneath the pavements of a burgeoning Paris. Today, the network of sewers is 1,300 miles long. It contains freshwater mains, compressed air pipes, telephone cables, and pneumatic tubes. Every day, 1.2 million cubic meters of wastewater are collected and processed by a plant in the suburb of Achères. One of the largest in Europe, it's capable of treating more than 2 million cubic meters of sewage per day.

The city's *égouts* are constructed around four principal tunnels, one 18 feet wide and 15 feet high. As Hugo observed, it's like an underground city, with the street names clearly labeled. Further, each branch pipe bears the number of the building to which it's connected. These underground passages are truly mammoth. Sewer tours begin at pont de l'Alma on the Left Bank, where a stairway leads into the city's bowels. However, you often have to wait in ine as much as half an hour. Visiting times might change during bad weather, as a storm can make the sewers dangerous. The tour consists of a film on sewer history, a small museum visit, and then a short trip through the maze. *Be warned:* The smell is pretty bad, especially in summer.

Pont de l'Alma, 7th arr. (✆ 01-53-68-27-81. Admission 25F (3.80€, $3.65) adults, 20F (3.05€, $2.90) students/seniors/children 5–12, under 5 free. May–Oct Sat–Wed 11am–5pm; Nov–Apr Sat–Wed 11am–4pm. Closed 3 weeks in Jan. Métro: Alma-Marceau. RER: Pont de l'Alma.

8 Neighborhood Highlights

Paris's neighborhoods often turn out to be attractions unto themselves. The 1st arrondissement, for example, probably has a higher concentration of attractions per block than anywhere else. Though all Paris's neighborhoods are worth wandering, some are more interesting than others. What follow are some of our favorites.

ISLANDS IN THE STREAM: ILE DE LA CITE & ILE ST-LOUIS

ILE DE LA CITE ⭐⭐⭐   Medieval Paris, that blend of grotesquerie and Gothic beauty, bloomed on this island in the Seine (Métro: Cité). Ile de la Cité, which the Seine protects like a surrounding moat, has been known as "the cradle" of Paris ever since. As Sauval once observed, "The Island of the City is shaped like a great ship, sunk in the mud, lengthwise in the stream, in about the middle of the Seine."

Few have written more movingly about its heyday than Victor Hugo, who invited the reader "to observe the fantastic display of lights against the darkness of that gloomy labyrinth of buildings; cast upon it a ray of moonlight, showing the city in glimmering vagueness, with its towers lifting their great heads from that foggy sea." Medieval Paris was a city not only of legends and lovers but also of bloodcurdling tortures and brutalities. No story illustrates this better than the affair of Abélard and his charge Héloïse, whose jealous and unsettled uncle hired ruffians to castrate her lover. (The attack predictably quelled their ardor, and he became a monk, she an abbess.) You can see their graves at Père-Lachaise (see p. 136).

Because you'll want to see all the attractions on Ile de la Cité, here is the most logical way to proceed. Begin, of course, at the cathedral of Notre-Dame. Proceed next to the Ste-Chapelle moving west. After a visit there, you can head northeast to the Conciergerie. To cap your visit, and for the best scenic view, walk to the northwestern end of the island for a view of the bridge, pont Neuf, seen from Square du Vert Galant.

The island's undisputed stars, as mentioned, are **Notre-Dame, Ste-Chapelle,** and the **Conciergerie**—all described earlier in this chapter. Across from Notre-Dame is the **Hôtel Dieu,** built from 1866 to 1878 in neo-Florentine style. This is central Paris's main hospital, replacing the 12th-century hospital that ran the island's entire width. Go in the main entrance and take a break in the spacious neoclassical courtyard whose small garden and fountain make a quiet oasis.

Don't miss the ironically named **pont Neuf** ("New Bridge") at the tip of the island opposite from Notre-Dame. The span isn't new—it's actually Paris's oldest bridge, begun in 1578 and finished in 1604. In its day it had two unique features: It was paved and it wasn't flanked with houses and shops. Actually, with 12 arches, it's not one bridge but two (they don't quite line up)—one from the Right Bank to the island and the other from the Left Bank to the island. At the **Musée Carnavalet** (see p. 124), a painting called *The Spectacle of Buffoons* shows what the bridge was like between 1665 and 1669. Duels were fought on it; the nobility's great coaches crossed it; peddlers sold their wares on it; and entertainers like Tabarin went there to seek a few coins from the gawkers. As public facilities were lacking, the bridge also served as a de facto outhouse.

Just past pont Neuf is the "prow" of the island, the **square du Vert Galant.** Pause to look at the equestrian statue of the beloved Henri IV, who was assassinated by Ravaillac (see the entry for the

Conciergerie, p. 132). A true king of his people, Henri was also (to judge from accounts) regal in the boudoir—hence the nickname "Vert Galant" (Old Spark). Gabrielle d'Estrées and Henriette d'Entragues were his best-known mistresses, but they had to share him with countless others, some of whom would casually catch his eye as he was riding along the streets. In fond memory of the king, the little triangular park continues to attract lovers. If at first it appears to be a sunken garden, that's because it remains at its natural level; the rest of the Cité has been built up during the centuries.

ILE ST-LOUIS 👣👣 Cross pont St-Louis, the iron footbridge behind Notre-Dame, to Ile St-Louis, and you'll find a world of tree-shaded quays, aristocratic town houses with courtyards, restaurants, and antiques shops. (You can also take the Métro to Sully-Morland or Pont Marie and cross the bridge.) The fraternal twin of Ile de la Cité, Ile St-Louis is primarily residential; nearly all the houses were built from 1618 to 1660, lending the island a remarkable architectural unity. Plaques on the facades identify the former residences of the famous. **Marie Curie** lived at 36 quai de Béthune, near pont de la Tournelle, and sculptor **Camille Claudel** (Rodin's mistress) lived and worked in the Hôtel de Jassaud, 19 quai de Bourbon.

The most exciting mansion—though perhaps also the one with the saddest history—is the 1656–57 **Hôtel de Lauzun,** 17 quai d'Anjou, built for Charles Gruyn des Bordes. He married Geneviève de Mouy and had her initials engraved on much of the interior decor; their happiness was short-lived, however, because he was convicted of embezzlement and sent to prison in 1662. The next occupant was the duc de Lauzun, who resided there for only 3 years. He had been a favorite of Louis XIV until he asked for the hand of the king's first cousin, the duchesse de Montpensier. Louis refused and had Lauzun tossed into the Bastille. Eventually the duchesse pestered Louis into releasing her beloved, and they married secretly and moved here in 1682, but domestic bliss eluded them—they fought often and separated in 1684. Lauzun then sold the house to the grand-nephew of Cardinal Richelieu and his wife, the grand-niece of Cardinal Mazarin, who had such a grand time throwing parties they went bankrupt and separated. Baron Pichon bought it in 1842 and rented it out to a hashish club. Tenants Baudelaire and Gaultier regularly held hashish soirées in which Baudelaire did research for his *Les Paradis artificiels* and Gaultier for his *Le Club des hachichins.* Now the mansion belongs to the city and is used to house official guests. The interior is sometimes open for temporary exhibits, so call the tourist office.

The **Hôtel Lambert,** 2 quai d'Anjou, was built in 1645 for Nicholas Lambert de Thorigny. The portal on rue St-Louis-en-l'Ile gives some idea of the splendor within, but the house's most startling element is the oval gallery extending into the garden. Designed to feature a library or an art collection, it's best viewed from the beginning of quai d'Anjou. Voltaire and his mistress, Emilie de Breteuil, lived here at one time—their raucous quarrels were legendary. The mansion also housed the Polish royal family, the Czartoryskis, for over a century, before becoming the residence of actress Michèle Morgan. It now belongs to the Rothschild family and isn't open to the public.

Numbers 9, 11, 13, and 15 quai d'Anjou also belonged to the Lambert family. At **no. 9** stands the house where painter/sculptor/lithographer Honoré Daumier lived from 1846 to 1863, producing hundreds of caricatures satirizing the bourgeoisie and attacking government corruption. He was imprisoned for 6 months because of his 1832 cartoon of Louis-Philippe swallowing bags of gold that had been extracted from the people.

Near the Hôtel de Lauzun is the church of **St-Louis-en-l'Ile,** no. 19 bis rue St-Louis-en-l'Ile. Despite a dour exterior, the ornate interior is one of the finest examples of Jesuit baroque. Built between 1664 and 1726, this church has been and still is the site of many weddings—with all the white stone and gilt, you'll feel as if you're inside a wedding cake. Look for the 1926 plaque reading "In grateful memory of St. Louis in whose honor the city of St. Louis, Missouri, USA, is named."

RIGHT BANK HIGHLIGHTS

LES HALLES *✦* For 8 centuries, **Les Halles** (Métro: Les Halles; RER: Châtelet–Les Halles) was the city's major wholesale fruit, meat, and vegetable market. In the 19th century, Zola called it "the underbelly of Paris." The smock-clad vendors, beef carcasses, and baskets of vegetables all belong to the past, for the original market, with zinc-roofed Second Empire "iron umbrellas," has been torn down. Today the action has moved to a steel-and-glass edifice at Rungis, a suburb near Orly. In 1979, the area saw the opening of the **Forum des Halles,** 1–7 rue Pierre-Lescot, 1st arrondissement. This large complex, much of it underground, contains shops, restaurants, and movie theaters. Many of the shops are unattractive, but others contain a wide display of merchandise that has made the mall popular with both residents and visitors.

For many visitors, a night on the town still ends in the wee hours with a bowl of onion soup at Les Halles, usually at **Au Pied de Cochon (The Pig's Foot),** 6 rue Coquillière, 1st (see p. 71), or at **Au Chien Qui Fume (The Smoking Dog),** 33 rue du Pont-Neuf (© 01-42-36-07-42). One of the most classic scenes of old Paris was elegantly dressed Parisians (many fresh from Maxim's) standing at a bar drinking cognac with blood-smeared butchers. Some writers have suggested that 19th-century poet Gérard de Nerval introduced the custom of frequenting Les Halles at such an unearthly hour. (His life was considered "irregular," and he hanged himself in 1855.)

A newspaper correspondent described today's scene this way: "Les Halles is trying to stay alive as one of the few places in Paris where one can eat at any hour of the night."

LEFT BANK HIGHLIGHTS

ST-GERMAIN-DES-PRES 🌟🌟   This neighborhood in the 6th arrondissement (Métro: St-Germain-des-Prés) was the postwar home of existentialism, associated with Sartre, de Beauvoir, Camus, and an intellectual bohemian crowd that gathered at **Café de Flore, Brasserie Lipp,** and **Les Deux Magots** (see chapter 4). Among them, black-clad poet and singer Juliette Greco was known as *la muse de St-Germain-des-Prés,* and to Sartre she was the woman who had "millions of poems in her throat." Her long hair, black slacks, black sweater, and black sandals launched a fashion trend adopted by young women everywhere. In the 1950s, new names appeared, like Françoise Sagan, Gore Vidal, and James Baldwin, but by the 1960s, tourists became firmly entrenched.

St-Germain-des-Prés still retains an intellectually stimulating bohemian street life, full of many interesting bookshops, art galleries, *caveau* (basement) clubs, bistros, and coffeehouses. But the stars of the area are two churches, **St-Germain-des-Prés,** 3 place St-Germain-des-Prés, 6th (see p. 129), and **St-Sulpice,** rue St-Sulpice, 6th, and the **Musée National Eugène Delacroix,** 6 place de Furstemburg, 6th (© 01-44-41-86-50). Nearby, **rue Visconti** was designed for pushcarts and is worth visiting today. At **nos. 20–24** is the residence where dramatist Jean-Baptiste Racine died in 1699. And at **no. 17** is the house where Balzac established his printing press in 1825. (The venture ended in bankruptcy, forcing the author back to his writing desk.) Such celebrated actresses as Champmeslé and Clairon also lived here.

9 Organized Tours

BY BUS

Tours are offered by **Cityrama,** 147–149 rue St-Honoré, 1st (© 01-44-55-61-00; Métro: Palais Royal or Musée du Louvre), which operates double-decker red-and-yellow buses with oversize windows and multilingual recorded commentaries giving an overview of Paris's history and monuments.

By far the most popular tour is a 2-hour bus ride, with recorded commentary in your choice of 13 languages, through Paris' monumental heart. Departing from place des Pyramides, adjacent to rue de Rivoli, it's offered seven times a day between May and October, and four times a day between November and April. Cost for this is 150F (22.80€, $21.75) per person, free for children under 12. Other, more specialized (and detailed) tours include a 3½-hour "Artistic Tour" that encompasses the interiors of Notre-Dame and the Louvre (every day except Tues and Sun, and departing at 9:45am), priced at 310F (47.10€, $44.95). Tours to the mammoth royal palace at Versailles depart twice a day (at 9:30am and 2:45pm) year-round for a price of 330F (50.15€, $47.85) per person. And 5-hour jaunts to the majestic Gothic cathedral at Chartres depart every Tuesday, Thursday, and Saturday at 1:45pm for a per person price of 300F (45.60€, $43.50). Tours of Paris by night depart at 10pm for a price of 150F (22.80€, $21.75) per person. Any of these night tours can be supplemented—for an additional fee—with optional add-ons that include river cruises on the Seine and attendance at selected cabaret shows.

BY BOAT ON THE SEINE

A Seine boat tour provides sweeping vistas of the riverbanks and some of the best views of Notre-Dame. Many of the boats have open sundecks, bars, and restaurants. **Bateaux-Mouche** cruises (© 01-42-25-96-10 for reservations, 01-40-76-99-99 for schedules; Métro: Alma-Marceau) depart from the Right Bank, next to pont de l'Alma, and last about 75 minutes, costing 45F (6.85€, $6.55) adults and 20F (3.05€, $2.90) children 4 to 12. From May to October, tours leave daily at 30-minute intervals, beginning at 11am and ending at 11pm; from November to April, there are at least nine departures daily from 11am to 9pm, with a schedule that changes according to demand and the weather. Three-hour dinner cruises depart daily at 8:30pm and cost 500F to 800F (76€–121.60€, $72.50–$116), depending on which fixed-price menu you order; jackets and ties are required for men. Less formal lunch cruises, departing every day at 1pm and returning about 2 hours later, cost 300F (45.60€, $43.50) per person.

Some people prefer longer excursions on the Seine and its network of canals. The 3-hour **Seine et le Canal St-Martin** tour, offered by **Paris Canal** (© **01-42-40-96-97**), requires advance reservations. The tour begins at 9:30am on the quays in front of the Musée d'Orsay (Métro: Solférino) and at 2:30pm in front of the Cité des Sciences et de l'Industrie at Parc de La Villette (Métro: Porte de La Villette). Excursions negotiate the waterways and canals of Paris, including the Seine, an underground tunnel below place de la Bastille, and the Canal St-Martin. Tours are offered twice daily from mid-March to mid-November; the rest of the year, tours are only on Sunday. The cost is 100F (15.20€, $14.50) adults and children under 4 free. With the exception of trips on Sundays and holidays, prices are usually reduced to 75F (11.40€, $10.90) for passengers 12 to 25 and over 60, and to 55F (8.35€, $8) for children 4 to 11.

10 Spectacular Shopping

Shopping is a favorite pastime of Parisians; some would even say it reflects the City of Light's soul. This is one of the rare places in the world where you don't have to go to any special area to shop—shopping opportunities surround you wherever you may be. Each walk you take will immerse you in uniquely French styles. The windows, stores, and people (even their dogs) brim with energy, creativity, and a sense of visual expression found in few other cities.

You don't have to buy anything to appreciate shopping in Paris—just soak up the art form the French have made of rampant consumerism. Peer in the *vitrines* (display windows), absorb cutting-edge ideas, witness new trends, and take home with you a whole new education in style.

BEST BUYS

PERFUMES, MAKEUP & BEAUTY TREATMENTS A discount of 20% to 30% makes these items a great buy; qualify for a VAT refund (see below) and you'll save 40% to 45% off the Paris retail price, allowing you to bring home goods at half the U.S. price. Duty-free shops abound in Paris and are always less expensive than the ones at the airports.

For bargain cosmetics, try out French dime store and drugstore brands like **Bourjois** (made in the Chanel factories), **Lierac,** and

Galenic. Vichy, famous for its water, has a complete skin care and makeup line. The newest retail trend in Paris is the *parapharmacie,* a type of discount drugstore loaded with inexpensive brands, health cures, beauty regimes, and diet plans. These usually offer a 20% discount.

FOODSTUFFS   Nothing makes a better souvenir than a product of France brought home to savor later. Supermarkets are located in prime tourist neighborhoods; stock up on coffee, designer chocolates, mustards (try Maille or Meaux brand), and perhaps American products in French packages for the kids. However, to be sure you don't try to bring home a foodstuff that's prohibited, see "Entry Requirements & Customs Regulations" on p. 2.

FUN FASHION   Sure you can spend and spend on couture or *prêt-à-porter,* but French teens and trendsetters have their own stores where the latest looks are affordable. Even the dime stores in Paris sell designer copies and hotshot styles. In the stalls in front of the department stores on boulevard Haussmann, you'll find some of the latest accessories, guaranteed for a week's worth of small talk once you get home.

GETTING A VAT REFUND

In April 2000, the French **value-added tax** (**VAT**—**TVA** in French) came down from 20.6% to 19.6%, but you can get most of that back if you spend 1,200F (182.40€, $174) or more in any store that participates in the VAT refund program. Most stores participate.

Once you meet your required minimum purchase amount, you qualify for a tax refund. The amount of the refund varies with the way the refund is handled and the fee some stores charge you for processing it. So the refund at a department store may be 13%, whereas at a small shop it may be 15% or even 18%.

You'll receive **VAT refund papers** in the shop; some stores, like Hermès, have their own; others provide a government form. Fill in the forms before you arrive at the airport and expect to stand in line at the Customs desk for as long as half an hour. You're required by law to show the goods at the airport, so have them on you or visit the Customs office before you check your luggage. Once the papers have been mailed to the authorities, a credit will appear, often months later, on your credit-card bill. All refunds are processed at the final point of departure from the **European Union (EU),** so if you're going to another EU country, don't apply for the refund in France.

Be sure to mark the paperwork to request that your refund be applied to your credit card so you aren't stuck with a check in francs that's hard to cash. This also ensures the best rate of exchange. In some airports, you're offered the opportunity to get your refund back in cash, which is tempting. But if you accept cash in any currency other than francs, you'll be losing money on the conversion rate.

To avoid VAT refund hassles, ask for a Global refund form ("Shopping Checque") at a store where you make a purchase. When leaving an EU country, have it stamped by customs, then take it to the Global Refund counter (these can be found at more than 700 airports and border crossings in Europe), where your money is refunded on the spot. For information, contact **Global Refund,** 707 Summer St., Stamford, CT 06901 (© **800/566-9828;** www. globalrefund.com).

DUTY-FREE BOUTIQUES

The advantage of duty-free shops is that you never have to pay the VAT, so you avoid the red tape of getting a refund. Both Charles de Gaulle and Orly airports have shopping galore. (De Gaulle has a virtual shopping mall with crystal, cutlery, chocolates, luggage, wine, pipes and lighters, lingerie, silk scarves, perfume, knitwear, jewelry, cameras and equipment, cheeses, and even antiques.) You'll find lots of duty-free shops on the avenues branching out from the Opéra Garnier, in the 1st arrondissement. Sometimes there are bargains here, but most often not. Usually these stores jack up prices, so even though there's no duty, you'll find no bargain on most goods. In general, these duty-free shops are best left for last-minute buys or the impulsive shopper who feels he or she is leaving Paris without having bought enough.

BUSINESS HOURS

Usual shop hours are Monday to Saturday from 10am to 7pm, but the hours vary greatly, and Monday mornings in Paris don't run at full throttle. Small shops sometimes close for a 2-hour lunch break and may not even open until after lunch on Monday. Thursday is the best day for late-night shopping, with stores open until 9 or 10pm.

Sunday shopping is currently limited to tourist areas and flea markets, though there's growing demand for full-scale Sunday hours. The big department stores are now open on the five Sundays before Christmas. The **Carrousel du Louvre,** a mall adjacent to the

Louvre, is open and hopping on Sunday, but closed on Monday. The tourist shops lining rue de Rivoli across from the Louvre are all open on Sunday, as are the antiques villages, assorted flea markets, and specialty events. There are several good food markets in the streets on Sunday. The **Virgin Megastore** on the Champs-Elysées, a big teen hangout, pays a fine to stay open on Sunday.

SHIPPING IT HOME

Shipping charges will possibly double your cost on goods, and you may have to pay duties on the items (see "Getting a VAT Refund," above). The good news: The VAT refund is automatically applied to all shipped items, so there's no need to worry about the 1,200F (182.40€, $174) minimum. Some stores do have a $100 minimum for shipping, though. You can also walk into any post office and mail home a jiffy bag or small box of goodies. French do-it-yourself boxes can't be reopened once closed, so pack carefully. The clerk at the post office will help you assemble the box (it's tricky), seal it, and send it off.

GREAT SHOPPING NEIGHBORHOODS

When you're planning a day of combined sightseeing and shopping, check a map to see how the arrondissements connect so you can maximize your efforts. Though Paris is made up of 20 arrondissements, only a handful is prime real estate for shopping. What follow are our recommendations.

1ST & 8TH ARRONDISSEMENTS These two *quartiers* adjoin each other (invisibly) and form the heart of Paris's best Right Bank shopping strip—they're one big hunting ground. This area includes the famed **rue du faubourg St-Honoré,** where the big designer houses are, and the **Champs-Elysées,** where the mass market and teen scene are hot. At one end of the 1st is the **Palais Royal,** one of the best shopping secrets in Paris, where an arcade of boutiques flanks each side of the garden of the former palace.

Also here is **avenue Montaigne,** Paris's most glamorous shopping street, boasting 2 blocks of ultrafancy shops, where you simply float from big name to big name and in a few hours can see everything from Dior to Caron. Avenue Montaigne is also the address of **Joseph,** a British design firm, and **Porthault,** makers of the poshest sheets in the world.

2ND ARRONDISSEMENT Right behind the Palais Royal is the **Garment District** (Sentier), as well as a few sophisticated shopping secrets, such as **place des Victoires.**

In the 19th century, this area became known for its *passages,* literally glass-enclosed shopping streets—in fact, the world's first shopping malls. They were also the city's first buildings to be illuminated by gaslight. Many have been torn down, but, amazingly, a dozen or so have survived. Of them all, we prefer *Passage den Grand Cerf,* between 145 rue St-Denis and 10 rue Dussoubs, 2nd (Métro: Bourse), lying a few blocks from the Beaubourg. It's a place of wonder, filled with everything from retro-chic boutiques and (increasingly) Asian-themed shops. What's exciting is to come upon a discovery, perhaps a postage stamp shop with some special jeweler who creates unique products such as jewel-toned safety pins.

3RD & 4TH ARRONDISSEMENTS   The border between these two arrondissements gets fuzzy, especially around **place des Vosges,** center stage of the Marais. No matter. The districts offer several dramatically different shopping experiences.

On the surface, the shopping includes the "real people stretch" (where all the non-millionaires shop) of **rue de Rivoli** and **rue St-Antoine,** featuring everything from Gap and a branch of Marks & Spencer, to local discount stores and mass merchants. Two "real people" department stores are in this area, **Samaritaine** and **BHV;** there's also **Les Halles** and the **Beaubourg** neighborhood, which is anchored by the Centre Pompidou.

Meanwhile, hidden in the Marais is a medieval warren of tiny twisting streets chockablock with cutting-edge designers and up-to-the-minute fashions and trends. Start by walking around place des Vosges for art galleries, designer shops, and special little finds, then dive in and lose yourself in the area leading to the Musée Picasso.

Finally, the 4th is also the home of the **Bastille,** an up-and-coming area for artists and galleries where you'll find the newest entry on the retail scene, the **Viaduc des Arts** (which actually stretches into the 12th). It's a collection of about 30 stores occupying a series of narrow vaulted niches under what used to be railroad tracks. They run parallel to avenue Daumesnil, centered around boulevard Diderot.

6TH & 7TH ARRONDISSEMENTS   Though the 6th is one of the most famous shopping districts in Paris—it's the soul of the Left Bank—a lot of the really good stuff is hidden in the zone that turns into the wealthy residential district of the 7th. **Rue du Bac,** stretching from the 6th to the 7th in a few blocks, stands for all that wealth and glamour can buy.

9TH ARRONDISSEMENT   To add to the fun of shopping the Right Bank, the 9th sneaks in behind the 1st, so if you choose not to walk toward the Champs-Elysées and the 8th, you can head to the city's big department stores, all built in a row along **boulevard Haussmann** in the 9th. Department stores include not only the two big French icons, **Au Printemps** and **Galeries Lafayette,** but also a large branch of Britain's **Marks & Spencer** and a branch of the Dutch answer to Kmart, low-priced **C&A.**

11 Side Trips from Paris

VERSAILLES
13 miles SW of Paris, 44 miles NE of Chartres

For centuries, the name of the Parisian suburb of Versailles resounded through the consciousness of every aristocratic family in Europe. The palace here outdazzled every other kingly residence in Europe—it was a horrendously expensive scandal and a symbol to later generations of a regime obsessed with prestige above all else.

Back in the *grand siècle,* all you needed was a sword, a hat, and a bribe for the guard at the gate. Providing you didn't look as if you had smallpox, you'd be admitted to the Château de Versailles, where you could stroll through salon after glittering salon—watching the Sun King rise and dress and dine and do even more intimate things while you gossiped, danced, plotted, flirted, and trysted.

Today, Versailles needs the return of Louis XIV and his fat treasury. You wouldn't believe it when looking at the glittering Hall of Mirrors, but Versailles is down-at-the-heels. It suffers from a lack of funds, which translates into a shortage of security forces; this budget crunch was made even worse on Christmas Day in 1999, when a horrendous windstorm wreaked havoc here.

You get to see only half of the palace's treasures; the rest are closed to the public. Some 3.2 million visitors arrive annually, and on average, they spend 2 hours viewing the palace.

ESSENTIALS
GETTING THERE   To get to Versailles, 13 miles southwest of Paris, catch the **RER** line C at the Gare d'Austerlitz, St-Michel, Musée d'Orsay, Invalides, Ponte de l'Alma, Champ de Mars, or Javel stop and take it to the Versailles Rive Gauche station, from which there's a shuttle bus to the château. The 35F (5.30€, $5.15) trip takes 35 to 40 minutes; Eurailpass holders travel free on the train but pay 20F (3.05€, $2.90) for a ride on the shuttle bus. Regular

SNCF trains make the run from central Paris to Versailles: One train departs from Gare St-Lazare for the Versailles Rive Droite RER station, a 15-minute walk from the château. If you can't or don't want to walk, you can take bus B from Versailles Chantiers to the château for 8F (1.20€, $1.15) each way.

As a last resort, you can use a combination of **Métro** and **city bus.** Travel to the pont de Sèvres stop by Métro, then transfer to bus 171 for a westward trek that'll take 20 to 45 minutes, depending on traffic. The bus will cost you three Métro tickets and deposit you near the château gates. If you have a **car,** take N-10, following the signs to Versailles, and then proceed along avenue de Général-Leclerc. Park on place d'Armes in front of the château.

VISITOR INFORMATION   Three main avenues radiate from place d'Armes in front of the palace. The **tourist office** is at 7 rue des Réservoirs (✆ **01-39-24-88-88**).

TOURING VERSAILLES

Château de Versailles ✰✰✰   Within 50 years, this residence was transformed from Louis XIII's simple hunting lodge into an extravagant palace. Begun in 1661, the construction of the château involved 32,000 to 45,000 workmen, some of whom had to drain marshes—often at the cost of their lives—and move forests. Louis XIV set out to build a palace that would be the envy of all Europe, and he created a symbol of pomp and opulence that was to be copied, yet never quite duplicated, all over Europe and even in America.

So he could keep an eye on the nobles of France (and with good reason), Louis XIV summoned them to live at his court. Here he amused them with constant entertainment and lavish banquets and balls, and amused himself with a roster of mistresses, the most important of which was Mme de Maintenon (he secretly married her after his queen, Marie-Thérèse of Spain, died). To some, he awarded such vital tasks as holding the hem of his ermine-lined robe. While the aristocrats frivolously played away their lives, often in silly intrigues and games, the peasants on the estates, angered by their absentee landlords, sowed the seeds of the Revolution.

When Louis XIV died in 1715, he was succeeded by his great-grandson, Louis XV, who continued the outrageous pomp, though he's said to have predicted the outcome: *"Après moi, le déluge"* (After me, the deluge). His wife, Marie Leszcynska of Poland, was shocked by the court's blatant immorality. When her husband tired of her, she lived as a nun, and the king's attention turned to Mme de Pompadour, who was accused of running up a debt far beyond that of a full-scale war. Mme de Pompadour handpicked her successor, Mme du Barry, who was just about as foolhardy with the nation's treasury.

Louis XVI found his grandfather's and father's behavior scandalous—in fact, on gaining the throne in 1774 he ordered that the "stairway of indiscretion" (secret stairs leading up to the king's bedchamber) be removed. This dull, weak king (who was virtuous and did have good intentions) and his Austrian-born queen, Marie Antoinette, were well-liked at first, but the queen's excessive frivolity and wild spending soon led to her downfall. Louis and Marie Antoinette were at Versailles on October 6, 1789, when they were notified that mobs were marching on the palace. As predicted, *le déluge* had arrived.

Napoléon stayed at Versailles but never seemed fond of it. Louis-Philippe prevented the destruction of the palace by converting it into a museum dedicated to the glory of France. To do that, he had to surrender some of his own not-so-hard-earned currency. Many years later, John D. Rockefeller contributed heavily toward the restoration of Versailles and work continues to this day.

The six magnificent **Grands Appartements** are in the Louis XIV style, each named after the allegorical painting on the room's ceiling. The best known and largest is the **Hercules Salon,** with a ceiling painted by François Lemoine, depicting the Apotheosis of Hercules. In the **Mercury Salon** (with a ceiling by Jean-Baptiste Champaigne), the body of Louis XIV was put on display in 1715; his 72-year reign was one of the longest in history.

The most famous room at Versailles is the 236-foot-long **Hall of Mirrors**, built to link the north and south apartments. Begun in 1678 by Mansart in the Louis XIV style, it was decorated by Le Brun and his team with 17 large arched windows matched by corresponding beveled mirrors in simulated arcades, plus amazing chandeliers and gilded lamp bearers. The vaulted ceiling is covered with paintings in classic allegorical style depicting the story of Louis XIV. On June 28, 1919, the treaty ending World War I was signed in this corridor. Ironically, the German Empire was also proclaimed here in 1871.

The royal apartments were for show, but Louis XV and Louis XVI retired to the **Petits Appartements** to escape the demands of court etiquette. Louis XV died in his bedchamber in 1774, a victim of smallpox. In the second-floor **King's Apartments,** which you can visit only with a guide, he stashed away first Mme de Pompadour and then Mme du Barry. Attempts have been made to return the **Queen's Apartments** to their appearance in the days of Marie Antoinette, when she played her harpsichord in front of specially invited guests.

Her king, Louis XVI, had an impressive **Library,** designed by Gabriel, which was sumptuous. Its panels are delicately carved, and the room has been restored and refurnished. The **Clock Room** contains Passement's astronomical clock, encased in gilded bronze. Twenty years in the making, it was completed in 1753 and is supposed to keep time until the year 9999. At the age of 7, Mozart played for the court in this room.

Gabriel designed the **Opéra** ✶✶ for Louis XV in 1748, though it wasn't completed until 1770. In its heyday, it took 3,000 candles to light the place. With gold-and-white harmony, Hardouin-Mansart built the **Royal Chapel** ✶✶✶ in 1699, dying before its completion. Louis XVI, when still the dauphin (crown prince), married Marie Antoinette here in 1770. Both the bride and the groom in this arranged marriage were teenagers.

After having been closed for years, the **Musée de France** (✆ **01-39-67-07-73**), has now reopened and is accessible via Porte D (Door D) in the château. The museum traces the history of the parliamentary process in France following the collapse of the monarchy in 1789, with exhibits describing the processes whereby laws and the democratic process are made and enforced. Admission is 20F (3.05€, $2.90) adults and half-price for children under 18, and rental of a prerecorded audio guide (English or French) is 25F (3.80€, $3.65). It's open Tuesday to Saturday from 9am to 5:30pm.

Place d'Armes. (✆ **01-30-83-78-00.** Admission to the château 46F (7€, $6.65) adults, 35F (5.30€, $5.10) ages 18–25; under age 18/over 60 free. Reduced rates for adults after 3:30pm. May 2–Sept 30 Tues–Sun 9am–6:30pm (to 5pm the rest of the year).

Gardens of Versailles ✶✶✶

Spread across 250 acres, the Gardens of Versailles were laid out by the great landscape artist Le Nôtre, who created a Garden of Eden using ornamental lakes and canals, geometrically designed flower beds, and avenues bordered with statuary. At the peak of their glory, 1,400 fountains spewed forth. *The Buffet* is an exceptional one, having been designed by Mansart. One fountain depicts Apollo in his chariot pulled by four horses, surrounded by tritons emerging from the water to light the world. On the mile-long Grand Canal, Louis XV—imagining he was in Venice—used to take gondola rides with his favorite of the moment.

On Christmas Day 1999, the most violent windstorm in France's history thundered through Paris, causing extensive damage to parks and gardens in the Ile-de-France. At Versailles, the wind toppled 10,000 trees and blew out some windows at the magnificent château. The palace has now reopened, but the difficult task of replanting the thousands of trees will take some time, and it'll be years before they return to their lush grandeur. Nonetheless, there is still much that remains to enchant, and the gardens get better and better every month.

Place d'Armes (behind the Palace of Versailles). © 01-30-83-78-00. Free admission. Daily 7am–dusk (between 5:30 and 9:30pm).

The Trianons & The Hamlet   A long walk across the park will take you to the Grand Trianon 🖈🖈, in pink-and-white marble. Le Vau built a Porcelain Trianon here in 1670, covered with blue and white china tiles, but it was fragile and soon fell into ruin. So, in 1687, Louis XIV commissioned Hardouin-Mansart to build the Grand Trianon. Traditionally, it has been a place where France has lodged important guests, though de Gaulle wanted to turn it into a weekend retreat. Nixon once slept here in the room where Mme de Pompadour died. Mme de Maintenon also slept here, as did Napoléon. The original furnishings are gone, of course, with mostly Empire pieces there today.

Gabriel, the designer of place de la Concorde in Paris, built the **Petit Trianon** 🖈🖈 in 1768 for Louis XV. Louis used it for his trysts with Mme du Barry. When he died, his son, Louis XVI, presented it to his wife, and Marie Antoinette adopted it as her favorite residence, a place to escape the rigid life at the main palace. Many of the current furnishings, including a few in her rather modest bedchamber, belonged to the ill-fated queen.

Rousseau's theories about recapturing the natural beauty of life were much in favor in the late 18th century, and they prompted Marie Antoinette to have Mique build her a 12-house **Hamlet** on the banks of the Grand Trianon Lake in 1783. She wanted a chance to experience the simplicity of peasant life—or at least peasant life as seen through the eyes of a frivolous queen. Dressed as a shepherdess, she would come here to watch sheep being tended and cows being milked, men fishing and washerwomen beating their laundry in the lake, and donkey carts bringing corn to be ground at the mill.

Place d'Armes (to the immediate right after entering the Palace of Versailles). ℂ 01-30-83-78-00. Grand Trianon 25F (3.80€, $3.65) adults, 15F (2.35€, $2.25) ages 18–25, under age 18 free. Petit Trianon 15F (2.35€, $2.25) adults, 10F (1.50€, $1.45) ages 18–25, under age 18 free. Both Trianons 30F (4.55€, $4.35) adults, 20F (3.05€, $2.90) ages 18–25, under age 18 free. Reduced rates for adults after 3:30pm. May 2–Sept 30 Tues–Sun 10am–6:30pm (to 5pm the rest of the year). Hamlet free; daily 7am–dusk (between 5:30 and 9:30pm).

WHERE TO DINE

Le Potager du Roy 𝒶 FRENCH   Philippe Letourneur cooks from the heart, specializing in a simple cuisine with robust flavors. His attractive restaurant occupies an 18th-century building in a neighborhood known during the days of the French monarchs as the Parc des Cerfs ("Stag Park," where courtiers could find paid companionship with B- and C-list courtesans). The skillfully prepared menu is reinvented with the seasons and may include foie gras with vegetable-flavored vinaigrette; roasted duck with a navarin of vegetables; macaroni ragout with a persillade of snails; and roasted cod with roasted peppers in the style of Provence. For something unusual, order the fondant of pork jowls with a confit of fresh vegetables. Try to save room for the chocolate cake, flavored with orange and served with coconut ice cream.

1 rue du Maréchal-Joffre. ℂ **01-39-50-35-34.** Reservations required. Fixed-price menu 145F (22.05€, $21.05) at lunch, 189F–285F (28.75€–43.30€, $27.40–$41.35) at dinner. AE, V. Tues–Fri noon–2:30pm and 7–10:30pm, Sat 7–10:30pm.

Les Trois Marches 𝒶𝒶𝒶 FRENCH   This is one of the best restaurants not only in Versailles but in the Ile-de-France. The Hôtel Trianon Palace became famous in 1919 when it served as headquarters for signatories to the Treaty of Versailles, and the dining room retains an old-world splendor. Gérard Vié is the most talented and creative chef in town, attracting a discerning crowd that doesn't mind paying the high prices. His *cuisine moderne* is subtle, often daring, and the service is smooth. Begin with the lobster salad with fresh herbs, served with onion soufflé; the galette of potatoes with bacon, chardonnay, and sevruga caviar; or the citrus-flavored scallop bisque. Stars among the main courses are the pigeon roasted and flavored with rosé and accompanied by celeriac and truffles, and the celeriac fashioned into ravioli, filled with foie gras, and topped by a thick slice of black truffle. If you arrive in late autumn, you may find penne-like pasta, tossed with morels, mushrooms, and Parmesan and blended in a butter sauce with white Alba truffles. For dessert, opt for the signature assortment.

In the Hôtel Trianon Palace, 1 bd. de la Reine. ℂ **01-39-50-13-21.** Reservations required far in advance. Fixed-price menu 350F (53.20€, $50.75) at lunch Mon–Fri,

650F–850F (98.80€–129.20€, $94.25–$123.25) at lunch Sat–Sun and at dinner. AE, DC, MC, V. Daily noon–2pm and 7:30–10pm. Closed Aug.

DISNEYLAND PARIS
20 miles E of Paris

After provoking some of the most controversial reactions in recent French history, the multimillion-dollar Euro Disney Resort opened in 1992 as one of the world's most lavish theme parks, situated on a 5,000-acre site (about one-fifth the size of Paris) in the suburb of Marne-la-Vallée. In 1994, it unofficially changed its name to Disneyland Paris. The early days of this megascale project weren't particularly happy: European journalists delighted in belittling it and accusing it of everything from cultural imperialism to the death knell of French culture. But after financial jitters and goodly amounts of public relations and financial juggling, the resort is on track.

In fact, it's now the number-one attraction in France, with 50 million annual visitors. MONSIEUR MICKEY TRIUMPHS! the French press headlined. Disney surpasses the Eiffel Tower and the Louvre in numbers of visitors and accounts for 4% of the tourism industry's foreign currency sales. Disneyland Paris looks, tastes, and feels like its parents in California and Florida—except for the European flair (the use of pastel colors rather than primary colors) and the $10 cheeseburgers *"avec pommes frites."* Allow a full day to see the park.

ESSENTIALS
GETTING THERE   The resort is linked to the **RER** commuter express rail network (Line A), which maintains a stop within walking distance of the park. Board the RER at such Paris stops as Charles de Gaulle–Etoile, Châtelet–Les Halles, or Nation. Get off at Line A's last stop, Marne-la-Vallée/Chessy, 45 minutes from central Paris. The round-trip fare from central Paris is 80F (12.15€, $11.60). Trains run every 10 to 20 minutes, depending on the time of day.

Each of the hotels in the resort connects by **shuttle bus** to both Orly and Charles de Gaulle. Buses depart from both airports at intervals of 45 minutes. One-way transportation to the park from either airport costs 85F (12.90€, $12.35).

If you're coming by **car**, take A-4 east from Paris, getting off at exit 14, marked PARC EURO DISNEYLAND. Guest parking at any of the thousands of parking spaces is 40F (6.10€, $5.80) per day. An interconnected series of moving sidewalks speeds up pedestrian transit from the parking areas to the theme park's entrance. Parking for guests at any of the resort's hotels is free.

SPENDING THE DAY AT DISNEY

Disneyland Paris ✮✮✮   The resort was designed as a total vacation package: Included within one enormous unit are the Disneyland Park with its five entertainment "lands," six large hotels, a campground, an entertainment center (Village Disney), a 27-hole golf course, and dozens of restaurants, shows, and shops. Peak season is mid-June to mid-September, as well as Christmas and Easter weeks. Entrance to Village Disney is free, though there's usually a cover charge for the dance clubs.

One of the attractions, **Main Street, U.S.A.,** features horse-drawn carriages and street-corner barbershop quartets. From the "Main Street Station," steam-powered railway cars leave for a trip through a Grand Canyon Diorama to **Frontierland,** with paddle-wheel steamers reminiscent of the Mississippi Valley described by Mark Twain. The park's steam trains chug past **Adventureland—** with swashbuckling 18th-century pirates, the tree house of the Swiss Family Robinson, and a roller coaster, Indiana Jones and the Temple of Peril . . . Backwards!, that travels in reverse—to **Fantasyland.** Here you can see the symbol of the theme park, the Sleeping Beauty Castle (*Le Château de la belle au bois dormant*), whose soaring pinnacles and turrets are a spectacular idealized interpretation of the châteaux of France.

Visions of the future are displayed at **Discoveryland,** whose tributes to human invention and imagination are drawn from the works of Leonardo da Vinci, Jules Verne, H. G. Wells, the modern masters of science fiction, and the *Star Wars* series. Discoveryland has proven among the most popular of all the areas and is one of the few that was enlarged (in 1995) after the park's inauguration. A noteworthy addition was a new roller coaster called **Space Mountain,** which emulates an earth-to-moon transit as conceived by Jules Verne. Another popular attraction here is an in-theater experience, **Honey, I Shrunk the Kids,** where 3-D and animation gives the illusion that the audience has been shrunk.

As Disney continues to churn out animated blockbusters, look for its newest stars to appear in the theme park. The fact that the characters from such films as *Aladdin, The Lion King,* and *Pocahontas* are actually made of celluloid hasn't kept them out of the Ice Capades, and it certainly won't keep them out of Disneyland Paris.

Disney also maintains an entertainment center, **Village Disney,** whose indoor/outdoor layout is a cross between a California mall and the Coney Island boardwalk. Scattered on either side of a pedestrian walkway, illuminated by overhead spotlights, it's just outside the boundaries of the fenced-in acreage containing the bulk of Disneyland's attractions. The complex accommodates dance clubs, snack bars, restaurants, souvenir shops, and bars for adults who want to escape from the children for a while. Unlike the rest of the park, admission to **Village Disney** is free, so it attracts night owls from Paris and its suburbs who wouldn't otherwise be particularly interested in the park itself.

Disneyland Paris recognizes that long lines tend to frustrate families. In 2000, the park inaugurated the **Fast Pass** system, whereby participants show up at the various rides, and receive a reservation for a 1-hour time block within which they should return. Within that 1-hour period, waiting times are usually no more than 8 minutes. This system is presently used for five of the most popular rides: Space Mountain (Discoveryland); Indiana Jones and the Temple of Peril . . . Backwards! (Adventureland); Big Thunder Mountain (Frontierland); Star Tours (Discoveryland); and Peter Pan's Flight (Fantasyland).

The park places height restrictions on only three rides, each of which involves some kind of scary roller-coaster experience. Riders of **Big Thunder Mountain** roller coaster must be at least 1 meter (3 ft., 3 in.) tall; and riders of both **Space Mountain** and **Indiana Jones and the Temple of Peril . . . Backwards!** must be at least 1 meter 40 centimeters (4 ft., 7 in.) tall.

Guided 3½-hour tours for 20 or more people can be arranged for 50F (7.60€, $7.25) for adults and 35F (5.30€, $5.15) for children 3 to 11. In view of the well-marked paths leading through the park and the availability of ample printed information in any language, the guided tours aren't really necessary. You can rent coin-operated lockers for 10F (1.50€, $1.45) and can store larger bags for 15F (2.30€, $2.20) per day. Children's strollers and wheelchairs rent for 30F (4.55€, $4.35) per day, with a 20F (3.05€, $2.90) deposit. Baby-sitting is available at any of the hotels if 24-hour advance notice is given.

Marne-la-Vallée. (*C*) **01-60-30-60-53** (Disneyland Paris Guest Relations office, in City Hall on Main Street, U.S.A.). www.disneylandparis.com. Admission to park for 1 day, depending on season, 170F–220F (25.85€–33.45€, $24.65–$31.90) adults, 140F–175F (21.35€–26.60€, $20.30–$25.45) children 3–12, children 2 and under always admitted free. July–Aug daily 9am–11pm; Sept–June Mon–Fri 10am–6pm, Sat–Sun 9am–8pm. Hours vary with the weather and the season.

WHERE TO STAY

The resort's six theme hotels share a reservation service. In North America, call (*C*) **407/W-DISNEY.** In France, contact the **Central**

Reservations Office, Euro Disney Resort, S.C.A., B.P. 105, F-77777 Marne-la-Vallée Cedex 4 (© **01-60-30-60-30**).What follow are our recommendations.

Disneyland Hotel ✿✿

Mouseketeers who have rich daddies and mommies check in here at Disney's poshest resort, which charges Paris Ritz tariffs. At the park entrance, this flagship four-story hotel is Victorian, with red-tile turrets and jutting balconies. The spacious guest rooms are plushly furnished but evoke the image of Disney, with cartoon depictions and a candy-stripe decor. The beds are king, double, or twin; in some rooms, armchairs convert to daybeds. Paneled closets, large mirrors, and safes are found in some units. Accommodations in the rear overlook Sleeping Beauty's Castle and Big Thunder Mountain. Some less desirable units open onto a parking lot. The luxurious combination baths have marble vanities and twin basins. On the Castle Club floor, you get free newspapers, all-day beverages, and access to a well-equipped private lounge.

Disneyland Paris, B.P. 105, F-77777 Marne-la-Vallée Cedex 4. © **01-60-45-65-00**. Fax 01-60-45-65-33. www.disneylandparis.com. 496 units. 2,260F–3,320F (343.50€–504.65€, $327.70–$481.40) double; from 4,950F (752.40€, $717.75) suite. Rates include 2-day pass and breakfast. AE, DC, DISC, MC, V. **Amenities:** 2 restaurants; 2 bars; health club with indoor/outdoor pool; whirlpool; sauna; room service; babysitting; laundry/dry cleaning. *In room:* A/C, TV, minibar, hair dryer.

Hotel Cheyenne/Hotel Santa Fe *Kids*

Next door to each other near a re-creation of Texas's Rio Grande and evoking the Old West, these are the resort's least expensive hotels. The Cheyenne accommodates visitors in 14 two-story buildings along Desperado Street; the Santa Fe, sporting a desert theme, encompasses four "nature trails" winding among 42 adobe-style pueblos. The Cheyenne is a particular favorite among families, offering a double bed and bunk beds. An array of activities are offered for children, including a play area in a log cabin with a lookout tower and a section where you can explore the "ruins" of an ancient Anasazi village. There's a mariachi atmosphere in the Rio Grande Bar, and country music in the Red Garter Saloon Bar. The only disadvantage, according to some parents with children, is the absence of a pool. Tex-Mex specialties are offered at La Cantina (Santa Fe), and barbecue and smokehouse specialties predominate at the Chuck Wagon Cafe (Cheyenne).

Disneyland Paris, B.P. 115, F-77777 Marne-la-Vallée Cedex 4. © **01-60-45-62-00** (Cheyenne) or 01-60-45-78-00 (Santa Fe). Fax 01-60-45-62-33 (Cheyenne) or 01-60-45-78-33 (Santa Fe). 2,000 units. Hotel Cheyenne 1,200F–1,850F (182.40€–281.20€, $174–$268.25) double; Hotel Santa Fe 1,100F–1,760F (167.20€–267.50€, $159.50–$255.20) double. Rates include 2-day pass and breakfast.

AE, DC, DISC, MC, V. **Amenities:** 2 restaurants; bar; 2 tennis courts; health club; sauna; hammock; ice-skating rink in winter; room service; massage; babysitting. *In room:* A/C, TV, minibar, hair dryer, safe.

Hotel New York ✦   Picture an Art-Deco New York of the 1930s. Inspired by the Big Apple, this hotel is designed around a nine-story central "skyscraper" flanked by the Gramercy Park Wing and the Brownstones Wing. (The exteriors of both wings resemble row houses.) More interested in convention bookings, this hotel is less family-friendly than the others previously recommended. Guest rooms are comfortable, with Art-Deco accessories, New York–inspired memorabilia, and roomy combination baths with twin basins. The most desirable units are called Castle Club and lie on the upper floors. Try for one of the units fronting Lake Buena Vista instead of those opening onto the parking lot.

Disneyland Paris, B.P. 100, F-77777 Marne-la-Vallée Cedex 4. ✆ **01-60-45-73-00.** Fax 01-60-45-73-33. www.disneylandparis.com. 563 units. 1,650F–2,420F (250.80€–367.85€, $239.25–$350.90) double; from 3,350F (509.20€, $485.75) suite. Rates include 2-day pass and breakfast. AE, DC, DISC, MC, V. **Amenities:** 2 restaurants; bar; pool; exercise room; sauna; room service; babysitting. *In room:* A/C, TV, minibar, hair dryer, safe.

WHERE TO DINE

Within the resort are at least 45 restaurants and snack bars, each trying hard to please millions of European and North American palates. Here are a few recommendations.

Auberge de Cendrillon FRENCH (TRADITIONAL)   This is a fairy-tale version of Cinderella's sumptuous country inn, with a glass couch in the center. A master of ceremonies, in a plumed tricorner hat and wearing an embroidered tunic and lace ruffles, welcomes you. There are corny elements here, but the chefs do go out of their way to make a big deal out of French cuisine. For the most part, they succeed admirably. The tone is set by the appetizers. Our favorites are their warm goat-cheese salad with lardons and their smoked salmon platter. Either choice will put you in the mood for some of the classics of the French table, especially loin of lamb roasted under a zesty mustard coating or tender sautéed veal medallions that are like nuggets of flavor. An aromatic chicken is also perfectly roasted in puff pastry. Because the restaurant follows the park's seasonal schedules, lunches are usually easier to arrange than dinners.

In Fantasyland. ✆ **01-64-74-24-02.** Reservations recommended. Main courses 110F–140F (16.70€–21.30€, $15.95–$20.30); fixed-price menu 175F (26.60€, $25.40). AE, DC, DISC, MC, V. Daily 11:30am–90 min. before park closing.

California Grill 🍴🍴 CALIFORNIAN/FRENCH   This is the showcase restaurant of this vast Disney world. At the California Grill, chef Eric Leaty, a well-known cookbook author, prepares food that's the equivalent of a one-Michelin-star restaurant. Focusing on the lighter specialties for which the Golden State is famous, with many concessions to French palates, this elegant restaurant manages to accommodate both adults and children gracefully. Even French food critics are impressed with the chef's oysters prepared with leeks and salmon. We also embrace the appetizer of foie gras with roasted red peppers, and rate as "Simply fabulous" the entree of roasted pigeon with braised Chinese cabbage and black-rice vinegar. Another winning selection is fresh salmon roasted over beechwood and served with a sprinkling of walnut oil, sage sauce, asparagus, and fricassée of forest mushrooms. Many items, such as "Mickie's pizzas," spaghetti Bolognese, and grilled ham with fries, are specifically for children. If you want a quiet, mostly adult venue, go here as late as your hunger pangs allow.

In the Disneyland Hotel. ℂ 01-60-45-65-00. Reservations required. Main courses 55F–205F (8.35€–31.15€, $8–$29.75); children's menu 85F (12.90€, $12.35). AE, DC, MC, V. Sun–Fri 7–11pm, Sat 6–11pm.

6

Paris After Dark

When darkness falls, the City of Light certainly lives up to its name—all the monuments and bridges are illuminated, and the glow of old-fashioned and modern street lamps, the blaze of sidewalk cafe windows, and the glare of huge neon signs flood the avenues and boulevards. Parisians start the serious part of their evenings just as Anglos stretch, yawn, and announce it's time for bed. Once a Paris workday is over, most people go straight to a cafe to meet with friends over a drink and perhaps a meal; then they may head home or proceed to a restaurant or the theater; and much later they may grace a nightclub, a bar, or a disco.

In this chapter, we describe Paris's many after-dark diversions—from attending a Molière play at the Comédie-Française to catching a cancan show at the Moulin Rouge to sipping a sidecar at Harry's New York Bar to partying at Le Queen with all the boys.

1 The Performing Arts

LISTINGS Announcements of shows, concerts, and operas are plastered on kiosks all over town. You'll find listings in the weekly *Pariscope,* an entertainment guide with a section in English, or the English-language bimonthly *Boulevard.* Performances start later in Paris than in London or New York—from 8 to 9pm—and Parisians tend to dine after the theater. You may not want to do the same, because many of the less-expensive restaurants close as early as 9pm.

TICKETS There are many ticket agencies in Paris, most of them near the Right Bank hotels. *Avoid them, if possible.* You can buy the cheapest tickets at the box office of the theater itself or at discount ticket agencies that sell tickets for cultural events and plays at discounts of up to 50%. One is the **Kiosque Théâtre,** 15 place de la Madeleine, 8th arr. (no phone; Métro: Madeleine), offering leftover tickets for about half price on the performance day. Tickets for evening shows are sold Tuesday to Friday from 12:30 to 8pm and Saturday from 2 to 8pm. Tickets for matinees are sold Saturday from 12:30 to 2pm and Sunday from 12:30 to 4pm. Other branches are in the basement of the Châtelet–Les Halles Métro station and in front of Gare Montparnasse.

Students with ID can often get last-minute tickets by applying at the box office an hour before curtain time.

Of course, the most effortless way to get tickets, especially if you're staying in a first-class or deluxe hotel, is to ask your concierge to arrange them. This is also the most expensive way and a service fee is added, but it's a heck of a lot easier if you don't want to waste precious hours in Paris trying to secure tickets, especially hard-to-get ones.

For easy availability of tickets for festivals, concerts, and the theater, try one of these locations of the **FNAC** record store chain: 136 rue de Rennes, 6th arr. (*©* **01-49-54-30-00;** Métro: Montparnasse-Bienvenue), or in the Forum des Halles, 1–7 rue Pierre-Lescot, 1st arr. (*©* **01-40-41-40-00;** Métro: Châtelet–Les Halles).

THEATER
Comédie-Française   Those with even a modest understanding of French can still delight in a sparkling production of Molière at this national theater, established to keep the classics alive and promote the most important contemporary authors. Nowhere else will you see the works of Molière and Racine so beautifully staged. The box office is open daily from 11am to 6pm, but the hall is dark mid-July to early September. In 1993, a Left Bank annex was launched, the **Comédie Française–Théâtre du Vieux-Colombier,** 21 rue du Vieux-Colombier, 4th arr. (*©* **01-44-39-87-00**). Though its repertoire varies, it's known for presenting some of the most serious French dramas in town. Tickets are 160F (24.30€, $23.20) or 65F (9.90€, $9.45) age 26 and under. Discounts are available if you reserve in advance. 2 rue de Richelieu, 1st arr. *©* 01-44-58-15-15. Tickets 70F–190F (10.65€–28.90€, $10.15–$27.55). Métro: Palais Royal or Musée du Louvre.

OPERA, DANCE & CLASSICAL CONCERTS
Cité de la Musique   This testimony to the power of music has been the most widely applauded, the least criticized, and the most innovative of late François Mitterrand's half-dozen *grands projets*. At the city's northeastern edge in what used to be a run-down and depressing neighborhood, this $120-million stone-and-glass structure incorporates a network of concert halls, a library and research center for the study of all kinds of music, and a museum. The complex hosts a rich variety of concerts, ranging from Renaissance music through 19th- and 20th-century works, including jazz and traditional music from nations around the world. 221 av. Jean-Jaurès, 19th

---

Tips A Stateside Ticket Agency

Selling tickets to just about any Paris show, **Globaltickets** has an office in the States at 1270 Ave. of the Americas, Suite 2414, New York, NY 10020 (© **800/223-6108** or 914/328-2150; www.globaltickets.com). The Paris office is at 19 rue des Mathurins, 9th arr. (© **01-42-65-39-21**; Métro: Havre-Caumartin). A personal visit isn't necessary. The company will mail tickets to your home, fax you a confirmation, or leave tickets at the box office in Paris. There's a markup of 10% to 20% (excluding opera and ballet) over box-office prices, plus a U.S. handling charge of $8. Hotel-and-theater packages are also available.

---

arr. © **01-44-84-45-00**, or 01-44-84-44-84) for tickets. Tickets 80F–200F (12.15€–30.40€, $11.60–$29) for 4:30 and 8pm concerts.

Musée de Radio France   This is the site of many of the performances of the **Orchestre Philharmonique de Radio France** and the somewhat more conservative **Orchestre National de France.** The concert hall's box office is open Monday to Saturday from 11am to 6pm. 116 av. Président-Kennedy, 16th arr. © **01-56-49-21-80.** Tickets 25F (3.80€, $3.65). Métro: Passy-Ranelagh.

Opéra Bastille   This controversial building—it has been called a "beached whale"—was designed by Canadian architect Carlos Ott, with curtains by Japanese designer Issey Miyake. Since the house's grand opening in July 1989 for the French Revolution's bicentennial, the Opera National de Paris has presented works like Mozart's *Marriage of Figaro* and Tchaikovsky's *Queen of Spades.* The main hall is the largest of any French opera house, with 2,700 seats, but music critics have lambasted the acoustics. The building contains two other concert halls, including an intimate 250-seat room that usually hosts chamber music. Both traditional opera performances and symphony concerts are presented here, as well as both classical and modern dance. Several concerts are given for free in honor of certain French holidays. Write ahead for tickets. Place de la Bastille, 120 rue de Lyon. © **01-43-43-96-96.** Tickets 60F–670F (9.10€–101.85€, $8.70–$97.15) opera, 60F–660F (9.10€–100.30€, $8.70–$95.70) dance. Métro: Bastille.

Opéra Comique   This is a particularly charming venue for light opera, on a smaller scale than Paris's major opera houses. Built in the late 1890s in an ornate style that might remind you of the Opéra

Garnier, it's the site of small productions of operas like *Carmen, Don Giovanni, Tosca,* and *Palleas & Melisande.* There are no performances from mid-July to late August. The box office, however, is open year-round Monday to Saturday from 11am to 7pm. 5 rue Favart, 2nd arr. ✆ **01-42-44-45-45.** Tickets 50F–610F (7.60€–92.70€, $7.25–$88.45). Métro: Richelieu-Drouot.

Opéra Garnier   The Opéra Garnier, once the haunt of the ill-fated Phantom, is the premier stage for dance and, once again, for opera. This 1875 rococo wonder was designed as a contest entry by architect Charles Garnier during the heyday of the French Empire; the facade is adorned with marble and sculpture, including *The Dance* by Carpeaux. Following a year-long renovation, during which the famous Chagall ceiling was cleaned and air-conditioning was added, the facade is gleaming as it did for its patron, Napoléon III. You can see the original gilded busts and statues, the rainbow-hued marble pillars, and the delicate mosaics. The Opéra Garnier combines ballet and opera, and still offers one of the most elegant evenings you can spend in the City of Light. Because of the competition from the Bastille, the Garnier has made great efforts to present more up-to-date dance works, like choreography by Jerome Robbins, Twyla Tharp, Agnes de Mille, and George Balanchine. The box office is open Monday to Saturday from 11am to 6:30pm. Place de l'Opéra, 9th arr. ✆ **01-40-01-17-89.** Tickets 60F–670F (9.10€–101.85€, $8.70–$97.15) opera, 30F–420F (4.55€–63.85€, $4.35–$60.90) dance. Métro: Opéra.

Théâtre National de Chaillot   Part of the architectural complex facing the Eiffel Tower, this is one of the city's largest concert halls, hosting a variety of cultural events that are announced on billboards in front. Sometimes (rarely) dance is staged here, or you might see a brilliantly performed play by Marguerite Duras. The box office is open Monday to Saturday from 11am to 7pm and Sunday from 11am to 5pm. 1 place du Trocadéro, 16th arr. ✆ **01-53-65-30-00.** Tickets 160F (24.30€, $23.20) adults, 120F (18.25€, $17.40) over 60, 80F (12.15€, $11.60) under age 25. Métro: Trocadéro.

2 The Club & Music Scene

Paris is still a late-night mecca, though some of the once-unique attractions now glut the market. The fame of Parisian nights was established in those distant days when the British and Americans still gasped at the sight of a bare bosom in a chorus line. The fact is that contemporary Paris boasts less vice than London, Hamburg, or San Francisco.

Nonetheless, both the quantity and the variety of Paris nightlife still exceed that of other cities. Nowhere else will you find such a huge and mixed array of nightclubs, bars, dance clubs, cabarets, jazz dives, music halls, and honky-tonks.

A MUSIC HALL

Olympia Charles Aznavour and other big names frequently appear in this cavernous hall. The late Yves Montand appeared once, and the performance was sold out 4 months in advance. (Nowadays, he performs at Père-Lachaise cemetery.) Today you're more likely to catch Gloria Estefan. A typical lineup might include an English rock group, showy Italian acrobats, a well-known French singer, a dance troupe, juggling American comedians (doing much of their work in English), and the featured star. A witty MC and an on-stage band provide a smooth transition. Performances usually begin at 8:30pm Tuesday to Sunday, with Saturday matinees at 5pm. 28 bd. des Capucines, 9th arr. ℭ **01-47-42-25-49.** Tickets 150F–300F (22.80€–45.60€, $21.75–$43.50). Métro: Opéra or Madeleine.

CHANSONNIERS

Chansonniers (literally "songwriters") provide a bombastic musical satire of the day's events. This combination of parody and burlesque is a time-honored Gallic amusement and a Parisian institution. Songs are often created on the spot, inspired by the "disaster of the day."

Au Caveau de la Bolée To enter this bawdy *boîte,* you descend into the catacombs of the early14th-century Abbaye de St-André, once a famous cafe that attracted Verlaine and Oscar Wilde, who slowly snuffed out his life in absinthe here. The singing is loud and smutty, just the way the predominantly student audience likes it. Occasionally, the audience sings along. You'll enjoy this place a lot more if you can follow the thread of the French-language jokes and satire, but even if you can't, there are enough visuals (magic acts and performances by singers) to amuse. The fixed-price dinner is followed by a series of at least four entertainers, usually comedians. In lieu of paying admission for the cabaret, you can order dinner. If you've already had dinner, you can order just a drink. 25 rue de l'Hirondelle, 6th arr. ℭ **01-43-54-62-20.** Fixed-price dinner 300F (45.60€, $43.50) Mon–Fri, 300F (45.60€, $43.50) Sat. Cover 150F (22.80€, $21.75) Mon–Sat if you don't order dinner. Dinner Mon–Sat 8:30pm; cabaret 10:30pm. Métro: St-Michel.

Au Lapin Agile   Picasso and Utrillo patronized this little cottage near the top of Montmartre, then known as the Cabaret des Assassins, and it has been painted by many artists, including Utrillo. You'll sit at carved wooden tables in a dimly lit room with walls covered by bohemian memorabilia and listen to French folk tunes, love ballads, army songs, sea chanteys, and music-hall ditties. You're encouraged to sing along, even if it's only the *"oui, oui, oui—non, non, non"* refrain of "Les Chevaliers de la Table Ronde." The best singalongs are on weeknights after tourist season ends. 22 rue des Saules, 18th arr. ℭ **01-46-06-85-87.** Cover (including 1st drink) 130F (19.75€, $18.85). Tues–Sun 9pm–2am. Métro: Lamarck.

NIGHTCLUBS & CABARETS

Decidedly expensive, these places give you your money's worth by providing some of the most lavishly spectacular floor shows anywhere. With the exception of Café Concert Ailleurs, they generally attract an older crowd in their 40s or 50s. They are definitely not youth-oriented.

Café Concert Ailleurs   The young Juliette Greco or Simone de Beauvoir of today gravitates to this cafe/cabaret operated by a group of artists. Some of the latest and most experimental music is performed here nightly over dinner. You can also show up for the 9pm show if you don't plan on dining here. Surprisingly, the cover charge is what you tell them you can pay. 13 rue Jean-de-Beausire, 4th arr. ℭ **01-44-59-82-82.** Cover 30F (4.55€, $4.35), 50F (7.60€, $7.25), or 80F (12.15€, $11.60). Dinner nightly at 8pm. Métro: Bastille.

Chez Michou   The setting is blue, the MC wears blue, and the spotlights bathe performers in yet another shade of blue. The creative force behind the color coordination and a hearty dollop of cross-genderism is Michou, veteran impresario whose 20-odd cross-dressing belles bear names like Hortensia and DuDuche; they lip-synch in costumes from haute couture to haute concierge, paying tribute to Americans like Whitney Houston, Diana Ross, and Tina Turner, and French stars like Mireille Mathieu, Sylvie Vartan, "Dorothée," and Brigitte Bardot. If you don't want dinner, you'll have to stand at the bar, paying a compulsory 220F (33.45€, $31.90) for the first drink. 80 rue des Martyrs, 18th arr. ℭ **01-46-06-16-04.** Cover (including dinner, aperitif, wine, coffee, and show) 600F (91.20€, $87). Dinner nightly at 8:30pm (reservations required); show begins nightly at 10:30pm. Métro: Pigalle.

Crazy Horse Saloon   Since it opened in 1951, this sophisticated strip joint has thrived thanks to good choreography and a sly, coquettish celebration of the female form. The theme binding each of the 5-minute numbers (featuring gorgeous dancers in erotic costumes) is La Femme in her various emotional states: temperamental, sad, dancing/bouncy, or joyful. Dance numbers that endure season after season include "The Itch" and "The Erotic Lesson." Dinner is a tasteful event served at Chez Francis, a restaurant under separate management a few steps from the cabaret. Shows last just under 2 hours. 12 av. George V, 8th arr. ℂ **01-47-23-32-32.** Reservations recommended. Cover 450F–560F (68.40€–85.10€, $65.25–$81.20) including 2 drinks at a table; 290F (44.10€, $42.05) including 2 drinks at the bar; dinner spectacle 660F (100.30€, $95.70). Shows Sun–Fri 8:30 and 11pm; Sat 7:30, 9:45, and 11:50pm. Métro: George V or Alma-Marceau.

Folies-Bergère   The Folies-Bergère has been an institution for foreigners since 1886. Josephine Baker, the African-American singer who danced in a banana skirt and threw bananas into the audience, became "the toast of Paris" here. According to legend, the first GI to reach Paris at the 1944 Liberation asked for directions to the club. Don't expect the naughty and slyly permissive skin-and-glitter revues of the past. In 1993, all that ended with a radical restoration and reopening under new management. Today, it's a conventional 1,600-seat theater featuring musical revues with a sense of nostalgia for old Paris. You're likely to see an intriguing, often charming, but not exactly erotic repertoire of mostly French songs, interspersed with the banter of an MC. A restaurant serves fixed-price dinners in an anteroom. 32 rue Saulnier, 9th arr. ℂ **01-44-79-98-98.** Cover 150F–350F (22.80€–53.20€, $21.75–$50.75); dinner and show 370F–550F (56.25€–83.60€, $53.65–$79.75). Tues–Sat at 9pm, Sun at 3pm. Métro: Rue Montmartre or Cadet.

Lido de Paris   The Lido's $15-million current production, *C'est Magique,* is a dramatic reworking of the classic Parisian cabaret show, with eye-popping special effects and bold new themes, both nostalgic and contemporary, including aerial and aquatic ballets using more than 60,000 gallons of water per minute. The show, the most expensive ever produced in Europe, uses 80 performers, $4 million in costumes, and a $2-million lighting design with lasers. There's even an ice rink and a pool that magically appear and disappear. The legendary Bluebell Girls are still here, however. Now that celebrated chef Paul Bocuse is a consultant, the cuisine is better than ever. 116 bis av. des Champs-Elysées, 8th arr. ℂ **800/227-4884** or 01-40-76-56-10. Cover for 10pm or midnight show 460F–560F (69.90€–85.10€,

$66.70–$81.20) including half bottle of champagne; 8pm dinner dance, including half bottle of champagne, and 10pm show 815F–1,015F (123.95€–154.35€, $118.25–$147.25). Métro: George V.

Moulin Rouge This is a camp classic. Toulouse-Lautrec immortalized the Moulin Rouge and its habitués in his works, but he'd probably have a hard time recognizing it today. Colette created a scandal here by giving an on-stage kiss to Mme de Morny, but it's harder to shock today's audiences. Try to get a table, as the view is much better on the main floor than from the bar. The emphasis on the strip routines and saucy sexiness of the Belle Epoque and of promiscuous Paris between the world wars keeps drawing the crowds. Handsome men and women, virtually all topless, contribute to the appeal. The finale usually includes two dozen belles ripping loose with a topless cancan in a style that might've been appreciated by Gigi herself. Place Blanche, 18th arr. ✆ **01-53-09-82-82.** Cover 520F–580F (79.05€–88.15€, $75.40–$84.10) including champagne; dinner and show from 790F (120.10€, $114.55). Seats at the bar, cover 370F (56.25€, $53.65) includes 2 drinks. Dinner nightly at 7pm; shows nightly at 9 and 11pm. Métro: Blanche.

JAZZ, SALSA, ROCK & MORE

The great jazz revival that long ago swept America is still going strong here, with Dixieland or Chicago rhythms being pounded out in dozens of jazz cellars, mostly called *caveaux*. Most clubs are between rue Bonaparte and rue St-Jacques on the Left Bank. The crowds attending clubs to hear rock, salsa, and the like are definitely young, often in their late teens, 20s, or early 30s. The exception to that is in the clubs offering jazz nights. Lovers of jazz span all ages.

Baiser Salé This musically varied cellar club is lined with jazz-related paintings and has a large central bar and an ongoing roster of videos showing great jazz moments from the past. There's no food or even any particular glamour—everything is very mellow and laid-back. Genres featured include Afro-Caribbean, Afro-Latino, salsa, merengue, R&B, and sometimes fusion. 58 rue des Lombards, 1st arr. ✆ **01-42-33-37-71.** Cover 50F–100F (7.60€–15.20€, $7.25–$14.50) Wed–Sun. Daily 6pm–6am, music daily 10pm–3am. Métro: Châtelet.

Bus Palladium In a single room with a very long bar, this rock temple has varnished hardwoods and fabric-covered walls that barely absorb the reverberations of nonstop recorded music. You won't find techno, punk rock, jazz, blues, or soul. It's rock for hard-core, mostly heterosexual, rock wannabes ages 25 to 35. 6 rue Fontaine,

9th arr. ℂ **01-53-21-07-33.** Cover 100F (15.20€, $14.50) Fri–Sat. Tues–Sat 11pm–6am. Métro: Blanche or Pigalle.

Caveau de la Huchette This celebrated jazz *caveau,* reached by a winding staircase, draws a young crowd, mostly students, who dance to the music of well-known jazz combos. In pre-jazz days, Robespierre and Marat frequented the place. 5 rue de la Huchette, 5th arr. ℂ **01-43-26-65-05.** Cover 60F (9.10€, $8.70) Sun–Thurs, 75F (11.40€, $10.95) Fri–Sat; students 55F (8.35€, $8.05) Sun–Thurs, 75F (11.40€, $10.95) Fri–Sat. Sun–Thurs 9:30pm–2:30am, Fri–Sat and holidays 9:30pm–4am. Métro/RER: St-Michel.

La Chapelle des Lombards *(Finds* The club's proximity to the Opéra Bastille seems incongruous, considering the radically experimental African/Caribbean jazz and Brazilian salsa that's the norm. It's a magnet for South American and African expatriates, and the rhythms and fire of the music propel everyone onto the dance floor. 19 rue de Lappe, 11th arr. ℂ **01-43-57-24-24.** Cover 100F–120F (15.20€–18.25€, $14.50–$17.40) including 1st drink. Women free Thurs before midnight. Thurs–Sat 10:30pm–dawn. Métro: Bastille.

L'Arbuci The artists who perform here are likely to be lesser-known players, sometimes from Southeast Asia, Madagascar, or the Philippines. The venue is subterranean, smoky, and intimate, and the music and ambience are often more appealing than the entrance suggests. If you don't want dinner, you're charged 70F to 100F (10.65€–15.20€, $10.15–$14.50) per drink. The bar is open to 3am. 25–27 rue de Buci, 6th arr. ℂ **01-44-32-16-00.** No cover. Dinner 200F–250F (30.40€–38€, $29–$36.25). Tues–Sat dinner services at 7:30 and 10:30pm; live music begins at 10pm. Métro: Mabillon or St-Germain-des-Prés.

Le Bilboquet/Club St-Germain This restaurant/jazz club/piano bar, where the film *Paris Blues* was shot, offers some of the best music in Paris. Jazz is played on the upper level in the restaurant, **Le Bilboquet,** a wood-paneled room with a copper ceiling, brass-trimmed sunken bar, and Victorian candelabra. The menu is limited but classic French, specializing in lamb, fish, and beef. Dinner is 180F to 300F (27.35€–45.60€, $26.10–$43.50). Under separate management is the downstairs **Club St-Germain** disco, where entrance is free, but drinks cost 100F (15.20€, $14.50). You can walk from one club to the other but must buy a new drink each time you change venues. 13 rue St-Benoît, 6th arr. ℂ **01-45-48-81-84.** No cover. Le Bilboquet nightly 8pm–2:45am; jazz music 10:30pm–2:45am. Club St-Germain Tues–Sun 11pm–5am. Métro: St-Germain-des-Prés.

Les Etoiles   Since 1856, this red-swabbed music hall has shaken with the sound of performers at work and patrons at play. Its newest incarnation is as a restaurant discothèque where the music is exclusively salsa and the food Cuban. Expect hearty portions of fried fish, shredded pork or beef, white rice, beans, and flan as bands from Venezuela play to a crowd that dances to the rhythms. 61 rue du Château d'Eau, 10e. ✆ **01-47-70-60-56.** Cover 120F (18.25€, $17.40) including 1st drink. Métro: Château d'Eau.

New Morning   Jazz maniacs come to drink, talk, and dance at this long-enduring club. It remains on the see-and-be-seen circuit, so you may see Spike Lee or Prince. The high-ceilinged loft was turned into a nightclub in 1981. Many styles of music are played and performed, and the club is especially popular with jazz groups from Central and South Africa. A phone call will let you know what's going on the night you plan to visit. Sometimes it's open on Sunday. 7–9 rue des Petites-Ecuries, 10th arr. ✆ **01-45-23-51-41.** Cover 100F–180F (15.20€–27.35€, $14.50–$26.10). Call ahead, but hours are generally Mon–Sat 8pm–1:30am. Métro: Château d'Eau.

DANCE CLUBS

The nightspots below are among hundreds of places where young people in their 20s or early 30s go chiefly to dance—distinct from others where the main attraction is the music. The area around the church of **St-Germain-des-Prés** is full of dance clubs, but they come and go so quickly you could arrive to find a hardware store in the place of last year's white-hot disco—but, like all things in nature, the new spring up to take the place of the old. Check in *Time Out: Paris* or *Pariscope* to get a sense of the current trends. Most of these clubs don't really get going until after 10pm.

Batofar   The hippest after-dark dive in town is actually on a barge on the Seine. This boat was once a lighthouse, and from its innards a cavernous night club has been carved, including a spacious dance floor packed with a gyrating crowd mostly in their 20s. House, garage, techno, and "blue note groove" live jazz round out the bill. This music is spun by the city's best DJs. Tapes can be ordered costing 20F (3.05€, $2.90) each. Facing 11 Quai Francois Mauriuac, 13th arr. ✆ **01-56-29-10-33.** Summers only, Tues–Sun 6pm–am (no set time). Cover 100F (15.20€, $14.50). Métro: Quai de la Gare.

La Flèche d'Or *Value*   Part of the chic swing to East Paris, this is a particularly lively counterculture cafe/club. After you've visited Jim Morrison at Père-Lachaise, you can enjoy live concerts here on

Friday and Saturday, everything from Jamaican reggae to Celtic rock. Salsa or swing music from a live dance band enlivens Sundays at 5pm. Anything could be happening—art shows, political debates, video nights, whatever. 102 bis rue de Bagnolet, 20th arr. ✆ 01-43-72-06-87. Cover free to 50F (7.60€, $7.25). Tues–Sun 10pm–2am. Métro: Alexandre Dumas.

Le Saint Occupying three medieval cellars deep in Paris's university area, this place lures 20- and 30-somethings who dance and drink and generally feel happy to be in a Left Bank student dive. The music melds New York, Los Angeles, and Europe and often leads to episodes of "Young Love Beside the Seine." 7 rue St-Severin, 5th arr. ✆ 01-43-25-50-04. Cover 60F–90F (9.10€–13.70€, $8.70–$13.05) including 1st drink. Daily 11pm–6am. Métro: St-Michel.

Les Bains This chic enclave has been pronounced "in" and "out," but lately it's very "in," attracting more model types and gays, especially on Monday night. Everyone dresses more for show than for comfort. The name Les Bains comes from the place's old function as a Turkish bath attracting gays, none more notable than Marcel Proust. It may be hard to get in if the bouncer doesn't like your looks. A restaurant has been added. 7 rue du Bourg-l'Abbé, 3rd arr. ✆ 01-48-87-01-80. Cover 120F (18.25€, $17.40) including 1st drink. Daily 11:30pm–6am. Métro: Réaumur.

3 Bars, Pubs & Clubs

WINE BARS

Many Parisians now prefer the wine bar to the traditional cafe or bistro. The food is often better and the ambience more inviting.

Au Sauvignon This tiny place, with old ceramic tiles and frescoes done by Left Bank artists, has tables overflowing onto a covered terrace where wines range from the cheapest Beaujolais to the most expensive St-Emilion Grand Cru. A glass of wine is 22F to 32F (3.35€–4.85€, $3.25–$4.65), and it costs an extra 2F (.30€, 34¢) to consume it at a table. To accompany your wine, choose an Auvergne specialty, like goat cheese or a terrine. The fresh Poilâne bread is ideal with ham, paté, or goat cheese. 80 rue des Sts-Pères, 7th arr. ✆ 01-45-48-49-02. Mon–Sat 8:30am–10:30pm. Métro: Sèvres-Babylone.

Aux Négociants Ten minutes downhill from the north facade of Sacré-Coeur, this *bistro à vins* has flourished since 1980 as an outlet for wines produced in the Loire Valley. Artists, street vendors, and office workers come here, linked only by an appreciation of wine costing 16F to 28F (2.45€–4.25€, $2.30–$4.05) per glass and the allure of the hearty *plats du jour* costing 60F to 70F (9.10€–10.65€, $8.70–$10.15). 27 rue Lambert, 18th arr. ℭ **01-46-06-15-11.** Mon and Fri noon–8pm, Tues–Thurs noon–10:30pm. Métro: Lamarck-Caulincourt or Château Rouge.

La Tartine   Mirrors, brass detail, and frosted-globe chandeliers make La Tartine look like a movie set of old Paris. At least 60 wines are offered at reasonable prices, including 7 kinds of Beaujolais and a large selection of Bordeaux by the glass. Glasses of wine are 10F to 18F (1.50€–2.75€, $1.45–$2.60), and the charcuterie platter is 45F (6.85€, $6.55). We recommend the light Sancerre wine and goat cheese from the Loire Valley. 24 rue de Rivoli, 4th arr. ℭ **01-42-72-76-85.** Thurs–Mon 8:30am–10pm and Wed noon–10pm. Métro: St-Paul.

Le Sancerre   Produced in the Loire Valley in red, rosé, and especially white, Sancerre wine is known for its not-too-dry fruity aroma and legions of fans who believe it should be more celebrated than it is. That's all you'll find here, where the wine comes from several producers in the Sancerre district and is 14F to 26F (2.15€–3.95€, $2.05–$3.75) per glass. Simple platters of food cost 45F to 75F (6.85€–11.40€, $6.55–$10.95). 22 av. Rapp, 7th arr. ℭ **01-45-51-75-91.** Mon–Sat 8am–10pm. Métro: Alma-Marceau.

Willi's Wine Bar   Journalists and stockbrokers patronize this increasingly popular wine bar in the center of the financial district, run by Englishman Mark Williamson. About 250 kinds of wine are offered, including a dozen wine specials you can taste by the glass for 22F to 82F (3.35€–12.45€, $3.25–$11.95). Lunch is the busiest time—on quiet evenings you can better enjoy the warm ambience and 16th-century beams. Daily specials are likely to include lamb brochette with cumin and Lyonnaise sausage in truffled vinaigrette, plus spectacular desserts like chocolate terrine. 13 rue des Petits-Champs, 1st arr. ℭ **01-42-61-05-09.** Mon–Sat noon–11pm. Métro: Bourse, Pyramide, or Palais Royal.

BARS & PUBS

These "imported" places try to imitate American cocktail bars or masquerade as British pubs—most strike an alien chord. But that doesn't prevent fashionable Parisians from barhopping (not to be confused with cafe-sitting). In general, bars and pubs are open daily from 11am to 1:30am.

Académie de la Bière *Value*   The decor is paneled and rustic, an appropriate foil for an "academy" whose curriculum includes more than 150 kinds of beer from microbreweries. Stella Artois, Belgium's best-selling beer, isn't available, though more than half of the dozen on tap are from small-scale breweries in Belgium that deserve to be better known. Snack-style food is available, including platters of mussels, assorted cheeses, and sausages with mustard. 88 bis bd. du Port-Royal, 5th arr. ℂ **01-43-54-66-65.** Daily 11am–2:30am. Métro: Port Royal.

Barrio Latino　It would be easy to spend an entire evening at this multistoried emporium of good times, Gallic flair, and Latino charm. You won't be finished with this place until you've done a bit of exploring, so here's what you can expect: Tapas bars and dance floors on the street level (*rez-de-chausée*) and 3rd floor (*2eme étage*); a Latino restaurant on the 2nd floor (*1er étage*); and a private club on the top floor. Staff members roll glass-covered carts, loaded with tapas, around the floors, selling them like hotdogs at an American baseball game. The restaurant (open daily noon–3pm and 7:30pm–1am) specializes in food that jaded French palates sometimes find refreshing. Main courses range from 80F to 110F (12.15€–16.70€, $11.60–$15.95) and include Argentinian steaks, Brazilian *fejoiada,* and Mexican *chili con carne,* all of which taste wonderful with beer, *caipirinhas,* Cuba Libres, and/or rum punches. Everywhere, you'll be surrounded in a recorded cocoon of marvelous Latin music. Clientele is very mixed, mostly straight, partly gay, and 100% blasé about matters such as an individual's sexuality. 46 rue du Faubourg St-Antoine, 4th arr. ℂ **01-55-78-84-75.** Cover 50F (7.60, $7.25) but only for non-diners, non-VIPs, and only on Fri–Sat after 9pm. Daily 11am–2 am. Métro: Bastille.

China Club　Designed to recall France's 19th-century colonies in Asia or a bordello in 1930s Shanghai (on the ground floor) and England's empire-building zeal in India (upstairs), the China Club allows you to chitchat or flirt with the singles who crowd into the street-level bar, then escape to calmer, more contemplative climes upstairs. You'll see regulars from the worlds of fashion and the arts, along with a pack of postshow celebrants from the nearby Opéra Bastille. A street-level Chinese restaurant serves dinner daily from 7pm to 12:30am, and in the more animated (and occasionally raucous) cellar bar, live music is presented every Friday and Saturday from 10pm to 3am. 50 rue de Charenton, 12th arr. ℂ **01-43-43-82-02.** Daily 7pm–2am. Métro: Bastille or Ledru Rollin.

Le Forum　Its patrons, who include frequent business travelers, compare this place to a private club in London. Part of that comes from the carefully polished oak paneling and ornate stucco and part from its store of single-malt whiskeys. You can also try 150 cocktails, including many that haven't been popular since the jazz age. Champagne by the glass is common, as is that high-octane social lubricant, the martini. 4 bd. Malesherbes, 8th arr. ℂ 01-42-65-37-86. Daily 2pm–midnight. Métro: Madeleine.

Le Fumoir At Le Fumoir, the well-traveled crowd that lives or works in the district provides a kind of classy raucousness. The decor is a lot like that of an English library, with about 6,000 books providing an aesthetic backdrop to the schmoozing. A Danish chef prepares an international menu featuring meal-size salads (the one with scallops and lobster is great), roasted cod with zucchini, and roasted beef in red-wine sauce. More popular are the stiff mixed drinks, the wines and beers, and the dozen or so types of cigars for sale. 6 rue de l'Amiral-de-Coligny, 1st arr. ℂ 01-42-92-00-24. Daily 11am–2am. Métro: Louvre-Rivoli.

Le Web Bar Occupying a three-story space at the eastern edge of the Marais, Le Web Bar echoes with the sound of people schmoozing with one another and with silent computer partners thousands of miles away. On the street level is a restaurant, on the second floor is a battery of at least 25 computers you can use for free, and on the top floor is an art gallery. To keep things perking, there's daily entertainment beginning around 7pm. Menu items stress comfort food like *boeuf bourguignonne*. 32 rue de Picardie, 3rd arr. ℂ 01-42-72-66-55. www.webbar.fr. Mon–Fri 8:30am–2am, Sat–Sun 11am–2am. Métro: République or Temple.

Index

See also Accommodations and Restaurant indexes, below.

RESTAURANTS

FROMMER'S® COMPLETE TRAVEL GUIDES

Alaska
Amsterdam
Argentina & Chile
Arizona
Atlanta
Australia
Austria
Bahamas
Barcelona, Madrid & Seville
Beijing
Belgium, Holland & Luxembourg
Bermuda
Boston
British Columbia & the Canadian Rockies
Budapest & the Best of Hungary
California
Canada
Cancún, Cozumel & the Yucatán
Cape Cod, Nantucket & Martha's Vineyard
Caribbean
Caribbean Cruises & Ports of Call
Caribbean Ports of Call
Carolinas & Georgia
Chicago
China
Colorado
Costa Rica
Denmark
Denver, Boulder & Colorado Springs
England
Europe
European Cruises & Ports of Call
Florida
France
Germany
Great Britain
Greece
Greek Islands
Hawaii
Hong Kong
Honolulu, Waikiki & Oahu
Ireland
Israel
Italy
Jamaica
Japan
Las Vegas
London
Los Angeles
Maryland & Delaware
Maui
Mexico
Montana & Wyoming
Montréal & Québec City
Munich & the Bavarian Alps
Nashville & Memphis
Nepal
New England
New Mexico
New Orleans
New York City
New Zealand
Nova Scotia, New Brunswick & Prince Edward Island
Oregon
Paris
Philadelphia & the Amish Country
Portugal
Prague & the Best of the Czech Republic
Provence & the Riviera
Puerto Rico
Rome
San Antonio & Austin
San Diego
San Francisco
Santa Fe, Taos & Albuquerque
Scandinavia
Scotland
Seattle & Portland
Shanghai
Singapore & Malaysia
South Africa
South America
Southeast Asia
South Florida
South Pacific
Spain
Sweden
Switzerland
Texas
Thailand
Tokyo
Toronto
Tuscany & Umbria
USA
Utah
Vancouver & Victoria
Vermont, New Hampshire & Maine
Vienna & the Danube Valley
Virgin Islands
Virginia
Walt Disney World & Orlando
Washington, D.C.
Washington State

FROMMER'S® DOLLAR-A-DAY GUIDES

Australia from $50 a Day
California from $70 a Day
Caribbean from $70 a Day
England from $70 a Day
Europe from $70 a Day
Florida from $70 a Day
Hawaii from $80 a Day
Ireland from $60 a Day
Italy from $70 a Day
London from $85 a Day
New York from $90 a Day
Paris from $80 a Day
San Francisco from $70 a Day
Washington, D.C., from $70 a Day

FROMMER'S® PORTABLE GUIDES

Acapulco, Ixtapa & Zihuatanejo
Alaska Cruises & Ports of Call
Amsterdam
Aruba
Australia's Great Barrier Reef
Bahamas
Baja & Los Cabos
Berlin
Big Island of Hawaii
Boston
California Wine Country
Cancún
Charleston & Savannah
Chicago
Disneyland
Dublin
Florence
Frankfurt
Hong Kong
Houston
Las Vegas
London
Los Angeles
Maine Coast
Maui
Miami
New Orleans
New York City
Paris
Phoenix & Scottsdale
Portland
Puerto Rico
Puerto Vallarta, Manzanillo & Guadalajara
San Diego
San Francisco
Seattle
Sydney
Tampa & St. Petersburg
Vancouver
Venice
Virgin Islands
Washington, D.C.

FROMMER'S® NATIONAL PARK GUIDES

Family Vacations in the National Parks
Grand Canyon
National Parks of the American West
Rocky Mountain
Yellowstone & Grand Teton
Yosemite & Sequoia/ Kings Canyon
Zion & Bryce Canyon

FROMMER'S® MEMORABLE WALKS

Chicago
London

New York
Paris

San Francisco

FROMMER'S® GREAT OUTDOOR GUIDES

Arizona & New Mexico
New England

Northern California
Southern New England

Vermont & New Hampshire

SUZY GERSHMAN'S BORN TO SHOP GUIDES

Born to Shop: France
Born to Shop: Hong Kong,
  Shanghai & Beijing

Born to Shop: Italy
Born to Shop: London

Born to Shop: New York
Born to Shop: Paris

FROMMER'S® IRREVERENT GUIDES

Amsterdam
Boston
Chicago
Las Vegas
London

Los Angeles
Manhattan
New Orleans
Paris
Rome

San Francisco
Seattle & Portland
Vancouver
Walt Disney World
Washington, D.C.

FROMMER'S® BEST-LOVED DRIVING TOURS

Britain
California
Florida
France

Germany
Ireland
Italy

New England
Scotland
Spain

HANGING OUT™ GUIDES

Hanging Out in England
Hanging Out in Europe

Hanging Out in France
Hanging Out in Ireland

Hanging Out in Italy
Hanging Out in Spain

THE UNOFFICIAL GUIDES®

Bed & Breakfasts and Country
Inns in:
  California
  New England
  Northwest
  Rockies
  Southeast
Beyond Disney
Branson, Missouri
California with Kids
Chicago
Cruises
Disneyland

Florida with Kids
Golf Vacations in the
  Eastern U.S.
The Great Smokey &
  Blue Ridge Mountains
Inside Disney
Hawaii
Las Vegas
London
Mid-Atlantic with Kids
Mini Las Vegas
Mini-Mickey
New England & New York
  with Kids

New Orleans
New York City
Paris
San Francisco
Skiing in the West
Southeast with Kids
Walt Disney World
Walt Disney World for
  Grown-ups
Walt Disney World for Kids
Washington, D.C.
World's Best Diving Vacations

SPECIAL-INTEREST TITLES

Frommer's Adventure Guide to Australia & New
  Zealand
Frommer's Adventure Guide to Central America
Frommer's Adventure Guide to India & Pakistan
Frommer's Adventure Guide to South America
Frommer's Adventure Guide to Southeast Asia
Frommer's Adventure Guide to Southern Africa
Frommer's Britain's Best Bed & Breakfasts and
  Country Inns
Frommer's France's Best Bed & Breakfasts and
  Country Inns
Frommer's Italy's Best Bed & Breakfasts and Country
  Inns
Frommer's Caribbean Hideaways

Frommer's Exploring America by RV
Frommer's Gay & Lesbian Europe
Frommer's The Moon
Frommer's New York City with Kids
Frommer's Road Atlas Britain
Frommer's Road Atlas Europe
Frommer's Washington, D.C., with Kids
Frommer's What the Airlines Never Tell You
Israel Past & Present
The New York Times' Guide to Unforgettable
  Weekends
Places Rated Almanac
Retirement Places Rated